An Introduction
Comparative
Mythology

Third Edition
Jennifer Taylor, Ph.D.
Valencia College—East

Kendall Hunt
publishing company

Cover images courtesy of the author

Kendall Hunt
publishing company

www.kendallhunt.com
Send all inquiries to:
4050 Westmark Drive
Dubuque, IA 52004-1840

DEDICATION

This edition is dedicated to the Muses, the patron goddesses of the arts and sciences and the inspiration of poets. Without them, this book would not be possible.

And to Robert, my navamsha, my counter part, my other half.

CONTENTS

Chapter 4 ■ Supreme Being Archetype   71

Chapter 5 ■ The Great Goddess Archetype   119

Chapter 6 ▪ The Dying and Rising God Archetype   171

Chapter 7 ▪ Trickster Archetype   197

Chapter 8 ▪ Hero Archetype   221

Chapter 9 ▪ Pantheons

CHAPTER 1
INTRODUCTION TO COMPARATIVE MYTHOLOGY

There are many types of stories and not all stories qualify as myths, academically speaking. Myths are a very specific type of story that involve gods and goddesses, or just a god or goddess, which have been traditionally passed down through the generations by storytellers until finally written down. Myths attempt to answer the big questions, like "Why are we here?" and "What happens when we die?". This means that they are anonymous in origin and with the passage of time the stories may have changed. Mythology is a branch of Folklore, which also contains categories such as Legends, Folk Tales, Fairy Tales, Fables, etc. These other types of stories really focus on human or sometimes even animal characters and the gods play minor or no roles at all. The only exception to this is in legends.

In legends, human heroes are the main characters, but those human heroes are often the sons and daughters of the gods. Therefore, some interaction with gods and goddesses may occur, but the heroes will be the focus of the story. There is also a kernel of truth to a legend, even if it is a small kernel. Two examples of legends would be the story of the Fall of Troy and the story of King Arthur. Historically, there is evidence that a city on the coast of Asia Minor was besieged by the Mycenaean Greeks and burned sometime in the early twelfth century BCE. There is also evidence that a man name Artorius Castus helped unite the Britons as their war leader after the Roman legions were withdrawn from Britain and the British were left to defend themselves against waves of various invaders from the continent, sometime in the third or fourth century CE.

It is much harder to speak about historical truth when working with myths. Myths speak in the language of metaphor and often cannot be taken literally without destroying their original intent. Exactly what their original intent was is open to much debate. Many scholars in the last few centuries have developed theories concerning myths and their purposes. Of these scholars, the most important to understand for the organization of this book are Sigmund Freud, Carl Jung, Joseph Campbell, and the post-Jungian, archetypal, and depth psychologists such as James Hillman. My training has been along those lines and it is how I tend to view the myths and how I tend to retell the stories. My goal is to focus on what is universal among the myths while at the same time honoring the local expressions of universal themes.

Carl Jung coined the term archetype to describe what he saw as universal images from the collective unconscious. These images express common human experiences going all the way back to earliest man. The collective unconscious represents the unconscious layer of the psyche that is common to all humans. The archetypal images appear in myth under the guise of characters such as the Supreme Being, the Great Goddess, the Dying and Rising God, the Trickster and the Hero; and as themes such as the Flood, the Creation, the Afterlife, and the Apocalypse. Each of the archetypal characters exists as a possibility or potentiality inherent in the human psyche that has a full range of possibilities from good to bad characteristics. However, a particular culture (or even an individual psyche) will often emphasize some characteristics of the archetype over others in its depiction of a particular expression of that archetype. Archetypes, because they spring from the collective unconscious of humankind, can be read psychologically to reflect back to the reader valuable information about human nature. Often, it is much easier to read about a hero fighting monsters than to face our own inner demons on our own heroic quest into the undiscovered countries of the deeper levels of the unconscious. James Hillman, an archetypal psychologist, describes archetypes thus in *Archetypal Psychology:* "From Jung comes the idea that the basic and universal structures of the psyche, the formal patterns of its relational modes, are archetypal patterns. These are like psychic organs, congenitally given with the psyche (yet not necessarily genetically inherited), even if somewhat modified by historical and geographical factors. These patterns or *archai* appear in the arts, religions, dreams, and social customs of all people and they manifest spontaneously in mental disorders" (11). He goes on to say, "The primary and irreducible language of these archetypal patterns is the metaphorical discourse of myths. These can therefore be understood as the most fundamental patterns of human existence" (11). Studying mythology is a way to tap into these fundamental patterns and gain insights into the nature of humans.

Archetypal psychology helps us read myths with depth and to see into the depths of those myths. All the gods become aspects of our own psyches, which we learn (according to Depth Psychology/Archetypal Psychology) are polytheistic, not monotheistic in nature. All the gods are within us. Which voices do you honor? Which do you repress? Which gods have you demonized? Which gods have you idealized? What exists in the unconscious that has been suppressed? What needs to be faced? What is already present and honored? Do you glorify the ego to the detriment of all the other gods? Are you monotheistic in your approach to your psyche? Is the ego supreme? Or do you honor all the voices of the psyche? Do you have a polytheistic psyche? For example, let's say that someone has a bad relationship with alcohol. If we use a Greek metaphor for alcohol consumption we might employ the god Dionysos as our metaphor. If we have a healthy relationship with Dionysos, we honor the wine that he represents, and knowing his myths, we recognize that it is necessary to treat Dionysos respectfully, not to abuse him or dismiss him for he has a way of paying back such disrepect (which the

Greeks named Hubris). If we ignore Dionysos (alcohol) completely, we are liable to have a breakdown at some future point where that god finds a trap door out of our psyche and we wake up after a binge of drinking feeling ill.

The myths that follow are from cultures from all over the world. In essence, a myth is a sacred story and these exist everywhere. Humans are mythmakers. Myths do not belong only to the ancient world or the past, but are very much a part of most cultures. When we use the term myth in this book, it does not refer to a lie or untruth. Instead it refers to something metaphorical, a higher Truth and not one that needs to be believed literally. In fact, reading myths literally will often diminish their metaphorical value, besides leading to conflict over religious beliefs. Since myths are very much a part of culture and often of religion, you will find myths from still living traditions from around the world included in this book. The following four functions provide a lens by which we may better view these myths.

Joseph Campbell's Four Functions of Myth

1. The **mystic or metaphysical** function: the reconciliation of consciousness with the preconditions of its own existence (for example, the notion that life feeds on life); redeeming human consciousness from its sense of guilt in life; beyond the realization of and horror at life's monstrous nature; finding a way to say "yes" to life even with all the horror.
2. The **cosmological** function: formulating a cosmic image; that is, creating an image of the universe such that, within its range, all things—the trees, the rocks, the animals, sun, moon, and stars—should be recognized as parts of a great sacred whole, all opening back to the transcendent mystery and thus serving as agents of the first function, as vehicles of the teaching.
3. The **sociological** function: validating the social order—validating and maintaining some specific social order, authorizing its moral code as a construct beyond criticism or human emendation. "Man is not free, according to either of these [Hebrew and Indian] mythic views, to establish for himself the social aims of his life and to work, then, toward these through institutions of his own devising; but rather, the moral, like the natural order, is fixed for all time . . ."
4. The **psychological** function: shaping individuals to the course of life; shaping individuals to the aims and ideals of their various social groups, bearing them on from birth to death through the course of a human life.

■ ■ ■

See Joseph Campbell. "Mythological Themes in Creative Literature and Art." In: *Myths, Dreams, and Religion.* New York: Society for the Arts, Religion, and Contemporary Culture, 1968. 138–175.

Not only do most myths fit into at least one of the Four Functions of myths, some are also what are called etiological myths. These are myths that give explanations for certain things. They could be explanations for names, explanations for customs, even explanations for ritual practices. For example, the story of Daphne, a Greek nymph (a nymph is a minor Greek goddess of water, trees, meadows, etc.) who preferred to be turned into a laurel tree after being shot by Eros with a lead tipped arrow rather than be the wife of Apollo, whom Eros had shot with a good tipped arrow, explains why and how the laurel tree became sacred to the god Apollo.

There are have been many attempts to study and interpret myths. One of the earliest scholars of myth, Euhemerus, writing around 300 BCE, felt that most myths had evolved from stories about amazing human beings. Through the centuries as they were honored, they were elevated to the status of gods. Another approach to the study of myth is structuralism. This study feels that the meaning of the myths can be determined by the structural oppositions that occur in the myth. These may include things like mortal/immortal, raw/cooked, city/nature, etc. This method of interpretation tends to be logical and empirically based. The most famous of the structuralists was Claude Levi-Strauss (1908-2009)

Another approach to the study of myth is the allegorical approach. Myths are interpreted as expressions of natural phenomenon. Max Muller (1823-1900), took the allegorical approach a step further in the late nineteenth century and believed that whatever the myth seemed to be about, it was actually connected to the conflict of sunlight and darkness. Sir James Frazer (1854-1941), a classicist, felt that myths were the basis for rituals. A more recent approach is the contextual approach. In this approach, followed by Walter Burkert (b. 1931), cultural and historical context are vital to understanding the myths.

CHAPTER 2
CREATION: THE BEGINNING OF ALL THINGS

Introduction

The ancient Greeks called the creation the cosmogony, the birth of the cosmos. The following are a collection of creation or cosmic birth myths from around the world. As birth is a feminine process, a feminine element is usually present at the beginning of the myth to start the process. Eggs, water, or a goddess are common motifs for the beginning of creation myths. Life comes from the waters so water is viewed as feminine. Life may hatch from an egg, so eggs are also regarded as feminine. Quite often, creation will begin with a goddess, perhaps the Earth herself, who will begin the birthing process. After the initial start to creation whether from a goddess or a primordial creator god, creation often continues with the help of a male/female pair. This pair may create or reproduce to create the rest of the gods, features of the world, and even humans.

Creation myths are vital to the cultures from which they sprang. They answer the fundamental human questions of "Why are we here?" "How did we get here?" and "What is our purpose?" In answering those archetypal questions, creation myths also provide culturally specific information for how to live among a certain people in a certain place and at a certain time in history (This serves the Sociological Function of myth.). Thus, myths provide us with archetypal insights into the fundamental nature of humankind and at the same time provide us with culturally specific details about how a culture relates to the world around it, how it personifies its gods, and how it views its role in the world. The myths are important because they give a sense of place and purpose to the cultures that engendered them, and were often ritually enacted to remind members of the culture of its origins. The ritual enactments could take place yearly as a way to publicly remind people of the order of their world and the place of humans within that scheme. For example, many scholars believe that the creation myths of Mesopotamia were reenacted in Babylon on the New Year's festival to remind citizens of their origins.

Creation usually starts in darkness and progresses through to light. In the beginning, all is dark and often void, and nothing is visible. As creation continues and light emerges, things can be seen. Establishing light in the myths becomes a metaphor for establishing order. The deep waters of creation are dark and unfathomable, and symbolically represent the unconscious. What happens within them is not clear, and may even be chaotic. Light, especially in the form of the sun, gives order and structure to creation, and also comes to represent consciousness. Each of the following creation myths are an attempt by the respective culture to give order and bring clarity to the world around them.

As you read through the following ten creation myths, notice their beginnings, notice the order that creation takes, notice what happens first, second, third, etc. At the end of each myth are some names and characters to know. At the end of the chapter there are study questions over the myths.

Types of Creation Myths

Emergence myths

These types of myths describe the creation of the cosmos with metaphors of gestation and birth. The most prominent symbol is the earth as mother. She is depicted as the source of all powers and potencies. Inside the earth is her womb and all the seeds and eggs of the world exist there in embryonic form. These forms reach maturity before they appear on the earth's surface. The emphasis in Emergence Myths is much more on the feminine principle and pays little attention to the masculine principle.

Creation from chaos

In these myths, creation arises out of apriori matter or stuff that is either negative or confused. The chaotic condition may be symbolized as water, a monster, or a serpent. Chaos may have qualities of coldness, sterility, quiescence, repression, and restraint.

Cosmic egg

The creation from chaos may involve the metaphor of a cosmic egg out of which creation or the first created being emerges. The egg is a symbol of fertility that contains potency for creation. The incubation of the egg implies a time-ordered creation and a specific determination of created order. The egg symbolizes a state of primordial perfection out of which the created order proceeds.

Creation from nothing

The autonomous and self-created deity exists in the void in himself and by himself. The creator deity appears out of the void or out of nothingness, which are understood to be potent realities. The creator deity is often symbolized by the sky or sky deities. Sky symbolism shows that the creator deity is not contingent upon the world, (he is transcendent from it) although the created order is contingent upon the deity. The creation is not a mere ordering or even founding of the world, but a powerful religious-magical evocation from a powerful supreme being.

World-parent myths

Creation is the result of the reproductive powers of primordial world parents. The conception and birth of offspring from world parents is often portrayed as an indifferent or unconscious activity. The world parents often come after a phase of chaos or indeterminacy. The offspring of world parents tend to be unknown to, or undiscovered by, their parents. Tension arises from this alienation and the offspring become the agents of the separation of the world parents.

Earth-diver myths

The water or earth constitutes the primordial stuff of the beginning. Water, in its undifferentiated indeterminacy, covers everything in the manner of chaos. A culture hero, usually an animal, dives into the primordial waters and brings up a particle of sand, mud, or earth, any substantial form of matter out of which a more stable mode of order might be established. The matter expands to great proportions, thus constituting the landmass of the world on which all beings reside.

In the following pages, we will look as examples of creation myths from eleven different cultures. As you read through each myth, see if you can figure out which type or types of creation myths it is. Some of the myths may have elements from more than one type of creation myth.

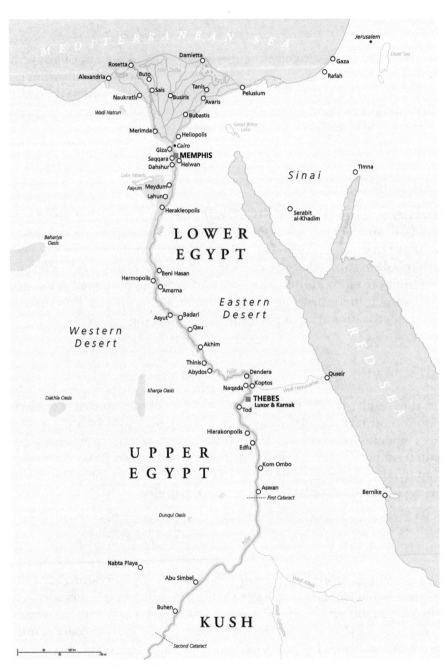

© Peter Hermes Furian/Shutterstock.com

Egyptian Creation: Heliopolis

This myth comes from the Greek named Heliopolis, the City of the Sun in Egypt. It reflects merely one version of Creation as it was believed to have happened in ancient Egypt. Many other versions existed that had different gods as the creators depending on the time period and which city was dominate at that time. All of the Egyptian myths have water as their starting point, probably out of recognition of how important the life giving waters of the Nile were in the daily lives of the ancient Egyptians.

In the beginning there was the primordial deity Khepri and the endless waters of the Nun. Khepri wanted to begin creation and did two things simultaneously. First, he caused a mound of earth to rise up from the endless waters and he took the form of the sun on top of that mound. His sun form was called Re. Second, Khepri created two offspring, a male and a female, to help continue creation. They were called Shu and Tefnut. He spat them out into the endless waters. Shu became the god of atmosphere (or some say moisture) and Tefnut became the goddess of cosmic order. Shu and Tefnut, as husband and wife, continued creation by having children, Geb and Nut. Geb, a male, was the Earth, and Nut, a female, was the sky. Father Earth and Mother Sky fell deeply in love. In fact, they were so in love that they refused to be parted from each other and left no space between them for creation to continue. Their father, Shu, had to separate the couple by raising up the body of his daughter, Nut, so that only her fingers and her toes touched the body of her husband, Geb. After the separation of Sky from Earth, Nut was able to give birth to their four (some say five) children: Osiris, Isis, Seth, and Nephthys—and creation continued.

Osiris became the first king of Egypt and was a god of fertility. He took Isis as his wife. She was the goddess of magic and healing, and the two were very happy together. They traveled throughout the land and taught the arts of civilization to mortals, which included agriculture and the brewing of beer. Their siblings, Seth and Nephthys, also married. Seth was the god of the desert and chaos and Nephthys was the goddess of dusk and death. The child of Osiris and Isis was Horus. His story is told later in the book. The most important gods in this myth are nine in number (The Ennead of Heliopolis): Khepri/Ra, Shu, Tefnut, Geb, Nut, Osiris, Isis, Seth, Nephthys.

Figure 2.1
© Bruce Rolff, 2010. Used under license from Shutterstock, Inc.

An alternate creation story came from the city of Memphis and made Ptah the creator god. This story stated that in the beginning there were Ptah, the high god, and Ptah-Nun, the watery chaos. Ptah caused a mound to rise out of the waters, the Ptah-Ta-Tanen, and he took the form of the sun on top of the mound as Ptah-Atum. "By the effort of his heart and mind, Ptah created Nun and his female counterpart, Nunet. In their turn Nun and Nunet brought forth Atum, who became the Thought of Ptah. Then Thoth came into being as the Tongue of Ptah" (Watterson, 164). Everything else came into creation as a combined act of thought and command from Atum and Thoth who were the heart/thought and mouth of the great god Ptah. All the other gods made up parts of Ptah who was above and beyond and part of all of the rest of the company of the gods. Thus, the myth from Memphis made Ptah above even the creator gods from Heliopolis. Khepri and Ra were regarded as merely aspects of the great god, Ptah, who was the craftsman of the gods.

■ ■ ■

Watterson, Barbara. *Gods of Ancient Egypt*. Phoenix Mill: Sutton Publishing Limited, 2000.

Egyptian names and characters to know:

Khepri
Re
Shu
Tefnut
Geb
Nut
Osiris
Isis
Seth
Ptah
Thoth

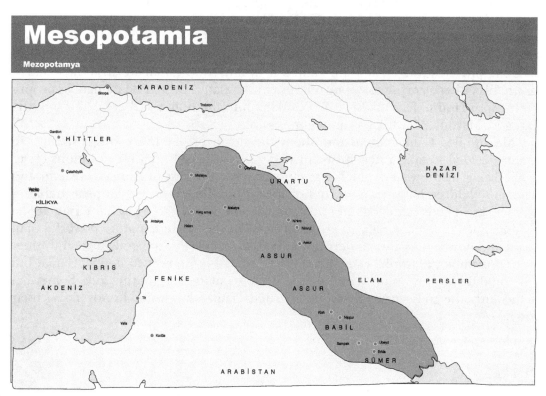

© Emir Kaan/Shutterstock.com

Mesopotamian Myth

The myths from Mesopotamia have origins in the city of Sumer around three thousand BCE where they were written in cuneiform on clay tablets. Eventually, the city of Sumer was conquered by the Akkadians who essentially kept the myths of those they had conquered but changed the names of the gods to match their own gods. The Akkadians were in turn conquered by the Babylonians who also kept the creation myth that was ultimately from Sumer, but changed all the names to match their gods. The Babylonian version, from approximately fifteen hundred BCE, is the best preserved of these myths and therefore the easiest to retell.

In the beginning there were Tiamat, the goddess of salt water, and Apsu, the god of fresh water. The two water gods were all that existed; however, water is extremely fertile so the two gods quickly multiplied their numbers, creating offspring who were also water gods who also produced offspring until the numbers and the noise in the waters became intolerable and Apsu could not sleep. Grumpily, Apsu spoke to his wife and their chief advisor, their son Mummu, and said that he was going to wipe out the rest of their children and grandchildren in order to have some peace. Tiamat wasn't too pleased by this idea but Mummu was very supportive. Encouraged by Mummu, Apsu attacked his offspring.

Unfortunately for Apsu his plan backfired and one of his sons, Ea, the god of wisdom, proved stronger than him and killed him. After Ea killed Apsu, he decided to use his father's corpse to create a house in the waters, which he named, appropriately, Apsu House. Ea took his wife Damkina into the house and created a son, the sun god, Marduk. Marduk was quite impressive.

Meanwhile, Tiamat found out about the death of her husband, Apsu, and in anger decided to take a new husband (Kingu) and breed up a race of monsters to make living in the waters much less enjoyable for the rest of the gods. Kingu and Tiamat's children harassed her other offspring and life was no longer pleasurable.

The great gods came together in a council and decided to try to fight Tiamat one by one. Each of the big male gods fought her, but she was much more powerful than Apsu and no one was able to defeat her. At their wits' end, the gods turned to their newest member, Marduk, who claimed that he had the power to defeat Tiamat but he would do so only on one condition: that he be made king of the gods. Somewhat reluctantly, the gods agreed that if he defeated Tiamat they would honor him as their king.

From *The Fourth Tablet of the Enuma Elish*
The Epic of Creation
L. W. King, Translator
The Seven Tablets of Creation

After the gods his fathers had decreed for the lord his fate,
They caused him to set out on a path of prosperity and success.
He made ready the bow, he chose his weapon,
He slung a spear upon him and fastened it . . .
He raised the club, in his right hand he grasped it,
The bow and the quiver he hung at his side.
He set the lightning in front of him,
With burning flame he filled his body.
He made a net to enclose the inward parts of Tiamat,
The four winds he stationed so that nothing of her might escape;
The South wind and the North wind and the East wind and the West wind
He brought near to the net, the gift of his father Anu.
He created the evil wind, and the tempest, and the hurricane,
And the fourfold wind, and the sevenfold wind, and the whirlwind, and the wind
which had no equal;
He sent forth the winds which he had created, the seven of them;
To disturb the inward parts of Tiamat, they followed after him.
Then the lord raised the thunderbolt, his mighty weapon,
He mounted the chariot, the storm unequaled for terror,
He harnessed and yoked unto it four horses,
Destructive, ferocious, overwhelming, and swift of pace;
. . . were their teeth, they were flecked with foam;
They were skilled in . . . , they had been trained to trample underfoot.
. . . . mighty in battle,
Left and right . . . .
His garment was . . . , he was clothed with terror,
With overpowering brightness his head was crowned.
Then he set out, he took his way,
And toward the raging Tiamat he set his face.
On his lips he held . . . ,
. . . he grasped in his hand.
Then they beheld him, the gods beheld him,
The gods his fathers beheld him, the gods beheld him.
And the lord drew nigh, he gazed upon the inward parts of Tiamat,
He perceived the muttering of Kingu, her spouse.

As Marduk gazed, Kingu was troubled in his gait,
His will was destroyed and his motions ceased.
And the gods, his helpers, who marched by his side,
Beheld their leader's . . . , and their sight was troubled.
But Tiamat . . . , she turned not her neck,
With lips that failed not she uttered rebellious words:
". . . thy coming as lord of the gods,
From their places have they gathered, in thy place are they!"
Then the lord raised the thunderbolt, his mighty weapon,
And against Tiamat, who was raging, thus he sent the word:
Thou art become great, thou hast exalted thyself on high,
And thy heart hath prompted thee to call to battle.
. . . their fathers . . . ,
. . . their . . . thou hatest . . .
Thou hast exalted Kingu to be thy spouse,
Thou hast . . . him, that, even as Anu, he should issue decrees.
thou hast followed after evil,
And against the gods my fathers thou hast contrived thy wicked plan.
Let then thy host be equipped, let thy weapons be girded on!
Stand! I and thou, let us join battle!
When Tiamat heard these words,
She was like one posessed, .she lost her reason. [sic]
Tiamat uttered wild, piercing cries,
She trembled and shook to her very foundations.
She recited an incantation, she pronounced her spell,
And the gods of the battle cried out for their weapons.
Then advanced Tiamat and Marduk, the counselor of the gods;
To the fight they came on, to the battle they drew nigh.
The lord spread out his net and caught her,
And the evil wind that was behind him he let loose in her face.
As Tiamat opened her mouth to its full extent,
He drove in the evil wind, while as yet she had not shut her lips.
The terrible winds filled her belly,
And her courage was taken from her, and her mouth she opened wide.
He seized the spear and burst her belly,
He severed her inward parts, he pierced her heart.
He overcame her and cut off her life;
He cast down her body and stood upon it.
When he had slain Tiamat, the leader,
Her might was broken, her host was scattered.
And the gods her helpers, who marched by her side,
Trembled, and were afraid, and turned back.

They took to flight to save their lives;
But they were surrounded, so that they could not escape.
He took them captive, he broke their weapons;
In the net they were caught and in the snare they sat down.
The . . . of the world they filled with cries of grief.
They received punishment from him, they were held in bondage.
And on the eleven creatures which she had filled with the power of striking terror,
Upon the troop of devils, who marched at her . . . ,
He brought affliction, their strength he . . . ;
Them and their opposition he trampled under his feet.
Moreover, Kingu, who had been exalted over them,
He conquered, and with the god Dug-ga he counted him.
He took from him the Tablets of Destiny that were not rightly his,
He sealed them with a seal and in his own breast he laid them.
Now after the hero Marduk had conquered and cast down his enemies,
And had made the arrogant foe even like
And had fully established Ansar's triumph over the enemy
And had attained the purpose of Nudimmud,
Over the captive gods he strengthened his durance,
And unto Tiamat, whom he had conquered, he returned.
And the lord stood upon Tiamat's hinder parts,
And with his merciless club he smashed her skull.
He cut through the channels of her blood,
And he made the North wind bear it away into secret places.
His fathers beheld, and they rejoiced and were glad;
Presents and gifts they brought unto him.
Then the lord rested, gazing upon her dead body,
While he divided the flesh of the . . . , and devised a cunning plan.
He split her up like a flat fish into two halves;
One half of her he stablished as a covering for heaven.
He fixed a bolt, he stationed a watchman,
And bade them not to let her waters come forth.
He passed through the heavens, he surveyed the regions thereof,
And over against the Deep he set the dwelling of Nudimmud.
And the lord measured the structure of the Deep,
And he founded E-sara, a mansion like unto it.
The mansion E-sara which he created as heaven,
He caused Anu, Bel, and Ea in their districts to inhabit.

After Marduk defeated Tiamat and raised up half her body as the heavens, he made the other half into the Earth. He also gave all the other gods their duties and ordered the movement of the stars, the sun, and the moon. The gods, at first, praised

Marduk's division of labor, but as time passed, they began to complain about the work they had to do especially on the Earth. Their complaints reached Marduk's ears and he devised a plan in order to free the gods from their labors: he would create a race of slaves to tend the Earth that the gods might be at ease. Marduk gave the order for their creation and Ea, his father, the god of wisdom, carried it out. The new race that was created by Ea were humans and he fashioned them from the blood of the captive god, Kingu, Tiamat's second husband, who had been defeated in battle by Marduk. The humans were created to serve the gods, keep the temple fires going and tend the Earth. The gods' ways were changed and they were at peace and they honored Marduk for saving them from Tiamat and restoring peace to their world.

■ ■ ■

The Fourth Tablet of the Enuma Elish, The Epic of Creation, translated by L. W. King, London, 1902. Located on www.sacred-texts.com

Mesopotamian names and characters to know:

Tiamat
Apsu
Mummu
Ea
Marduk
Kingu

Hebrew Creation: Genesis Chapters 1–3 and the Story of Lilith

The Hebrew Creation story is unique among those included in this chapter in that there is only one god and that god creates by the spoken word rather than by physically making the universe. Although there is only one god present in this story, water, a feminine element, is still present at the beginning of the narrative.

Genesis Chapter 1 was composed sometime in the sixth century BCE and was probably originally a hymn sung to thank the Hebrew God Y-hw-h for delivering the Hebrews out of captivity in Babylon. This is evident from the sing-song quality to the writing that includes many repetitions of lines. Pay attention to the order of creation, especially the creation of humans.

Genesis Chapters 2–3 were composed sometime in the tenth century BCE and were concerned more with human beings and the Garden of Eden than the creation of the world. Note the differences in the creation of humans and the order of creation

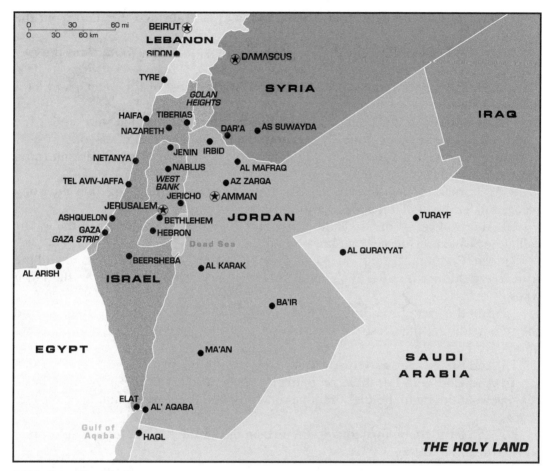

© Globe Turner/Shutterstock.com

in Chapter 2 from Chapter 1. Also introduced in Chapter 2 is the one forbidden thing, a common motif in world mythology. Chapter 3 explains why humans no longer live in Eden, which was like an earthly paradise, and why humans suffer.

Genesis chapters 1–3, from King James Version. Located on www.sacred-texts.com

King James Version: Genesis Chapter 1

1 In the beginning God created the heaven and the earth.

2 And the earth was without form, and void; and darkness was upon the face of the deep. And the Spirit of God moved upon the face of the waters.

3 And God said, Let there be light: and there was light.

4 And God saw the light, that it was good: and God divided the light from the darkness.

5 And God called the light Day, and the darkness he called Night. And the evening and the morning were the first day.

6 And God said, Let there be a firmament in the midst of the waters, and let it divide the waters from the waters.

7 And God made the firmament, and divided the waters which were under the firmament from the waters which were above the firmament: and it was so.

8 And God called the firmament Heaven. And the evening and the morning were the second day.

9 And God said, Let the waters under the heaven be gathered together unto one place, and let the dry land appear: and it was so.

10 And God called the dry land Earth; and the gathering together of the waters called he Seas: and God saw that it was good.

11 And God said, Let the earth bring forth grass, the herb yielding seed, and the fruit tree yielding fruit after his kind, whose seed is in itself, upon the earth: and it was so.

12 And the earth brought forth grass, and herb yielding seed after his kind, and the tree yielding fruit, whose seed was in itself, after his kind: and God saw that it was good.

13 And the evening and the morning were the third day.

14 And God said, Let there be lights in the firmament of the heaven to divide the day from the night; and let them be for signs, and for seasons, and for days, and years:

15 And let them be for lights in the firmament of the heaven to give light upon the earth: and it was so.

16 And God made two great lights; the greater light to rule the day, and the lesser light to rule the night: he made the stars also.

17 And God set them in the firmament of the heaven to give light upon the earth,

18 And to rule over the day and over the night, and to divide the light from the darkness: and God saw that it was good.

19 And the evening and the morning were the fourth day.

20 And God said, Let the waters bring forth abundantly the moving creature that hath life, and fowl that may fly above the earth in the open firmament of heaven.

21 And God created great whales, and every living creature that moveth, which the waters brought forth abundantly, after their kind, and every winged fowl after his kind: and God saw that it was good.

22 And God blessed them, saying, Be fruitful, and multiply, and fill the waters in the seas, and let fowl multiply in the earth.

23 And the evening and the morning were the fifth day.

24 And God said, Let the earth bring forth the living creature after his kind, cattle, and creeping thing, and beast of the earth after his kind: and it was so.

25 And God made the beast of the earth after his kind, and cattle after their kind, and every thing that creepeth upon the earth after his kind: and God saw that it was good.

26 And God said, Let us make man in our image, after our likeness: and let them have dominion over the fish of the sea, and over the fowl of the air, and over the cattle, and over all the earth, and over every creeping thing that creepeth upon the earth.

27 So God created man in his own image, in the image of God created he him; male and female created he them.

28 And God blessed them, and God said unto them, Be fruitful, and multiply, and replenish the earth, and subdue it: and have dominion over the fish of the sea, and over the fowl of the air, and over every living thing that moveth upon the earth.

29 And God said, Behold, I have given you every herb bearing seed, which is upon the face of all the earth, and every tree, in the which is the fruit of a tree yielding seed; to you it shall be for meat.

30 And to every beast of the earth, and to every fowl of the air, and to every thing that creepeth upon the earth, wherein there is life, I have given every green herb for meat: and it was so.

31 And God saw every thing that he had made, and, behold, it was very good. And the evening and the morning were the sixth day.

King James Version: Genesis Chapter 2

1 Thus the heavens and the earth were finished, and all the host of them.

2 And on the seventh day God ended his work which he had made; and he rested on the seventh day from all his work which he had made.

3 And God blessed the seventh day, and sanctified it: because that in it he had rested from all his work which God created and made.

4 These are the generations of the heavens and of the earth when they were created, in the day that the LORD God made the earth and the heavens,

5 And every plant of the field before it was in the earth, and every herb of the field before it grew: for the LORD God had not caused it to rain upon the earth, and there was not a man to till the ground.

6 But there went up a mist from the earth, and watered the whole face of the ground.

7 And the LORD God formed man of the dust of the ground, and breathed into his nostrils the breath of life; and man became a living soul.

8 And the LORD God planted a garden eastward in Eden; and there he put the man whom he had formed.

9 And out of the ground made the LORD God to grow every tree that is pleasant to the sight, and good for food; the tree of life also in the midst of the garden, and the tree of knowledge of good and evil.

10 And a river went out of Eden to water the garden; and from thence it was parted, and became into four heads.

11 The name of the first is Pison: that is it which compasseth the whole land of Havilah, where there is gold;

12 And the gold of that land is good: there is bdellium and the onyx stone.

13 And the name of the second river is Gihon: the same is it that compasseth the whole land of Ethiopia.

14 And the name of the third river is Hiddekel: that is it which goeth toward the east of Assyria. And the fourth river is Euphrates.

15 And the LORD God took the man, and put him into the garden of Eden to dress it and to keep it.

16 And the LORD God commanded the man, saying, Of every tree of the garden thou mayest freely eat:

17 But of the tree of the knowledge of good and evil, thou shalt not eat of it: for in the day that thou eatest thereof thou shalt surely die.

18 And the LORD God said, It is not good that the man should be alone; I will make him an help meet for him.

19 And out of the ground the LORD God formed every beast of the field, and every fowl of the air; and brought them unto Adam to see what he would call them: and whatsoever Adam called every living creature, that was the name thereof.

20 And Adam gave names to all cattle, and to the fowl of the air, and to every beast of the field; but for Adam there was not found an help meet for him.

21 And the LORD God caused a deep sleep to fall upon Adam, and he slept: and he took one of his ribs, and closed up the flesh instead thereof;

22 And the rib, which the LORD God had taken from man, made he a woman, and brought her unto the man.

23 And Adam said, This is now bone of my bones, and flesh of my flesh: she shall be called Woman, because she was taken out of Man.

24 Therefore shall a man leave his father and his mother, and shall cleave unto his wife: and they shall be one flesh.

25 And they were both naked, the man and his wife, and were not ashamed.

King James Version: Genesis Chapter 3

1 Now the serpent was more subtil than any beast of the field which the LORD God had made. And he said unto the woman, Yea, hath God said, Ye shall not eat of every tree of the garden?

2 And the woman said unto the serpent, We may eat of the fruit of the trees of the garden:

3 But of the fruit of the tree which is in the midst of the garden, God hath said, Ye shall not eat of it, neither shall ye touch it, lest ye die.

4 And the serpent said unto the woman, Ye shall not surely die:

5 For God doth know that in the day ye eat thereof, then your eyes shall be opened, and ye shall be as gods, knowing good and evil.

6 And when the woman saw that the tree was good for food, and that it was pleasant to the eyes, and a tree to be desired to make one wise, she took of the fruit thereof, and did eat, and gave also unto her husband with her; and he did eat.

7 And the eyes of them both were opened, and they knew that they were naked; and they sewed fig leaves together, and made themselves aprons.

8 And they heard the voice of the LORD God walking in the garden in the cool of the day: and Adam and his wife hid themselves from the presence of the LORD God amongst the trees of the garden.

9 And the LORD God called unto Adam, and said unto him, Where art thou?

10 And he said, I heard thy voice in the garden, and I was afraid, because I was naked; and I hid myself.

11 And he said, Who told thee that thou wast naked? Hast thou eaten of the tree, whereof I commanded thee that thou shouldest not eat?

12 And the man said, The woman whom thou gavest to be with me, she gave me of the tree, and I did eat.

13 And the LORD God said unto the woman, What is this that thou hast done? And the woman said, The serpent beguiled me, and I did eat.

14 And the LORD God said unto the serpent, Because thou hast done this, thou art cursed above all cattle, and above every beast of the field; upon thy belly shalt thou go, and dust shalt thou eat all the days of thy life:

15 And I will put enmity between thee and the woman, and between thy seed and her seed; it shall bruise thy head, and thou shalt bruise his heel.

16 Unto the woman he said, I will greatly multiply thy sorrow and thy conception; in sorrow thou shalt bring forth children; and thy desire shall be to thy husband, and he shall rule over thee.

17 And unto Adam he said, Because thou hast hearkened unto the voice of thy wife, and hast eaten of the tree, of which I commanded thee, saying, Thou shalt not eat of it: cursed is the ground for thy sake; in sorrow shalt thou eat of it all the days of thy life;

18 Thorns also and thistles shall it bring forth to thee; and thou shalt eat the herb of the field;

19 In the sweat of thy face shalt thou eat bread, till thou return unto the ground; for out of it wast thou taken: for dust thou art, and unto dust shalt thou return.

20 And Adam called his wife's name Eve; because she was the mother of all living.

21 Unto Adam also and to his wife did the LORD God make coats of skins, and clothed them.

22 And the LORD God said, Behold, the man is become as one of us, to know good and evil: and now, lest he put forth his hand, and take also of the tree of life, and eat, and live for ever:

23 Therefore the LORD God sent him forth from the garden of Eden, to till the ground from whence he was taken.

24 So he drove out the man; and he placed at the east of the garden of Eden Cherubims, and a flaming sword which turned every way, to keep the way of the tree of life.

Jewish Midrash

There is a story concerning Adam's first wife that exists in a Jewish oral tradition known as midrash. The story goes that the first wife of Adam was created from the dust of the ground just as Adam had been and life was breathed into her nostrils. Her name was Lilith. Yahweh had created her for Adam when Adam could not find a helpmate among all the animals that Yahweh had made and paraded before him. Adam named the animals, but none worked as a mate so Yahweh created Lilith as his companion. Adam was very excited about his new companion and desired her greatly, but he was not really interested in conversation. Lilith questioned why she had to be on the bottom and when Adam didn't have an answer for her, she spoke one of the secret names of Yahweh and rose up off the ground and flew out of Eden. When Yahweh realized that Lilith had not worked out, he put Adam to sleep and removed one of his ribs to create Adam's second wife, Eve. After leaving Eden, Lilith met up with demons and bred up a race of demons to steal the seed and lives of the descendents of Adam. These demons were the succubi and incubi.

© Creative Lab/Shutterstock.com

Hebrew names and characters to know:

Yahweh
Adam
The serpent
Eve
Lilith

Greek Creation

The following is a condensed version of the Greek Creation that highlights the main story of the creation and the strife amongst the gods. It is based on Hesiod's *Theogony,* which was written around seven hundred BCE and includes a detailed family tree for the Greek gods, too detailed to go over in full here. I've omitted many of the side stories including the creation of the monsters.

In the beginning there was a void, the first deity to emerge from the Void was Gaia, Mother Earth. Also from the void came Darkness and Night, who beget Light and Day. Gaia continued creation by producing the features of the Earth, her sons: the sea, the mountains, and the heavens. Of her sons, she chose her son, Ouranos, the Heavens, as her mate. The Heavens lay on top of her and impregnated her with three Cyclopes, three Hecatonchires, and the twelve Titans. However, Ouranos was a tyrant and would not move off of Gaia so that she could give birth. In agony, she appealed to her children and asked for their help. Only the youngest of the Titans, Kronos, was willing to help her. Following Gaia's instructions, Kronos castrated his father, Ouranos, which caused his parents to separate creating space between the Earth and the Sky. After Kronos had castrated Ouranos, he cast his father's genitals into the Sea where a foam developed around them. Shortly thereafter, a beautiful goddess, Aphrodite, stepped out from the foam surrounding the genitals of Ouranos. "First she approached holy Cythera; then from there she came to sea-girt Cyprus. And out stepped a modest and beautiful goddess, and the grass began to grow all round beneath her slender feet. Gods and men call her Aphrodite because she was formed in foam,* and Cytherea, because she approached Cythera, and Cyprus-born, because she was born in wave-washed Cyprus, and 'genial',* because she appeared out of genitals. Eros and fair Desire attended her birth and accompanied her as she went to join the famliy of gods," (9).

After the separation of Heaven from Earth, Gaia was able to give birth to all of her eighteen children. As Ouranos was no longer fertile he could not rule the gods and Gaia was worn out from the birth of her children so the rulership of the gods passed to Kronos and his sister-wife, Rhea. It became a golden age for the Titans as

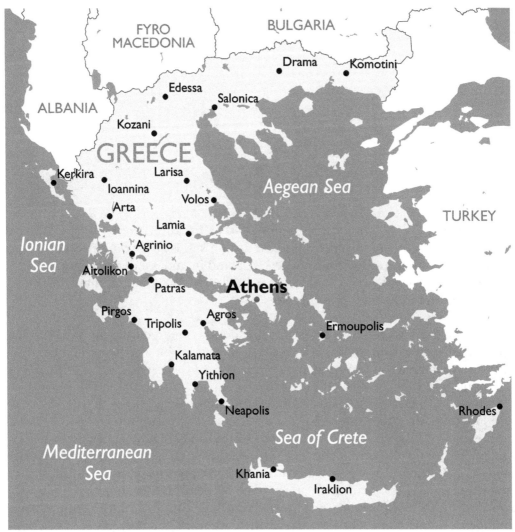

© lynx_v/Shutterstock.com

Kronos and his wife were of their number and treated the other Titans well. Many married and had children. However, the Cyclopes and Hecatonchires were cast into the underworld by Kronos.

The Titans included the river that wrapped around the edges of the world, Okeanos, and his sister-wife, Tethys, a water goddess. Together they had six thousand Okeanids, who made up many of the bodies of water on the earth. Three thousand were males and three thousand were females.

Hyperion, the first sun god, married Theia, the first moon goddess, and they had three children: Helios, Selene, and Eos. Helios took over the job of the Sun from his father and retained the job even after Apollo later joined him as a sun god. Selene took over for her mother, Theia, becoming the second moon goddess, which she later shared with Apollo's sister, Artemis. Eos, the third child, was the goddess of the dawn and had the job of pushing Helios' chariot into the sky each morning. Helios and Selene took over from their parents peacefully and there was never any struggle between them.

Mnemosyne, the goddess of memory, also a Titan, did not marry another Titan, but later became the lover of Zeus and the mother of the Nine Muses, the patron goddesses of the arts and sciences. The Titan, Themis, the goddess of justice, likewise, had offspring with Zeus, the Three Fates.

The other four titans were Kreios, Phoebe, Koios, and Iapetos. They too married and had children although little remains concerning their natures. They are, perhaps, more famous for their children. Iapetos united with Clymene, an Okeanid, and they had the famous children Atlas, Menoitios, Prometheus, and Epimetheus.

While the majority of the Titans enjoyed Kronos' reign as king of the gods, Rhea was not so happy. Kronos had received a prophecy from his parents that what he had done to his father, one of his children would do to him. Each time that Rhea gave birth to one of their children, Kronos swallowed it in order to prevent the prophecy. He swallowed Hades, Poseidon, Hestia, Demeter, and Hera. By the time Rhea was pregnant with their sixth child, she had had enough. "Rhea suffered terrible grief. But when she was about to give birth to Zeus, Father of gods and men, then she begged her dear parents, Earth and starry Heaven, to devise a plan so that she could bear her child in secrecy and make Kronos pay her father's furies* and those of the children he had been swallowing, great Kronos the crooked-scheming" (17). Gaia told Rhea to substitute a large rock wrapped in baby clothes and to have it handy for Kronos when he came to swallow the newborn child while the actual baby would be kept safe by Gaia, hidden away on the island of Krete until Zeus was strong enough to face his father. Rhea followed her mother's advice and gave baby Zeus to her mother, Gaia, who raised him in secrecy while Kronos received a rock wrapped in swaddling clothes, which he swallowed without even looking at it.

Zeus was raised by Gaia until he was old enough to face his father. He needed allies before he could confront Kronos. He went to the underworld and freed the Cyclopes and the Hecatonchires who supported him. Then he and Rhea, his mother, contrived to cause Kronos to throw up Zeus' siblings either with a potion or a feather down his throat. Kronos threw up Hades, Poseidon, Hestia, Hera, and Demeter as well as the large rock that had been wrapped in swaddling clothes. The large rock was placed at Delphi to mark the center of the world and became "a monument thereafter and a thing of wonder for mortal men," (18). Hades, Poseidon, Hestia, Demeter and Hera all sided with Zeus and a ten year war against Kronos and the majority of the Titans ensued called the War or Battle of the Titans (Titanomachy). The Cyclops made Zeus thunder bolts, which gave his side the upper hand and they won the battle against Kronos and the Titans. After the victory, any of the Titans who accepted Zeus and his siblings as the new rulers of the world were allowed to retain their positions. Any of the Titans who did not accept Zeus and his siblings, were cast into the underworld. Kronos, too, was locked in the underworld or put out on an island in the west where he remained.

Zeus and his brothers and sisters took up residence on top of Greece's highest mountain, Mt. Olympos, and were thereafter called the Olympians. After they took over as rulers of the world, Gaia woke and realized that some of her children were locked away in the underworld. In anger, she sent a race of Giants to attack the Olympians, (The Gigantomachy). This plot failed and the Olympians defeated the giants rather easily even though the war was said to last ten years. After the giants were defeated, Gaia was angered that they had been hurt and she sent a dragon, Typhon, to attack the Olympians. Zeus, with the aid of his siblings and sometimes others, managed to subdue the dragon by throwing a mountain on top of it. That mountain was Mt. Etna on Sicily.

Finally, after all the wars and conflict, the Olympians settled down to divvy up the world. The three males drew lots to determine who would rule what in the world. Hades drew the lot for the Underworld, Poseidon drew the lot for the Sea, and Zeus drew the lot for the Sky, which made him the King of the Gods. Zeus chose Hera as his wife, which made her Queen of the Gods. She was also in charge of marriage and morality. Demeter was goddess of grain and agriculture and the third sister, Hestia, a virgin goddess, was in charge of the home and the hearth. After the Olympians were settled, or possibly before all the wars began, they invited Aphrodite to join them on Mt. Olympos. She became the goddess of love, sex, and beauty, although she retained ties to the sea and to the islands that she first had come to after her birth, Cythera and Cyprus.

From these first Olympians came many other gods, but only the sons or daughters of Zeus were allowed to make their home on top of Mt. Olympos and number themselves among the Olympian pantheon. The rest of the Olympians included: Ares, god of bloodthirsty war, son of Zeus and Hera; Hephaestos, god of metallurgy, lame or club-footed, he was the butt of many jokes on Mt. Olympos, but he was also a skilled smith. He fashioned not only armor and weapons for the gods, but also beautiful works of art and delicate works of gold. He, too, was a son of Zeus and Hera, or some say just Hera.

Athena sprang from the head of Zeus after he swallowed his pregnant lover, Metis, fearing that her child would overthrow him. Athena was the goddess of war and wisdom and all women's household handicrafts, i.e., weaving. She was a virgin goddess and a great patron of heroes and warriors. She was her father's favorite and personified his wisdom. Artemis and Apollo were twins born to Leto, another of Zeus' lovers. Artemis was also a virgin goddess who preferred the wilderness and the hunt to more civilized pursuits. She was the patron of wild animals as well as the huntress of them and became associated with the moon (which she shared with Selene), and childbirth as she was born first to Leto and had helped her mother through her labor with Apollo. Apollo became the god of medicine, music, prophecy, and sunlight (which he shared with Helios). Next was Dionysos, born from Zeus' thigh after the death of his human mother, Semele, who died from the overwhelming glory of Zeus' revealed godhood. Zeus rescued the embryo of their son from her womb and placed it in his thigh. Dionysos was born from Zeus and was therefore a god. He was the potent god of the grapevine, grapes, and wine who led his followers into sweet intoxication and ecstasy while his detractors faced madness and even dismemberment. Those who followed him knew well the necessity of moderation, Greek wine was always blended with water to reduce its strength. The last of the Olympians was Hermes, the trickster, son of Zeus and a nymph named Maia. Hermes became the god of thieves and travelers, and the messenger of the gods because of his successful theft of his brother's cattle on the very day that Hermes had been born.

Many were the children of the gods. Many are the names of those who were created beyond those named here. There are some scholars who do not number Hades among the Olympians or the goddess Hestia. I, however, feel that it is hubris to omit either name from the list, which brings my Olympian count to fourteen instead of twelve.

ZEUS | JUPITER   GERA | JUNO   POSEIDON | NEPTUNE   HADES | PLUTO   DEMETER | CERES   APOLLO | PHOEBUS   NIKE | VICTORIA

HESTIA | VESTA   DIONYSUS | BACCHUS   THEMIS | JUSTISE   APHRODITE | VENUS   HEPHAESTUS | VULCAN   HEKATE | TRIVIA   ARES | MARS

ARTEMIS | DIANA   ATHENA | MINERVA   HYMENAIOS | HYMEN   HELIOS | SOL   EROS | CUPID   PERSEPHONE | PROSERPINA   HERMES | MERCURY   PAN | FAUNUS

Greek names and characters to know:

Gaia
Ouranos
Cyclops
Hecatonchires
Titans
Kronos
Rhea
Oceanos
Tethys
Hyperion
Theia
Helios
Selene
Eos
Mnemosyne
Themis
Hades
Poseidon
Hestia
Demeter
Hera
Zeus
Aphrodite
Ares
Hephaestos
Athena
Artemis
Apollo
Dionysos
Hermes

Japanese Creation Myth: Izanagi and Izanami

The Japanese creation myth dates to around seven hundred CE. There are various forms of this myth, but I have streamlined them and also cut down the names to make them easier to follow.

The gods on high came into existence and decide that they needed to get creation going on a more physical plane so they sent Izanagi and Izanami down to the cosmic sea on the heavenly bridge with the heavenly spear, which the two gods used to stir the sea. When they raised the spear from the waters, a tiny bit of land dropped off the tip and fell into the sea, becoming the first island of Japan. Izanagi and Izanami descended the bridge to the island, Onogra, and there they built a pillar dedicated to the heavens in the middle of the island. Afterward, they performed a ritual where they walked from opposite sides of the island toward the pillar. When they met at the middle by the pillar, they circled it and then Izanami, the goddess, spoke to Izanagi and said, "How pleasant it is to meet such a handsome youth here." Izanagi responded, "It is equally pleasant to meet such a lovely maiden." The two realized that they were shaped differently with different parts and decided to experiment. They made a child, but the child was limp, without any bones, like a leech. The couple called on the heavenly deities and asked what went wrong. The heavenly gods informed them that the reason for the misborn child was because the goddess had spoken first to the god. The couple determined to repeat the ritual but this time

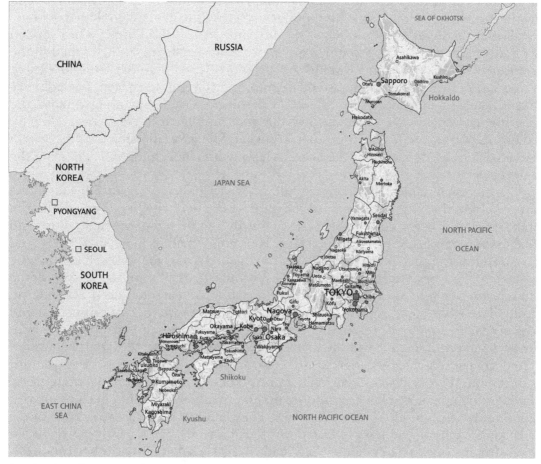

© Bardocz Peter/Shutterstock.com

Izanagi spoke first to Izanami. The result was that she gave birth to the islands of Japan, all the nature spirits/gods/goddesses. Eventually, in giving birth to the fire deity, she was scorched severely and died.

Izanagi was inconsolable. He was miserable without his wife and decided to retrieve her from the underworld. We went to the cave that had a deep tunnel into the underworld and began his descent. Eventually he was met by his wife, whom he recognized by her voice because she was covered in veils. She asked him why he had ventured into the land of the dead and he replied that he had come to retrieve her if he could. Izanami had to ask the lords of the underworld if she could leave but she made Izanagi promise that while she was busy he would not try to look upon her but wait for her return. Izanagi agreed. Unfortunately, he began to miss her so much that he snuck up on her and got a look at her face. He was horrified: she was a rotting corpse. Izanami was so angry that her husband had broken his word to her and had seen her in her unsightly condition that she chased him up out of the underworld, demons from the dark places accompanying her. Izanagi eluded the pursuit by casting peaches at his wife's feet, which she slowed to pick up. He made it to the exit from the underworld and sealed it shut so that his estranged wife and the demons could not get out.

Feeling polluted, Izanagi went to a river to bathe and purify himself. As he dropped his filthy garments on the ground, many more gods sprang up. As he bathed in the river, many other gods came from his purification. Three were the most important. From his left eye came Amaterasu-no-mikoto, the sun goddess. From his right eye came Tskuki-no-mikoto, the moon god. From his nose came Susano-no-mikoto, the storm god. Izanagi gave rulership over the gods and earth to Amaterasu. He gave rulership over the night to her brother Tskuki and he gave rulership over the seas to Susano. Then he departed for the heavens leaving his chief children in charge of the world below.

Amaterasu immediately set out to build up the civiliation of Japan. She taught the arts of civilization: the cultivation of the earth, irrigation, city building, administration, etc. Japan began to flourish. Susano was of a more tempermental nature and like to mess up whatever his sister created. He caused earth tremors, tidal waves, and harsh storms to ravage her work and destroy the crops and the towns. Each time he destroyed her work, Amaterasu began all over until she finally got so fed up with the destruction she gave up and she withdrew herself into a cave and drew a boulder in front of it so that she remained undisturbed. Amaterasu's withdrawal caused fear and consternation among the rest of the gods. They punished Susano, stripped him of his powers and sent him to live in the forest in exile until he repented of his behaviour. Then the gods decided the only way to entice Amaterasu from her cave and return sunshine to the world was to trick her to come out by throwing an elaborate party. They strung up colored lanterns and set up entertainment and they began to have a good time right outside Amaterasu's cave. They laughed and they sang, they drank sake and Uzume (a goddess associated with the dawn) danced a bawdy dance, lifting her skirts and opening her blouse. This made the gods laugh uproariously. Inside her cave, Amaterasu wondered how the gods could be having so much fun in the dark. Her curiosity grew and grew until she decided to peek around the boulder blocking the entrance to her cave to see if she could discern what was causing all the ruckus. When Amaterasu looked around the boulder she saw the most beautiful light, which increased her curiosity. All should be in darkness without her, but there was light, beautiful, glowing light!

Amaterasu moved the boulder further away from the entrance to her cave in order to obtain a better view. More glorious, glowing light met her gaze. Intrigued, Amaterasu moved the boulder completely away from the entrance of her cave and was immediately captivated by her appearance in the large mirror that the gods had placed just outside the entrance. Seeing her own radiance for the first time, Amaterasu realized that removing herself was a mistake. Greeted by the gods, she joyfully resumed her position amongst them. Susano was brought to her and apologized for the error of his ways. He promised to stop destroying what she created and as a token of the peace between them the two gods exchanged gifts. Amaterasu gave Susano a sword from which he had children. Susano gave Amaterasu a necklace from which she had children. It was determined that Amaterasu's children would rule the islands of Japan and Susano's children would be their subjects. To this day, the Emperor of Japan traces his lineage back to the goddess Amaterasu.

Japanese names and characters to know:

Izanagi
Izanami
Amaterasu
Tskuki
Susano
Uzume

Chinese Creation: Pan Gu and Nu Gua

In China there are two forces called yin and yang that are the foundation for the existence of all things. Together they form the Tao. Yin is what is dark, moist, feminine, earthy, passive, and is associated with the Earth, while yang is what is light, warm, masculine, bright, active, and is associated with the sun. These two forces are not completely in opposition as each contains a bit of the other in order to relate. Together the two forces give birth to all things. Yin gives rise to Yang, which gives rise to Yin, which gives rise to Yang. They are never really separate forces; each one needs

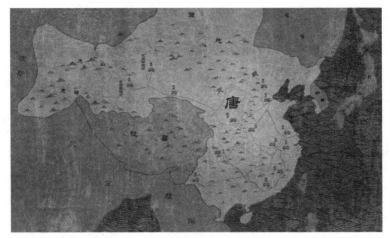

© Liu zishan/Shutterstock.com

Figure 2.2
© Olga A, 2010. Used under licence from Shutterstock,
Inc.

the other to exist. The Chinese creation myth of Pan Gu incorporates the idea of the these two forces into the tale establishing the existence of the opposites from the very beginning of the cosmos.

In the beginning there was a cosmic egg. Mixed together inside the cosmic egg were yin and yang. The light bright yang energy eventually filled up the top of the egg and the dark moist yin energy filled up the bottom of the egg. In the midst of yin and yang grew Pan Gu. Each day for eighteen thousand years, Pan Gu grew taller and taller until he cracked the egg. He continued to grow taller and taller until he had raised all the light bright yang energy up to form the heavens and pushed the dark moist yin energy down to make the earth. After separating Heaven and Earth, Pan Gu was worn out. His body collapsed to the earth and became all its features. His eyes became the sun and the moon. His breath became the wind and clouds and his sweat turned into the dew.

Humans were created a bit later by a goddess named Nu Gua. She is most often portrayed as having a woman's head on a snake's body. Nu Gua left the heavens and came down to earth where she felt something was missing. Inspired by her reflection, she created smaller versions of herself out of mud. After she had molded the creature, she placed it on the earth where it came to life joyfully. Inspired by her success, Nu Gua created many more people out of the mud, but soon realized that the job was too slow a process so changed her methods. The goddess used some vegetation dipped in mud to fling droplets off in every direction. All of the droplets of mud turned into people and Nu Gua's job of populating the earth was soon complete. All that remained was to teach the humans how to procreate and tend their offspring.

Chinese names and characters to know:

Pan Gu
Nu Gua

Indian Creation

There are many creation stories from India, but due to time and book size constraints, I have chosen to only include a small sampling of those myths here. The first myths come from the Rig Veda, one of the oldest scriptures in the world. It dates back to about two thousand BCE. The last myth is a further explanation of Puruṣa from the Indian Upanishads, which dates closer to the five hundreds BCE.

■ ■ ■

Rig Veda, translated by Ralph T. H. Griffith, 1896. Located on www.sacred-texts.com

© Vectomart/Shutterstock.com

HYMN XC. Puruṣa

1 A THOUSAND heads hath Puruṣa, a thousand eyes, a thousand feet. On every side pervading earth he fills a space ten fingers wide.

2 This Puruṣa is all that yet hath been and all that is to be; The Lord of Immortality which waxes greater still by food.

3 So mighty is his greatness; yea, greater than this is Puruṣa. All creatures are one-fourth of him, three-fourths eternal life in heaven.

4 With three-fourths Puruṣa went up: one-fourth of him again was here. Thence he strode out to every side over what eats not and what eats.

5 From him Virāj was born; again Puruṣa from Virāj was born. As soon as he was born he spread eastward and westward o'er the earth.

6 When Gods prepared the sacrifice with Puruṣa as their offering, Its oil was spring, the holy gift was autumn; summer was the wood.

7 They balmed as victim on the grass Puruṣa born in earliest time. With him the Deities and all Sādhyas and Ṛṣis sacrificed.

8 From that great general sacrifice the dripping fat was gathered up. He formed the creatures of the air, and animals both wild and tame.

9 From that great general sacrifice Ṛcas and Sāma-hymns were born: There from were spells and charms produced; the Yajus had its birth from it.

10 From it were horses born, from it all cattle with two rows of teeth: From it were generated kine, from it the goats and sheep were born.

11 When they divided Puruṣa how many portions did they make? What do they call his mouth, his arms? What do they call his thighs and feet?

12 The Brahman was his mouth, of both his arms was the Rājanya made. His thighs became the Vaiśya, from his feet the Sūdra was produced.

13 The Moon was gendered from his mind, and from his eye the Sun had birth; Indra and Agni from his mouth were born, and Vāyu from his breath.

14 Forth from his navel came mid-air the sky was fashioned from his head, Earth from his feet, and from his ear the regions. Thus they formed the worlds.

15 Seven fencing-sticks had he, thrice seven layers of fuel were prepared, When the Gods, offering sacrifice, bound, as their victim, Puruṣa.

16 Gods, sacrificing, sacrificed the victim, these were the earliest holy ordinances. The Mighty Ones attained the height of heaven, there where the Sādhyas, Gods of old, are dwelling.

■ ■ ■

Rig Veda, translated by Ralph T. H. Griffith, 1896. (from www.sacred-texts.com)

Figure 2.3
© Sverlova Mariya, 2010. Used under licence from Shutterstock, Inc.

HYMN CXXIX. Creation

THEN was not non-existent nor existent: there was no realm of air, no sky beyond it. What covered it, and where? and what gave shelter? Was water there, unfathomed depth of water?

Death was not then, nor was there aught immortal: no sign was there, the day's and night's divider. That One Thing, breathless, breathed by its own nature: apart from it was nothing whatsoever.

Darkness there was: at first concealed in darkness this All was indiscriminated chaos. All that existed then was void and form less: by the great power of Warmth was born that Unit.

Thereafter rose Desire in the beginning, Desire, the primal seed and germ of Spirit. Sages who searched with their heart's thought discovered the existent's kin-ship in the non-existent.

Transversely was their severing line extended: what was above it then, and what below it? There were begetters, there were mighty forces, free action here and energy up yonder

Who verily knows and who can here declare it, whence it was born and whence comes this creation? The Gods are later than this world's production. Who knows then whence it first came into being?

He, the first origin of this creation, whether he formed it all or did not form it, Whose eye controls this world in highest heaven, he verily knows it, or perhaps he knows not.

■ ■ ■

Rig Veda, translated by Ralph T. H. Griffith, 1896. Located on www.sacred-texts.com

HYMN CXC. Creation

1 FROM Fervour kindled to its height Eternal Law and Truth were born: Thence was the Night produced, and thence the billowy flood of sea arose.

2 From that same billowy flood of sea the Year was afterwards produced, Ordainer of the days nights, Lord over all who close the eye.

3 Dhātar, the great Creator, then formed in due order Sun and Moon. He formed in order Heaven and Earth, the regions of the air, and light.

■ ■ ■

The Upanishads, Part 2 (SBE15), by Max Müller, 1879. Located on www.sacred-texts.com

From the 4th Brahmana in the *Bradayanaka Upanishad* comes this story of Puruṣa

In the beginning Brahman took on the shape of a man and was called Puruṣa. Puruṣa thought "This is I" and therefore humans say "this is I," when speaking. Puruṣa was afraid after he became aware, but then he realized he was the only thing in existence and there was nothing to fear. After realizing that he was alone, Puruṣa became lonely. Puruṣa was large enough to split into two so he fell into two parts, a husband (pati) and wife (patni). Each was a half of the other and they were not alone. Husband and wife embraced and made children, humans.

After the husband and wife had made children, the wife was uncomfortable and thought to hide herself as a cow. Her husband, the male half of Puruṣa, turned into a bull and mated with her anyway and that is from where all the bovines come. The wife then turned herself into a mare, but her husband turned himself into a stallion and mated with her anyway. That is from where all the horses come. Next, she took the form of a female ass, but he took the form of the male ass and that is where solid hoofed animals came from. The two halves of Puruṣa progressed from goats to lambs all the way down to ants, the wife taking the female form to hide and her husband taking the male form and mating with her anyway leaving offspring behind in each form.

When all of creation had been created in this fashion, Puruṣa came back together as one entity and said, "I am all of this for I created all of this."

Indian names and characters to know:

Brahman
Puruṣa

Yoruba Creation, West Africa

This story comes from the Yoruba culture and explains the creation of Ife. There are many variants of the myth in which the objects and creatures that Obatala brings down from the heavens differ, but essentially they are the same.

In the beginning, there was water, sky, and marshy land near the water. The Supreme Being was Olorun and he ruled the heavens, while the goddess Olokun ruled everything below. Olorun gave permission to the god Obatala to create land that wasn't marshy that creatures could live on as well as all the various creatures. To cre-

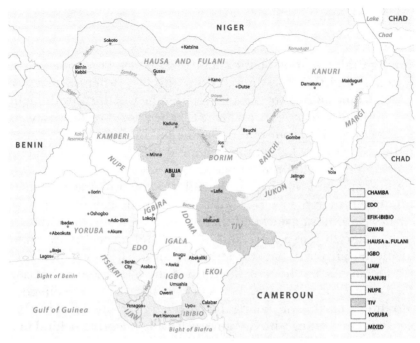

© Rainer Lesniewski/Shutterstock.com

ate the land and the creatures Obatala needed to take certain things with him down from the heavens to the waters below: a black cat, a white hen, a snail's shell full of sand, a palm nut, and a golden chain to suspend himself from the heavens. All of this was told to Obatala in a prophecy by Olorun's eldest son, Orunmila.

Obatala followed Orunmila's advice and descended the golden chain from the heavens carrying everything else in a bag. When Obatala reached the end of the chain, he was still above the waters, but Orunmila's words came to him and he sprinkled the sand from the snail's shell into the water where it formed a patch of earth, then he set down the white hen on the earth, which began to scratch at the earth spreading it far around. It gathered in heaps and made depressions, creating the hills and valleys of the earth. After the earth was formed, Obatala let loose of the chain and stood on the ground, which he named Ife, meaning wide.

After standing on the earth and naming the earth, Obatala planted the palm nut and it grew into a tree that dropped more palm nuts, which also grew into trees. After the trees grew, Obatala decided to entertain himself by making creatures from the clay of the earth. He formed many creatures, but he soon became distracted by the idea of making wine from the palm nuts. The wine tasted so good that he drank many bowls. While intoxicated, Obatala resumed the creation of creatures that were less than perfect due to his inebriation. After he sobered up, Obatala became the protector of all those who were not perfect and swore never to drink again. Under Obatala's protection, the people of Ife thrived.

The gods were pleased with Obatala's creations except for Olokun who was not pleased to lose so much of what lay below the heavens as her kingdom. In anger, she caused the ocean waves to smash into the earth and destroy much of what Obatala had created. The only way that people survived was by climbing the tallest mountains and praying to Eshu, the trickster god, to take news of their predicament up to the gods. Eshu agreed on condition that the humans sacrifice to him and to Obatala. The people did so and Eshu reported their troubles to the gods. Orunmila, Olorun's eldest son, came down from heaven on the golden chain and ended the flood by casting spells. The earth was restored and the people returned to the land.

African Yoruba names and characters to know:

Olorun
Olokun
Orunmila
Obatala
Eshu

Norse Creation

There are various versions of the Norse creation from the Eddas. I have chosen to follow Kevin Crossley-Holland's version from *The Norse Myths* because it is in plain language and easier to follow than some of the more poetic translations. The Eddas existed in oral tradition in Iceland and were not written down until somewhere between one thousand and thirteen hundred CE.

In the beginning there was ice and fire. The fire was in the south in a region called Muspell. The fires were so fierce that nothing endured them unless born to them. The fires will be used at the end of the world in the apocalypse.

The ice was in the north, in a region called Niflheim. In this snowy, cold, icy region there was a spring that was the source for eleven rivers.

In between Muspell and Niflheim lies Ginnungagap, an empty region that eventually filled with the frost and ice in the northern region, brought by the rivers out of Niflheim. The southern region was hot as it lay close to Muspell. In between north and south, Ginnungagap was comfortable, the ice there thawed and life began in the form of a frost giant named Ymir.

© Rainer Lesniewski/Shutterstock.com

As Ymir slept in the warming Ginnungagap, he began to sweat. His sweat turned into male and female frost giants. Even the sweat from his legs turned into more frost giants.

Along with Ymir, there was a cow, Audumla, which formed from the ice that melted in Ginnungagap. Audumla licked the ice and eventually a man (actually, a god) appeared named Buri. Buri had a son named Bor and Bor married Bestla, the daughter of Bolthor, a frost giant. Bor and Bestla had three children: Odin, Vili, and Ve.

The three sons of Bor and Bestla did not like Ymir. They killed him and used his body to fashion the world. The earth and its features were created from his flesh and bones. His blood became seas and lakes, his skull became the sky. From Muspell they took fire and raised it into the sky as the sun and the moon and the stars.

After the sun and moon and stars were created, the earth warmed and grew green. The three sons of Bor found two trees that had fallen and used their trunks to fashion the first man and woman. "Odin breathed into them the spirit of life; Vili offered them sharp wits and feeling hearts; and Ve gave them the gifts of hearing and sight. The man was called Ask and the woman Embla and they were given Midgard to live in. All the families and nations and races of men are descended from them" (Crossley-Holland, 5).

As creation continued, giants named Night and Day were born and Odin gave them the job of driving chariots through the sky to mark the days. Two humans, boldly named Sun and Moon, were removed from the earth and set to guide the chariots of the Sun and Moon across the sky.

From the maggots that crawled in Ymir's body, Odin, Vili, and Ve made dwarves who lived in the earth. They were shaped like men and had the same intellects, but remained mostly beneath the earth. The dwarves were skilled craftsmen and fashioned wondrous works, including Thor's famous hammer, Odin's spear, Sif's golden hair, and Freya's golden necklace.

The gods then built a home for themselves in the heavens, Asgard. From Asgard they created the rainbow bridge, Bifrost, to reach Midgard, middle earth, where men and dwarves lived. Odin ruled from Asgard and with him there were twelve main goddesses and twelve main gods as well as many other gods and goddesses.

Asgard lay among the roots of Yggdrasil, the cosmic world tree. Its trunk passed through Midgard and its branches ended in the underworld. Yggdrasil was the source of life, the world axis. It always existed and always will. Yggdrasil connects all nine realms in Norse mythology. It is the cosmic tree.

Note: Some versions place the tree right side up, in which case Asgard is among the branches of Yggdrasil and the underworld is located among the roots.

Norse names and characters to know:

Ymir
Audumla
Bor
Bestla
Odin
Vili
Ve
Asgard
Midgard
Yggdrasil

Cherokee Creation

Some myths consist of animals as the main characters and often in such cases it is an animal that is responsible for the beginnings of the world. These myths may take the form of Earth Diver myths where an animal or various animals dive into the primeval waters and return with a bit of mud or clay from which they can make the earth. The following myth comes from the Cherokee nation and was recorded by James Mooney from *Nineteenth Annual Report of the Bureau of American Ethnology 1897–98, Part I*, 1900 (located January-February, 2001 from www.sacred-texts.com).

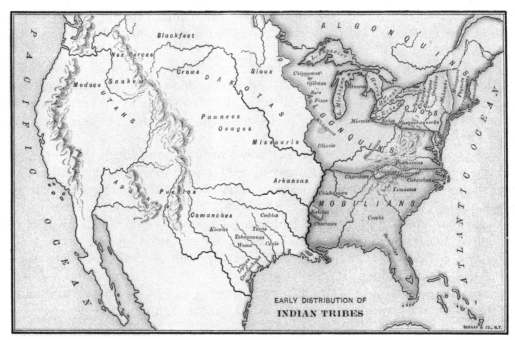

© North Wind Picture Archives/Alamy Stock Photo

1. How The World Was Made

The earth is a great island floating in a sea of water, and suspended at each of the four cardinal points by a cord hanging down from the sky vault, which is of solid rock. When the world grows old and worn out, the people will die and the cords will break and let the earth sink down into the ocean, and all will be water again. The Indians are afraid of this.

When all was water, the animals were above in Gälûñ′lätï, beyond the arch; but it was very much crowded, and they were wanting more room. They wondered what was below the water, and at last Dâyuni′sï, "Beaver's Grandchild," the little Water-beetle, offered to go and see if it could learn. It darted in every direction over the surface of the water, but could find no firm place to rest. Then it dived to the bottom and came up with some soft mud, which began to grow and spread on every side until it became the island which we call the earth. It was afterward fastened to the sky with four cords, but no one remembers who did this.

At first the earth was flat and very soft and wet. The animals were anxious to get down, and sent out different birds to see if it was yet dry, but they found no place to alight and came back again to Gälûñ′läti. At last it seemed to be time, and they sent out the Buzzard and told him to go and make ready for them. This was the Great Buzzard, the father of all the buzzards we see now. He flew all over the earth, low down near the ground, and it was still soft. When he reached the Cherokee country, he was very tired, and his wings began to flap and strike the ground, and wherever they struck the earth there was a valley, and where they turned up again there was a mountain. When the animals above saw this, they were afraid that the whole world would be mountains, so they called him back, but the Cherokee country remains full of mountains to this day.

When the earth was dry and the animals came down, it was still dark, so they got the sun and set it in a track to go every day across the island from east to west, just overhead. It was too hot this way, and Tsiska′gïlï′, the Red Crawfish, had his shell scorched a bright red, so that his meat was spoiled; and the Cherokee do not eat it. The conjurers put the sun another hand-breadth higher in the air, but it was still too hot. They raised it another time, and another, until it was seven handbreadths high and just under the sky arch. Then it was right, and they left it so. This is why the conjurers call the highest place Gûlkwâ′gine Di′gälûñ′lätiyûñ′, "the seventh height," because it is seven hand-breadths above the earth. Every day the sun goes along under this arch, and returns at night on the upper side to the starting place.

There is another world under this, and it is like ours in everything—animals, plants, and people—save that the seasons are different. The streams that come down from the mountains are the trails by which we reach this underworld, and the springs at their heads are the doorways by which we enter it, but to do this one must fast and, go to water and have one of the underground people for a guide. We know that the seasons in the underworld are different from ours, because the water in the springs is always warmer in winter and cooler in summer than the outer air.

When the animals and plants were first made—we do not know by whom—they were told to watch and keep awake for seven nights, just as young men now fast and keep awake when they pray to their medicine. They tried to do this, and nearly all were awake through the first night, but the next night several dropped off to sleep, and the third night others were asleep, and then others, until, on the seventh night, of all the animals only the owl, the panther, and one or two more were still awake. To these were given the power to see and to go about in the dark, and to make prey of the birds and animals which must sleep at night. Of the trees only the cedar, the pine, the spruce, the holly, and the laurel were awake to the end, and to them it was given to be always green and to be greatest for medicine, but to the others it was said: "Because you have not endured to the end you shall lose your hair every winter."

Men came after the animals and plants. At first there were only a brother and sister until he struck her with a fish and told her to multiply, and so it was. In seven days a child was born to her, and thereafter every seven days another, and they increased very fast until there was danger that the world could not keep them. Then it was made that a woman should have only one child in a year, and it has been so ever since.

Cherokee names and terms to know:

Gälûñ'läti
Dâyuni'sï, "Beaver's Grandchild," the little Water-beetle
Great Buzzard
Tsiska'gïlï', the Red Crawfish
Gûlkwâ'gine Di'gälûñ'lätiyûñ', "the seventh height"

Figure 2.4
© Andrei Marincas, 2010. Used under license from Shutterstock, Inc.

Study Questions for Chapter 2:
Creation: The Beginning of All Things

General Questions:

1. What are the most common types of Creation myths?
2. What elements are considered necessary for the birth of the cosmos to begin?
3. How does a creation myth express the idea of consciousness emerging from the unconscious?

Egyptian Creation: Heliopolis

1. Who was the primordial deity?
2. How did the primordial deity begin creation according to this myth?
3. Who were the first male and female pair in this myth and what were they in charge of?
4. Why wouldn't Geb and Nut separate?
5. Who were the offspring of Geb and Nut and what were they each in charge of?
6. What type of creation myth is this closest to? (see pages 6–7)

Egyptian Creation: Memphis

1. Who is the primordial deity according to this creation myth?
2. What was the first act of creation performed by the primordial deity?
3. How does this myth differ from the Heliopolitan creation?

Mesopotamian Creation

1. Who were the primordial couple according to this creation myth?
2. What was Mummu's role?
3. Why did Apsu want to attack all of their offspring?
4. What happened when Apsu faced Ea?
5. Who was the son of Ea? What did he look like?
6. How did Tiamat react to her husband's death?
7. Who defeated Tiamat? What was made from her body?
8. Why were humans made? How were they made?
9. What type of creation myth is this myth?

Hebrew Creation: Genesis Chapters 1–3

1. What existed in the beginning along with the Hebrew god?
2. How did this god create?
3. List the order of creation based on Genesis Chapter 1.
4. List the order of creation based on Genesis Chapter 2. What things differ?
5. What was the one thing forbidden to Adam in the Garden?
6. How were Adam, his wife, and the serpent punished after they did the one forbidden thing?
7. Why did the Hebrew god cast Adam and his newly named wife Eve out of the Garden at the very end of Chapter 3 of Genesis?
8. What type of creation myth is this myth?

Jewish Midrash: Lilith

1. Who is Lilith?
2. Why didn't Lilith work out as Adam's wife?

Greek Creation

1. Who was the first deity to emerge from the Void according to Hesiod?
2. Why did Gaia ask Kronos to castrate Ouranos?
3. Who was born from Ouranos' castrated genitals and the sea?
4. What did Kronos do to the Hecatonchires and the Cyclops?
5. What jobs did the following Titans have? Oceanos, Tethys, Hyperion, Theia, Helios, Selene, Eos, Mnemosyne, and Themis?
6. What prophecy did Gaia and Ouranos tell their son Kronos about his imminent children? What was Kronos' reaction to the prophecy?
7. How did Rhea protect her last child from Kronos?
8. How did Zeus defeat his father and the other Titans?
9. What other battles did Zeus and the Olympians have to fight before they could rule the cosmos?
10. What type of creation myths is this myth?

Japanese Creation

1. How did Izanagi and Izanami begin the creation process?
2. What ritual did they perform on the first island of Japan? What went wrong?
3. What happened when they repeated the ritual in its correct format?
4. Why did Izanami end up in the underworld?
5. Which gods were created from Izanagi's purification process after he returned from the underworld?
6. What type of creation myth is this myth?

Chinese Creation

1. What was the first thing in existence in the Chinese creation myth?
2. How did Pan Gu begin the creation process? How long did it take?
3. What happened to Pan Gu?
4. What did Nu Gua create and how did she create?
5. What type of creation myth is this myth?

Indian Creation

Hymn XC Puruṣa

1. How was Puruṣa responsible for creation according to this myth?
2. What was made from each of his body parts?
3. What type of creation myth is this myth?

Hymn CXXIX Creation

1. What existed in the beginning?
2. How were things created?

Hymn CXC Creation

1. In what order were things created in this myth?
2. Who was responsible for the creation?

The *Bhradayanaka Upanishad*

1. Who began creation according to this myth?
2. Who were pati and patni and what did they create?
3. Where is the divine located according to this myth?
4. What type of creation myth is this myth?

African Creation

1. Who began the creation and how?
2. Who completed the creation and how?
3. What type of creation myth is this myth?

Norse Creation

1. What two realms existed in the beginning?
2. What were the first two creatures in existence?
3. Who else was created?
4. What happened to Ymir?
5. How was the first human couple created?
6. Which three gods were the most responsible for creation? What all did they create?
7. What type of creation myth is this myth?

Cherokee Creation

1. Which animal was the first to investigate the waters and start the process of creation?
2. Which animal made the earth ready for the others to arrive?
3. What happened when the sun was first placed in the sky?
4. What rewards did the animals receive that stayed awake the longest?
5. What punishment did the animals receive that did not remain awake very long?
6. When were humans created? How did they increase in number at first?
7. What type of creation myth is this myth?

CHAPTER 3
FLOOD MYTHS

Introduction

While water is associated with life and birth there is also a destructive side to water. Too much water can drown farmland and make the soil too wet to produce life, yet even when water is destructive, it is still associated with birth. Even after a flood, new life emerges. Flood myths thus emphasize the connection between birth, death, and rebirth. There is no life without death, and no death without life.

Floods are like a cosmic cleansing; a way of washing out whatever is old, or outworn, or impure and leaving behind a cleansed surface or palate on which the gods or god may begin anew. In many ways, flood myths are re-creation myths. There is a return to the watery chaos of the beginning. The flood as it appears in a myth may be part of a natural cycle or it may be a punishment, justified or arbitrary. In either case, whatever is no longer needed is washed away; however, there is usually a survivor or several survivors whose job it is to repopulate the Earth after the flood.

The most common way to survive the flood is in a boat or some kind of floating object like a hollow gourd or even a barrel. The most common place for the boat to end up is on the side of a mountain, which often becomes a holy mountain. As the flood destroys not only human life, but also animals and plants, sometimes these will be included on the boat and other times it will be up to the survivors to find a way to recreate the animals and plants, as well as the humans, after the flood.

As you read the following flood myths, ask yourself the following questions. What do the methods used by the particular cultures suggest about them? Is the flood a punishment? If so, why? If not, why does it occur? How do the gods preserve humans? How do they preserve the animals?

Mesopotamian Flood

The earliest account of the Flood myth in Mesopotamia comes from ancient Sumer around three thousand BCE and features the survivor Ziuzudra. However, not enough of the myth remains intact to tell the story in full. A later version appeared in the *Epic of Gilgamesh* from the Babylonians around fifteen hundred BCE and was much better preserved. Here we see the usual motifs of a survivor, a boat, and a sacred mountain plus a few other items perhaps more familiar from later flood myths. See if you can pick them out.

The Mesopotamian gods became aggravated by the amount of noise that humans were making down on the earth. No longer able to sleep due to the racket, Enlil angrily approached the council of the gods demanding that they wipe out the humans with a flood. The other gods agreed except for Ea, the god of wisdom, who had an oath with the human Utnapishtim, whom he warned about the flood in a dream.

Ea told Utnapishtim to sell all his worldly possessions and build a boat in which he would take his family and two of every animal in preparation for the flood that was coming in seven days time. When Utnapishtim asked what to say if his neighbors question his strange behavior, Ea told him to say that he had angered one of the gods and was moving to a new city to avoid the god's wrath.

When the work on the boat was completed to the specifications given by Ea in Utnapishtim's dream, Utnapishtim loaded up the boat with his family, the animals, and all the craftsmen who had worked on the boat.

"The same evening, the louring clouds—those princes of darkness—sent a prodigious rain, and a storm blew up. I appointed a helmsman, and committed the craft to the waters. In the gray of the morning, a dense black cloud suddenly rolled up from the horizon, and all the gods began to let loose. Came Adad with his escorts and thundered; came Nergal and wrenched off the anchor; came Ninurta, bringing woe and disaster; came the Annunaki, flashing their lightning torches. Everything then turned black; you could not even see your neighbor. Even the gods in heaven were scared" (Gaster, 83–84).

Soon the rains began. The gods of the storm and sea released all the waters and they raged back and forth for six days and six nights. The water rose so high that not only was every living thing not in the boat drowned, even the gods themselves became worried by the high rising waters and fled to the highest heaven. Ishtar, the Queen of Heaven, bemoaned the day that the gods had agreed on such a dire event as a flood and swore by her necklace of many colored stones, especially lapis lazuli, that she would not forget these days.

As the waters stilled, Utnapishtim's boat came to rest on the side of a mountain, Mt. Nisir. There it remained fast. Utnapishtim sent out a dove to see if the water had receded but the dove came back to the boat. Next, he sent out a swallow, which also returned. Finally, he sent out a raven and the raven finding the world restored, flew away and did not return. Then Utnapishtim knew it was safe to leave the boat.

Immediately upon disembarking, Utnapishtim built an altar to the gods and made a sacrifice to them. The gods gathered around the sacrifice drinking in its sweet smell. As they gathered there like flies to honey, Enlil stormed up, angry that some humans had survived the flood. However, after it was made clear to Enlil that the survivors were making sacrifices, something all the gods desired, Enlil softened in his attitude toward them and in fact rewarded Utnapishtim and his wife with immortality and placed them at the mouth of the rivers, a place not quite of the mortal world, nor of the gods.

■ ■ ■

Gaster, Theodor H. *Myth, Legend, and Custom in the Old Testament.* New York: Harper & Row, 1969.

Names and characters to know:

Enlil
Ea
Utnapishtim
Mt. Nisir
Ishtar

Hebrew Flood

The Hebrew flood is found in the Hebrew Tanakh and was borrowed by the Christians and included in their Old Testament. It is very similar to the Mesopotamian story although several key things differ. The Hebrews were for a time held in Babylon (approx. 580–520 BCE) as captives, and some borrowing may have occurred between the two cultures. The version included here is from the old Testament in the King James Version of the Bible.

King James Version: Genesis Chapter 6

1 And it came to pass, when men began to multiply on the face of the earth, and daughters were born unto them,

2 That the sons of God saw the daughters of men that they were fair; and they took them wives of all which they chose.

Figure 3.1
© joyart/Shutterstock.com

3 And the LORD said, My spirit shall not always strive with man, for that he also is flesh: yet his days shall be an hundred and twenty years.

4 There were giants in the earth in those days; and also after that, when the sons of God came in unto the daughters of men, and they bare children to them, the same became mighty men which were of old, men of renown.

5 And God saw that the wickedness of man was great in the earth, and that every imagination of the thoughts of his heart was only evil continually.

6 And it repented the LORD that he had made man on the earth, and it grieved him at his heart.

7 And the LORD said, I will destroy man whom I have created from the face of the earth; both man, and beast, and the creeping thing, and the fowls of the air; for it repenteth me that I have made them.

8 But Noah found grace in the eyes of the LORD.

9 These are the generations of Noah: Noah was a just man and perfect in his generations, and Noah walked with God.

10 And Noah begat three sons, Shem, Ham, and Japheth.

11 The earth also was corrupt before God, and the earth was filled with violence.

12 And God looked upon the earth, and, behold, it was corrupt; for all flesh had corrupted his way upon the earth.

13 And God said unto Noah, The end of all flesh is come before me; for the earth is filled with violence through them; and, behold, I will destroy them with the earth.

14 Make thee an ark of gopher wood; rooms shalt thou make in the ark, and shalt pitch it within and without with pitch.

15 And this is the fashion which thou shalt make it of: The length of the ark shall be three hundred cubits, the breadth of it fifty cubits, and the height of it thirty cubits.

16 A window shalt thou make to the ark, and in a cubit shalt thou finish it above; and the door of the ark shalt thou set in the side thereof; with lower, second, and third stories shalt thou make it.

17 And, behold, I, even I, do bring a flood of waters upon the earth, to destroy all flesh, wherein is the breath of life, from under heaven; and every thing that is in the earth shall die.

18 But with thee will I establish my covenant; and thou shalt come into the ark, thou, and thy sons, and thy wife, and thy sons' wives with thee.

19 And of every living thing of all flesh, two of every sort shalt thou bring into the ark, to keep them alive with thee; they shall be male and female.

20 Of fowls after their kind, and of cattle after their kind, of every creeping thing of the earth after his kind, two of every sort shall come unto thee, to keep them alive.

21 And take thou unto thee of all food that is eaten, and thou shalt gather it to thee; and it shall be for food for thee, and for them.

22 Thus did Noah; according to all that God commanded him, so did he.

King James Version: Genesis Chapter 7

1 And the LORD said unto Noah, Come thou and all thy house into the ark; for thee have I seen righteous before me in this generation.

2 Of every clean beast thou shalt take to thee by sevens, the male and his female: and of beasts that are not clean by two, the male and his female.

3 Of fowls also of the air by sevens, the male and the female; to keep seed alive upon the face of all the earth.

4 For yet seven days, and I will cause it to rain upon the earth forty days and forty nights; and every living substance that I have made will I destroy from off the face of the earth.

5 And Noah did according unto all that the LORD commanded him.

6 And Noah was six hundred years old when the flood of waters was upon the earth.

7 And Noah went in, and his sons, and his wife, and his sons' wives with him, into the ark, because of the waters of the flood.

8 Of clean beasts, and of beasts that are not clean, and of fowls, and of every thing that creepeth upon the earth,

9 There went in two and two unto Noah into the ark, the male and the female, as God had commanded Noah.

10 And it came to pass after seven days, that the waters of the flood were upon the earth.

11 In the six hundredth year of Noah's life, in the second month, the seventeenth day of the month, the same day were all the fountains of the great deep broken up, and the windows of heaven were opened.

12 And the rain was upon the earth forty days and forty nights.

13 In the selfsame day entered Noah, and Shem, and Ham, and Japheth, the sons of Noah, and Noah's wife, and the three wives of his sons with them, into the ark;

14 They, and every beast after his kind, and all the cattle after their kind, and every creeping thing that creepeth upon the earth after his kind, and every fowl after his kind, every bird of every sort.

15 And they went in unto Noah into the ark, two and two of all flesh, wherein is the breath of life.

16 And they that went in, went in male and female of all flesh, as God had commanded him: and the LORD shut him in.

17 And the flood was forty days upon the earth; and the waters increased, and bare up the ark, and it was lift up above the earth.

18 And the waters prevailed, and were increased greatly upon the earth; and the ark went upon the face of the waters.

19 And the waters prevailed exceedingly upon the earth; and all the high hills, that were under the whole heaven, were covered.

20 Fifteen cubits upward did the waters prevail; and the mountains were covered.

21 And all flesh died that moved upon the earth, both of fowl, and of cattle, and of beast, and of every creeping thing that creepeth upon the earth, and every man:

22 All in whose nostrils was the breath of life, of all that was in the dry land, died.

23 And every living substance was destroyed which was upon the face of the ground, both man, and cattle, and the creeping things, and the fowl of the heaven; and they were destroyed from the earth: and Noah only remained alive, and they that were with him in the ark.

24 And the waters prevailed upon the earth an hundred and fifty days.

King James Version: Genesis Chapter 8

1 And God remembered Noah, and every living thing, and all the cattle that was with him in the ark: and God made a wind to pass over the earth, and the waters assuaged;

2 The fountains also of the deep and the windows of heaven were stopped, and the rain from heaven was restrained;

3 And the waters returned from off the earth continually: and after the end of the hundred and fifty days the waters were abated.

4 And the ark rested in the seventh month, on the seventeenth day of the month, upon the mountains of Ararat.

5 And the waters decreased continually until the tenth month: in the tenth month, on the first day of the month, were the tops of the mountains seen.

6 And it came to pass at the end of forty days, that Noah opened the window of the ark which he had made:

7 And he sent forth a raven, which went forth to and fro, until the waters were dried up from off the earth.

8 Also he sent forth a dove from him, to see if the waters were abated from off the face of the ground;

9 But the dove found no rest for the sole of her foot, and she returned unto him into the ark, for the waters were on the face of the whole earth: then he put forth his hand, and took her, and pulled her in unto him into the ark.

10 And he stayed yet other seven days; and again he sent forth the dove out of the ark;

11 And the dove came in to him in the evening; and, lo, in her mouth was an olive leaf pluckt off: so Noah knew that the waters were abated from off the earth.

12 And he stayed yet other seven days; and sent forth the dove; which returned not again unto him any more.

13 And it came to pass in the six hundredth and first year, in the first month, the first day of the month, the waters were dried up from off the earth: and Noah removed the covering of the ark, and looked, and, behold, the face of the ground was dry.

14 And in the second month, on the seven and twentieth day of the month, was the earth dried.

15 And God spake unto Noah, saying,

16 Go forth of the ark, thou, and thy wife, and thy sons, and thy sons' wives with thee.

17 Bring forth with thee every living thing that is with thee, of all flesh, both of fowl, and of cattle, and of every creeping thing that creepeth upon the earth; that they may breed abundantly in the earth, and be fruitful, and multiply upon the earth.

18 And Noah went forth, and his sons, and his wife, and his sons' wives with him:

19 Every beast, every creeping thing, and every fowl, and whatsoever creepeth upon the earth, after their kinds, went forth out of the ark.

20 And Noah builded an altar unto the LORD; and took of every clean beast, and of every clean fowl, and offered burnt offerings on the altar.

21 And the LORD smelled a sweet savour; and the LORD said in his heart, I will not again curse the ground any more for man's sake; for the imagination of man's heart is evil from his youth; neither will I again smite any more every thing living, as I have done.

22 While the earth remaineth, seedtime and harvest, and cold and heat, and summer and winter, and day and night shall not cease.

King James Version: Genesis Chapter 9

1 And God blessed Noah and his sons, and said unto them, Be fruitful, and multiply, and replenish the earth.

2 And the fear of you and the dread of you shall be upon every beast of the earth, and upon every fowl of the air, upon all that moveth upon the earth, and upon all the fishes of the sea; into your hand are they delivered.

3 Every moving thing that liveth shall be meat for you; even as the green herb have I given you all things.

4 But flesh with the life thereof, which is the blood thereof, shall ye not eat.

5 And surely your blood of your lives will I require; at the hand of every beast will I require it, and at the hand of man; at the hand of every man's brother will I require the life of man.

6 Whoso sheddeth man's blood, by man shall his blood be shed: for in the image of God made he man.

7 And you, be ye fruitful, and multiply; bring forth abundantly in the earth, and multiply therein.

8 And God spake unto Noah, and to his sons with him, saying,

9 And I, behold, I establish my covenant with you, and with your seed after you;

10 And with every living creature that is with you, of the fowl, of the cattle, and of every beast of the earth with you; from all that go out of the ark, to every beast of the earth.

11 And I will establish my covenant with you, neither shall all flesh be cut off any more by the waters of a flood; neither shall there any more be a flood to destroy the earth.

12 And God said, This is the token of the covenant which I make between me and you and every living creature that is with you, for perpetual generations:

13 I do set my bow in the cloud, and it shall be for a token of a covenant between me and the earth.

14 And it shall come to pass, when I bring a cloud over the earth, that the bow shall be seen in the cloud:

15 And I will remember my covenant, which is between me and you and every living creature of all flesh; and the waters shall no more become a flood to destroy all flesh.

16 And the bow shall be in the cloud; and I will look upon it, that I may remember the everlasting covenant between God and every living creature of all flesh that is upon the earth.

17 And God said unto Noah, This is the token of the covenant, which I have established between me and all flesh that is upon the earth.

18 And the sons of Noah, that went forth of the ark, were Shem, and Ham, and Japheth: and Ham is the father of Canaan.

19 These are the three sons of Noah: and of them was the whole earth overspread.

20 And Noah began to be an husbandman, and he planted a vineyard:

21 And he drank of the wine, and was drunken; and he was uncovered within his tent.

22 And Ham, the father of Canaan, saw the nakedness of his father, and told his two brethren without.

23 And Shem and Japheth took a garment, and laid it upon both their shoulders, and went backward, and covered the nakedness of their father; and their faces were backward, and they saw not their father's nakedness.

24 And Noah awoke from his wine, and knew what his younger son had done unto him.

25 And he said, Cursed be Canaan; a servant of servants shall he be unto his brethren.

26 And he said, Blessed be the LORD God of Shem; and Canaan shall be his servant.

27 God shall enlarge Japheth, and he shall dwell in the tents of Shem; and Canaan shall be his servant.

28 And Noah lived after the flood three hundred and fifty years.

29 And all the days of Noah were nine hundred and fifty years: and he died.

▨ ▨ ▨

Located on www.sacred-texts.com

Names and characters to know:

Hebrew God: Yahweh
Noah
Mt. Ararat

Greek Flood

There are many variations of the flood story from Greece. One of the most familiar versions is from the first century BCE-CE Roman poet, Ovid; however, it is a Roman adaptation and full of humor. Ovid was having a good time writing the story and probably did not believe in the events he was retelling. There are older Greek versions from various poets dating back into the fifth century BCE that remain in bits and pieces. Depending on when and where the story came from, the situations changed, the mountains that the boat landed on changed, and the reasons for the flood changed. Deucalion and Pyrrha's story remained one of the most popular versions of the Greek flood myth.

Figure 3.2
© Mark R, 2010. Used under license from Shutterstock, Inc.

Zeus came down to earth to visit among mortal men. When he visited the king, Lykaon, he was disgusted by the king's ignoble behavior. Lykaon wished to test Zeus' omniscience so he had a human killed and cooked to feed to the god. Zeus was so insulted by the barbaric act that he made the palace collapse and turned Lykaon into a werewolf to feed on human flesh. Then he stormed back up to Mt. Olympos where he convened the council of the gods. When he told the other Olympians of his experience on Earth he said that humans ought to be destroyed if Lykaon, who was a king and supposedly therefore more noble than the average person, could act so cruelly, surely the average person was even worse. The rest of the gods agreed that the humans had become wicked. Zeus decided to destroy them and first reached for his lightning bolts, but halted after remembering a prophecy that the world would end in fire. Upon remembering this prophecy, he put away his bolts and instead decided to use water to wipe out mankind. With the assistance of Poseidon, Zeus unleashed a massive flood.

According to the Roman poet Ovid, the sea life, particularly the dolphins and the sea nymphs, enjoyed the flood tremendously and were amazed to float above the once proud oak trees, farmlands and vineyards.

The only survivors of the flood were Deucalion, the son of Prometheus, and his wife, Pyrrha, the daughter of Epimetheus. The two survived the flood in a boat or a chest, loaded with supplies, and, according to Gaster, after "nine days and as many nights" (85) landed on the side of Mt. Parnassus. There, depending on the version, several different things may have happened. The couple may have made offerings to Zeus who blessed them with a gift. Deucalion chose to recreate humans by throwing rocks. In a different version, the place where they land in their boat was the location of the oracle of Themis. The world was covered with sludge from the aftermath of the flood and the couple did not know what they should do. Deucalion suggested that they visit Themis' oracle. The oracle told them to cover their heads and loosen their belts and throw the bones of Mother Earth behind them. After puzzling out the riddle, the couple complied. The stones that Deucalion threw behind him became men and those that Pyrrha threw became women. Thus humans were hard like stone.

The newly created humans set about tilling the earth and planting the fields. As they began to plough the fields they discovered something wondrous: the mixture of the damp earth and the heat from the sun caused new life to form under the surface of the earth. As the farmers ploughed furrows into Mother Earth they exposed the newly formed creatures, some only partially formed and others ready to emerge from the soil. Thus was the earth repopulated with animals and humans.

■ ■ ■

Gaster, Theodor H. *Myth, Legend, and Custom in the Old Testament.* New York: Harper & Row, 1969.

Names and characters to know:

Zeus
Poseidon
Deucalion
Pyrrha
Themis

Indian Flood

There are many variants of the Indian flood story from the various regions of Indian. In many versions it is Manu, the first human, who is saved by a fish that has the ability to grow very large. In some versions the human is unnamed but referred to as a *rishi* or *great sage.* Manu is mentioned in the Vedas (2,000–1,700 BCE) and elaborated on in the epic poem, the *Mahábhárata,* which dates to 200 BCE–200 CE. The first excerpt is from the Vedas, and the second excerpt is from the Mahabharata.

© PremiumStock/Shutterstock.com

Manu performed great yoga and eventually reached mokshan enlightenment. After reaching moksha and obtaining oneness with all things, the gods granted Manu any one thing that he asked. Manu's request was to save all things when the world was destroyed at the end of the age. It happened that one day as he was ritually washing, a fish fell into his hands. The fish, which was rather small, had the ability to grow as large as whatever container it was in and it asked Manu to save it. In return the fish warned Manu of the upcoming flood and told him to have a boat prepared in which he could load all living things. Manu did as the fish advised. When the flood waters came, Manu was ready in his boat with the animals and plants and the fish came to pull his boat to safety by having Manu tie it to the horn of the fish. The fish was so large it took up much of the occan and the rope that Manu used to tie his boat to the fish's horn was the cosmic serpent Shesh or Ananta. The fish, in actuality, was one of the gods, either Brahma or Vishnu, who came down to preserve man and all living things.

In the *Mahábhárata* the sage Markandeya refers to Manu as the great Rishi, who was equal unto Brahma in glory. He had practised rigid austerities in a forest for ten thousand years, standing on one leg with uplifted hand. One day while he brooded in wet clothes, a fish rose from a stream and asked for his protection against the greater fish that desired to swallow it, at the same time promising to reward him. Manu placed the fish in an earthen jar and tended it carefully until it increased in size then he put it in a tank. The fish continued to grow until the tank became small for it, and Manu heard it pleading to be transferred to the Ganges, "the favourite spouse of Ocean". He carried it to the river, and in time the fish spoke to him, saying: "I cannot move about in the river on account of my great length and bulk. Take me quickly to the Ocean." Manu was enabled to carry the fish from the Ganges to the sea, and then it spoke with a smile and said:

> "Know thou, O worshipful one, my protector, that the dissolution of the Universe is at hand. The time is ripe for purging the world. I will therefore advise thee what thou shouldst do, so that it may be well with thee. Build a strong and massive ark, and furnish it with a long rope; thou wilt ascend in it with the seven Rishis (the Celestial Rishis), and take with thee all the different seeds enumerated by Brahmans in days of yore, and preserve them carefully. Wait for me and I will appear as a horned animal. Act according to my instructions, for without mine aid thou canst not save thyself from the terrible deluge."

Manu gathered together all the different seeds and "set sail in an excellent vessel on the surging sea." He thought of the fish, and it arose out of the waters like an island; he cast a noose, which he fastened to the horns on its head, and the fish towed the ark over the roaring sea; tossed by the billows the vessel reeled about like one who was drunk. No land was in sight. "There was water everywhere, and the waters covered the heaven and the firmament also . . . . When the world was thus flooded none but Manu, the seven Rishis, and the fish could be seen."

After many long years the vessel was towed to the highest peak of the Himavat, which is still called Naubandhana (the harbour), and it was made fast there. The fish then spoke and said: "I am Brahma, the Lord of all Creatures; there is none greater than me. I have saved thee from this cataclysm. Manu will create again all beings—gods, Asuras, and men, and all those divisions of creation which have the power of locomotion and which have it not. By practising severe austerities he will acquire this power . . . ."

Then Manu set about creating all beings in proper and exact order.

■ ■ ■

Chapter VIII Divinities of the Epic Period from *Indian Myth and Legend* by Donald A. Mackenzie [1913]. Located on www.sacred-texts.com

Names and characters to know:

Manu
Ghasha fish
Brahma
Vishnu

Chinese Flood

There are many different flood stories from China. Here is one from Sui, southern Guizhou, China, along the Long and Duliu rivers:

© dedek/Shutterstock.com

There once was an old man and his wife who lived a meager life at the base of Mt. Sun. The old man, Xiang, purposefully startled an eagle that was carrying a little snake, which caused the eagle to drop the snake. The snake promptly disappeared. Xiang thought no more of it until he and his wife shared the same dream in which a golden dragon thanked Xiang for rescuing his daughter, the little red snake, and invited Xiang to meet him at his home. Husband and wife agreed and traveled across the difficult mountains until they were met by a lovely young lady who thanked Xiang for rescuing her from the eagle when she had been distracted by the rainbow.

The dragon's daughter invited the old couple to live on the slope of the mountain in a beautiful spot with a lovely pond full of delicious fish close to hand. The location was so ideal that the old couple became more youthful as they dwelled there and ate of the fish from the pond. Eventually, Xiang invited his former neighbors to live with him and his wife in the lovely spot. All went well for many years until one man became greedy and over fished the pond and eventually killed off all the fish.

Xiang was able to save one fish and in turn the fish told Xiang to build a wooden house. Everyone in the village followed suit except the greedy man who lived in a stone house. Eighty-one days passed and a terrible storm arose. Everyone who lived in wooden houses was okay because the wooden houses floated and survived the deluge that resulted from the heavy storm. However, the greedy man in his stone house did not survive. His demise was further ensured when the golden dragon caused the top part of Sun Mountain to collapse. The falling rocks buried the greedy man. All the villagers in their wooden houses floated until the flood receded. When the flood was over they created a statue of a giant, stone fish, which still stands to this day as a reminder of the flood.

■ ■ ■

Paraphrased from Miller, Lucien (ed). *South of the Clouds: Tales from Yunnan.* Seattle: University of Washington Press, 1994.

Names and characters to know:

Xiang
Xiang's wife
Red snake
Golden Dragon
Greedy man

Huichol Flood, Western Mexico

Here is a story from western Mexico with some other interesting variations on the standard motifs of a survivor who survives in a boat.

Grandmother Nakawe, the earth goddess, warned a man to forget clearing his fields because a flood was coming in five days. She told him to prepare a fig tree box and place in it corn kernels and every color bean, fire and fuel for the fire, and a female black dog. After the man had prepared all the things that she had told him, he climbed into the box and Grandmother Nakawe sealed him in so that the box would float during the flood. She kept watch over the man by sitting on top of the box as it floated on the surface of the flood. The man floated for five years in his box, going in all the cardinal directions. Eventually, his box landed on the side of a mountain.

After the box landed, the world was still covered in water, but the water was drained when various birds shifted the earth by removing mountains and making valleys into which the flood waters drained.

The man set up home in a cave with the female dog. During the day he began to cultivate the land and in the evening he would return home to find food ready for him. Growing suspicious, the man watched one day and found out that the female dog removed her fur and transformed into a human woman during the day. He cast her fur into a fire and bathed her in a special water and she stayed in human form. Together they created offspring and the earth was once again populated.

■ ■ ■

Gaster, Theodor H. *Myth, Legend, and Custom in the Old Testament,* Harper & Row: New York, 1969: 122–123.

Names and characters to know:

The man
Grandmother Nakawe
The female dog

Lithuanian Flood

Here, in this myth from Lithuania, we see some of the traditional motifs but with a slightly different twist.

The great god, Pramzinas, disgusted by the wickedness of a warring world, sent giants in the form of Wind and Water to destroy the world. For twenty days and nights the two giants, Wandu and Wejas, did their work with zeal. The world was covered in water and only a few creatures survived by climbing to the top of the tallest mountain. Pramzinas checked on the progress of the giants by looking out his heavenly window toward the earth. All he saw was water. It happened that when the great god looked out his window he was shelling nuts to eat. He tossed the shells onto the world below. The fall of the nutshells was a timely act, for the animals and humans on top of the mountain were able to climb aboard one such shell and ride out the remainder of the flood, until land reemerged. After Pramzinas was satisfied that the Earth was cleansed he stopped the flood and the waters receded. The animals and humans in the nutshell disembarked and went separate ways in order to repopulate the Earth. One couple who was elderly, remained in Lithuania. They were exhausted both physically and emotionally from the ordeal of the flood and too elderly to reproduce. "So to comfort them God sent the rainbow, which advised them to jump over the bones of the earth nine times . . ." (Gaster, 93). Each time the couple jumped over the bones of the earth, another couple sprang from the ground. Nine couples were created this way.

■ ■ ■

Paraphrased from Gaster, Theodor. *Myth, Legend, and Custom in the Old Testament. Vol. 1.* New York: Harper & Row, 1969.

Names and characters to know:

Pramzina
Wandu
Wejas

Maori (New Zealand)

Years ago, humans forgot to honor the creator, Tane, abandoned his teachings, ignored his prophets or made fun of them, and fought each other. Two of the prophets constructed a floating house on a raft and gathered dogs, sweet potatoes, and fern root on it. They prayed that Tane would demonstrate his powers to those who had mocked them and show them the error of their ways.

Two men and several women boarded the raft. One of the men acted as a priest and conducted the prayers for the rain to begin and end. The rains came when he prayed and stopped when he prayed for them to stop. This lasted four or five days. The waters rose and bore the raft down to the sea. The raft floated for many months. Eventually it landed at Hawaiki. The humans on the raft were the only humans that remained and they promptly worshipped the gods by building them each altars and giving thanks to the gods for their survival. The sites where they built these first altars to the gods after the end of the flood remained holy spots and are visited only by the chief priest.

■ ■ ■

Paraphrased from Gaster, Theodor H. *Myth, Legend, and Custom in the Old Testament: A Comparative Study with Chapters from Sir James G. Fraser's Folklore in the Old Testament.* Harper & Row: New York, 1969. (Most of the flood stories in this work are taken from Frazer, 1919.)

Names and characters to know:

Tane

Native American Flood from the Skokomish in Washington

Life on earth became wicked so the Great Spirit decided to wipe it out with a flood except for the good animals and one good man and his family. The man was instructed by the Great Spirit to shoot many arrows into a cloud so that they would form a rope or ladder. All the good people and animals were able to climb up the arrow rope but none of the bad ones were because the good man broke the rope behind the good animals.

After the good people had climbed up the rope, the Great Spirit sent a flood to kill off all the wicked creatures, snakes, and humans. The flood eventually dried up and the good people and animals climbed back down to repopulate the earth.

■ ■ ■

Paraphrased from Clark, Ella E. *Indian Legends of the Pacific Northwest.* Berkeley: University of California Press, 1953.

Names and characters to know:

The Great Spirit
One worthy survivor and his family

Summary

Flood myths are quite common throughout the world. One reason for so many of these myths is that many of the earliest cultures grew up on the banks of powerful rivers. In Mesopotamia, there were two mighty rivers, the Tigris and the Euphrates. However, other cultures, like the Greek, may have carried away memories of a time when they came from a place like Mesopotamia, since there really are not powerful rivers of that magnitude in Greece. However, the Greeks were surrounded by the sea on every side and they relied on the sea for trade and for food. The Hebrews had been enslaved in Babylon for at least three generations and may have taken those stories back with them to Judea.

Some scholars argue that the flood myth is so ubiquitous because it was disseminated around the globe from the earliest cultures. Other scholars suggest that the flood myths must echo the flooding that occurred when Pangaia, the one massive continent, split into the smaller continents. Whichever theory appeals the most to you, the three most common motifs found within the majority of flood myths are a survivor(s), a floating device, and a sacred mountain.

Study Questions for Chapter Three: Flood Myths

General Questions:

1. How are flood myths re-creation myths?
2. What element would be used to truly end all things?
3. What are the most common motifs found in flood myths?
4. How might a flood myth be read psychologically?

Mesopotamian Flood

1. Why did the Mesopotamian gods want to flood the earth?
2. Which god was the instigator?
3. Which god decided to warn a human? Who was the human?
4. What instructions were given to the human regarding surviving the flood?
5. Who all was allowed on the boat?
6. Where did the boat come to land?
7. How did the humans learn it was safe to leave their boat?
8. What was the first thing that the survivors did after leaving their boat?
9. What was the reaction of the gods to the flood?
10. What reward was given to the survivor?
11. How long did the Mesopotamian flood last?

Hebrew Flood

1. Why did the Hebrew god want to flood the earth?
2. Who did he warn and why?
3. What instructions were given to the human regarding surviving the flood?
4. Who all was allowed on the boat?
5. Where did the boat come to land?
6. How did the survivors know it was safe to leave the boat?
7. What was the first thing that the survivors did after leaving the boat?
8. What covenant was made between the Hebrew god and the survivors, and what became the symbol of the covenant?
9. How long did the Hebrew flood last?

Greek Flood

1. Why did the Greek gods decide to flood the earth?
2. Who survived the flood?
3. What was the reaction of the sea life to the extensive waters?
4. Where did the survivors' boat land?
5. How did they recreate the human race after the flood?
6. How were animals recreated after the flood?
7. How long was the flood?

Indian Flood

1. Why was there a flood? Why was there a flood according to the the Vedas? Why was there a flood according to the Mahabharata?
2. Who survived and why? Who survived the flood according to the Vedas? Who survived the flood according to the Mahabharata?
3. How were humans recreated after the flood? How were humans recreated after the flood in both versions of the myth?

Chinese Flood

1. Why was there a flood?
2. Who were the survivors?
3. How did they survive the flood?

Huichol Flood

1. Why was there a flood?
2. Who was the survivor?
3. How did he survive the flood?
4. Who warned him?
5. How was the human race recreated after the flood?

Lithuanian Flood

1. Why was there a flood?
2. Who were the survivors?
3. How did they survive the flood?
4. How was the human race recreated after the flood?

Maori Flood (New Zealand)

1. Why was there a flood?
2. Who were the survivors?
3. How did they survive the flood?
4. What did they do after the flood was over?

Skokomish Flood

1. Why was there a flood?
2. Who survived the flood?
3. How did they survive the flood?
4. How was the earth repopulated after the flood?

CHAPTER 4
SUPREME BEING ARCHETYPE

First a word about Archetypes in general:

Archetypes are universal images from the collective unconscious that express common human experiences. The archetypes in themselves are like prototypes that include all possibilities within them, both the good characteristics and the bad characteristics. A particular culture will stress some characteristics over others, so the archetype itself is like a pattern with many variations existing around the world. However, when trying to determine a particular god's archetypal nature, the majority of the characteristics will fit, otherwise the god or goddess is not an example of that archetype.

Also—if a culture stresses only the good side of the archetype, the archetype by necessity will split and someone else in the collection of gods and/or demons will have to carry all the negative qualities of that archetype. For example, in Christianity, the more that God is considered all good, the more powerful the character of Satan becomes. Satan really is not very powerful in the myths from the Hebrew Tanakh, which are mostly present in the Christian Bible as the Old Testament, where Satan works for God.

Characteristics of the Supreme Being Archetype

The Supreme Being Archetype in mythology is a reflection of patriarchal authority and is always male or beyond gender. He often rules from the skies above as the sky itself or as the sun, providing the earth below it with what it needs to survive: rain, light, and heat. As his residence is in the sky, he is literally and metaphorically looked up to as the source for laws, values, order, and judgments. He is the head and usually the king of the family of gods, with life and death control over gods and mortals, much like a Roman paterfamilias. He is virile and, as the sky, impregnates the Earth and makes her fertile. He often marries the earth goddess, which creates a *hieros gamos*, or sacred marriage, between earth and sky, which is a very fertile union. If he does marry, his wife is subordinate to him. He is supreme.

As the Supreme Being he is most often wise and omniscient, omnipotent, and sometimes omnipresent or immanent like Brahman. He is transcendent and remote from the mortal realm, making his home in the heavens above. making his home in the heavens above, unapproachable due to the location, but also due to his radiant glory. The Supreme Being can be a wrathful and punishing, as well as a benevolent and loving, father figure. He is the human experience of the all-powerful father figure writ large onto the heavens.

The Supreme Being is often associated with the eagle or other high-flying birds and with powerful, fertile land animals like the bull or stallion stressing the Supreme Being's virility and power. The Supreme Being may be the creator and originator of all things or he may come along after Creation has begun. He decides the fate of gods and mortals, and the world below.

Mesopotamia: Marduk

Marduk was the chief god of the city of Babylon in Mesopotamia. He is the sun god, son of the god of wisdom, Ea, and his wife, Damkina. Marduk was the only god powerful enough to defeat the angry great mother goddess, Tiamat, goddess of salt waters. He killed her and made the heavens and the earth from her divided corpse. Afterward, Marduk ruled from the heavens where he gave all the other gods their duties, including his own father. He set the stars and moon in the sky and told them their courses. Finally, he ordered the creation of humans to serve the gods because the gods did not like having to tend the newly made earth.

The Enuma Elish, the creation myth of the Babylonians, describes Marduk's appearance after his birth:

"Alluring was his figure, sparkling the lift in his eyes.
Lordly was his gait, commanding from of old.
When Ea saw him, the father who begot him,
He exulted and glowed, his heart filled with gladness.
He rendered him perfect and endowed him with a double godhead.
Greatly exalted was he above them, exceeding throughout.
Perfect were his members beyond comprehension,
Unsuited for understanding, difficult to perceive.
Four were his eyes, four were his ears;
When he moved his lips, fire blazed forth.
Large were all hearing organs,

And the eyes in like number, scanned all things.
He was the loftiest of the gods, surpassing was his stature;
His members were enormous, he was exceeding tall.
'My little son, my little son!'
My son, the Sun! Sun of the heavens!'
Clothed with the halo of ten gods, he was strong to the utmost,
As their awesome flashes were heaped upon him" (Eliade, 100–101).

When Tiamat proved too difficult for the elder gods to defeat, Marduk offered to fight and defeat her in exchange for the kingship of the gods. The gods were so glad to have a champion that they offered him many things. Here is a brief excerpt from the Fourth Tablet of *The Enuma Elish*.

▪ ▪ ▪

Eliade, Mircea. *Essential Sacred Writings from Around the World*. Harper: San Francisco, 1967.

The Fourth Tablet

1. They prepared for him a lordly chamber,
2. Before his fathers as prince he took his place.
3. "Thou art chiefest among the great gods,
4. "Thy fate is unequalled, thy word is Anu!
5. "O Marduk, thou art chiefest among the great gods,
6. "Thy fate is unequalled, thy word is Anu!
7. "Henceforth not without avail shall be thy command,
8. "In thy power shall it be to exalt and to abase.
9. "Established shall be the word of thy mouth, irresistible shall be thy command;
10. "None among the gods shall transgress thy boundary.
11. "Abundance, the desire of the shrines of the gods,
12. "Shall be established in thy sanctuary, even though they lack (offerings).
13. "O Marduk, thou art our avenger!
14. "We give thee sovereignty over the whole world.
15. "Sit thou down in night, be exalted in thy command.
16. "Thy weapon shall never lose its power, it shall crush thy foe.
17. "O lord, spare the life of him that putteth his trust in thee,
18. "But as for the god who began the rebellion, pour out his life."
19. Then set they in their midst a garment,
20. And unto Marduk their first-born they spake:
21. "May thy fate, O lord, be supreme among the gods,
22. "To destroy and to create; speak thou the word, and (thy command) shall be fulfilled.

23. "Command now and let the garment vanish;
24. "And speak the word again and let the garment reappear!"
25. Then he spake with his mouth, and the garment vanished;
26. Again he commanded it, and the garment reappeared.
27. When the gods, his fathers, beheld (the fulfilment of) his word,
28. They rejoiced, and they did homage (unto him, saying), "Marduk is king!"
29. They bestowed upon him the sceptre, and the throne, and the ring,
30. They give him an invincible weapon, which overwhelmeth the foe.

After Marduk's victory and coronation and the creation of all things, the gods praised Marduk. These praises make up the majority of the Seventh Tablet from *The Enuma Elish.*

The Seventh Tablet

1. O Asari, "Bestower of planting," "[Founder of sowing],"
2. "Creator of grain and plants," "who caused [the green herb to spring up]!"
3. O Asaru-alim, "who is revered in the house of counsel," "[who aboundeth in counsel],"
4. The gods paid homage, fear [took hold upon them]!
5. O Asaru-alim-nuna, "the mighty one," "the Light of [the father who begat him],"
6. Who directeth the decrees of Anu, Bel, [and Ea]!"
7. He was their patron, he ordained [their . . . .];
8. He, whose provision is abundance, goeth forth [. . .]!
9. Tutu [is] "He who created them anew;"
10. Should their wants be pure, then are they [satisfied];
11. Should he make an incantation, then are the gods [appeased];
12. Should they attack him in anger, he withstandeth [their onslaught]!
13. Let him therefore be exalted, and in the assembly of the gods [let him . . .];
14. None among the gods can [rival him]!
15. Tutu is Zi-ukkina, "the Life of the host [of the gods],"
16. Who established for the gods the bright heavens.
17. He set them on their way, and ordained [their path (?)]
18. Never shall his [. . .] deeds be forgotten among men.
19. Tutu as Zi-azag thirdly they named, "the Bringer of Purification,"
20. "The God of the Favouring Breeze," "the Lord of Hearing and Mercy,"
21. "The Creator of Fulness and Abundance," "the Founder of Plenteousness,"
22. "Who increaseth all that is small."
23. "In sore distress we felt his favouring breeze,"
24. Let them say, let them pay reverence, let them bow in humility before him!
25. Tutu as Aga-azag may mankind fourthly magnify!

26. "The Lord of the Pure Incantation," "the Quickener of the Dead,"
27. "Who had mercy upon the captive gods,"
28. "Who removed the yoke from upon the gods his enemies,"
29. "For their forgiveness did he create mankind,"
30. "The Merciful One, with whom it is to bestow life!"
31. May his deeds endure, may they never be forgotten
32. In the mouth of mankind whom his hands have made!
33. Tutu as Mu-azag, fifthly, his "Pure Incantation" may their mouth proclaim,
34. "Who through his Pure Incantation hath destroyed all the evil ones!"
35. Shag-zu, "who knoweth the heart of the gods," "who seeth through the innermost part!"
36. "The evil-doer he hath not caused to go forth with him!"
37. "Founder of the assembly of the gods," "[who . . .] their heart!"
38. "Subduer of the disobedient,"

Continuing to praise Marduk, Tablet Seven says:

110. "For the stars of heaven he upheld the paths,
111. "He shepherded all the gods like sheep!
112. "He conquered Tiamat, he troubled and ended her life,"
113. In the future of mankind, when the days grow old,
114. May this be heard without ceasing, may it hold sway for ever!
115. Since he created the realm (of heaven) and fashioned the firm earth,
116. "The Lord of the World," the father Bêl hath called his name.
117. (This) title, which all the Spirits of Heaven proclaimed,
118. Did Ea hear, and his spirit was rejoiced, (and he said):
119. "He whose name his fathers have made glorious,
120. "Shall be even as I, his name shall be Ea!
121. "The binding of all my decrees shall he control,
122. "All my commands shall he make known!"
123. By the name of "Fifty" did the great gods
124. Proclaim his fifty names, they made his path pre-eminent."

Epilogue

125. Let them be held in remembrance, and let the first man proclaim them;
126. Let the wise and the understanding consider them together!
127. Let the father repeat them and teach them to his son;
128. Let them be in the ears of the pastor and the shepherd!
129. Let a man rejoice in Marduk, the Lord of the gods,
130. That he may cause his land to be fruitful, and that he himself may have prosperity!

131. His word standeth fast, his command is unaltered;
132. The utterance of his mouth hath no god ever annulled.
133. He gazed in his anger, he turned not his neck;
134. When he is wroth, no god can withstand his indignation.
135. Wide is his heart, broad is his compassion;

■ ■ ■

The Seven Tablets of Creation, by Leonard William King. 1902. Located on www.sacred-texts.com

Hebrew God: Yahweh

Yahweh, according to Genesis Chapter 1, is the creator of heaven and earth, the lights in the sky, the sun and the moon and the stars, all the plants, animals, and, finally, humans. He gives humans dominion over the earth and all its creatures. In Chapters 2 and 3, Yahweh removes himself from the Garden of Eden where he first makes man after man disobeys his command not to eat of the tree of knowledge of good and evil. Yahweh returns to the heavens and lives there. He makes brief appearances throughout the rest of the Old Testament, most notably to Moses when he punishes the Egyptians and helps free the Israelites by guarding them as a pillar of fire by night. He speaks with Moses on the mountain and he speaks to Job from

© Masha Arkulis/Shutterstock.com

the whirlwind. He is all powerful and although in origin he was perhaps beyond gender, as the phrases "he created them in his image, male and female together he created them" (Genesis 1) suggest, over the course of time, Yahweh was referred to more and more with masculine pronouns. He became the supreme father figure.

The first example comes from Exodus: In this scene, Moses approaches Yahweh on the mountain to commune with him and receive his commands:

King James Version: Exodus Chapter 34

1 And the LORD said unto Moses, Hew thee two tables of stone like unto the first: and I will write upon these tables the words that were in the first tables, which thou brakest.

2 And be ready in the morning, and come up in the morning unto mount Sinai, and present thyself there to me in the top of the mount.

3 And no man shall come up with thee, neither let any man be seen throughout all the mount; neither let the flocks nor herds feed before that mount.

4 And he hewed two tables of stone like unto the first; and Moses rose up early in the morning, and went up unto mount Sinai, as the LORD had commanded him, and took in his hand the two tables of stone.

5 And the LORD descended in the cloud, and stood with him there, and proclaimed the name of the LORD.

6 And the LORD passed by before him, and proclaimed, The LORD, The LORD God, merciful and gracious, longsuffering, and abundant in goodness and truth,

7 Keeping mercy for thousands, forgiving iniquity and transgression and sin, and that will by no means clear the guilty; visiting the iniquity of the fathers upon the children, and upon the children's children, unto the third and to the fourth generation.

8 And Moses made haste, and bowed his head toward the earth, and worshipped.

9 And he said, If now I have found grace in thy sight, O LORD, let my LORD, I pray thee, go among us; for it is a stiffnecked people; and pardon our iniquity and our sin, and take us for thine inheritance.

10 And he said, Behold, I make a covenant: before all thy people I will do marvels, such as have not been done in all the earth, nor in any nation: and all the people among which thou art shall see the work of the LORD: for it is a terrible thing that I will do with thee.

11 Observe thou that which I command thee this day: behold, I drive out before thee the Amorite, and the Canaanite, and the Hittite, and the Perizzite, and the Hivite, and the Jebusite.

12 Take heed to thyself, lest thou make a covenant with the inhabitants of the land whither thou goest, lest it be for a snare in the midst of thee:

13 But ye shall destroy their altars, break their images, and cut down their groves:

14 For thou shalt worship no other god: for the LORD, whose name is Jealous, is a jealous God:

15 Lest thou make a covenant with the inhabitants of the land, and they go a whoring after their gods, and do sacrifice unto their gods, and one call thee, and thou eat of his sacrifice;

16 And thou take of their daughters unto thy sons, and their daughters go a whoring after their gods, and make thy sons go a whoring after their gods.

17 Thou shalt make thee no molten gods.

18 The feast of unleavened bread shalt thou keep. Seven days thou shalt eat unleavened bread, as I commanded thee, in the time of the month Abib: for in the month Abib thou camest out from Egypt.

19 All that openeth the matrix is mine; and every firstling among thy cattle, whether ox or sheep, that is male.

20 But the firstling of an ass thou shalt redeem with a lamb: and if thou redeem him not, then shalt thou break his neck. All the firstborn of thy sons thou shalt redeem. And none shall appear before me empty.

21 Six days thou shalt work, but on the seventh day thou shalt rest: in earing time and in harvest thou shalt rest.

22 And thou shalt observe the feast of weeks, of the firstfruits of wheat harvest, and the feast of ingathering at the year's end.

23 Thrice in the year shall all your menchildren appear before the LORD God, the God of Israel.

24 For I will cast out the nations before thee, and enlarge thy borders: neither shall any man desire thy land, when thou shalt go up to appear before the LORD thy God thrice in the year.

25 Thou shalt not offer the blood of my sacrifice with leaven; neither shall the sacrifice of the feast of the passover be left unto the morning.

26 The first of the firstfruits of thy land thou shalt bring unto the house of the LORD thy God. Thou shalt not seethe a kid in his mother's milk.

27 And the LORD said unto Moses, Write thou these words: for after the tenor of these words I have made a covenant with thee and with Israel.

28 And he was there with the LORD forty days and forty nights; he did neither eat bread, nor drink water. And he wrote upon the tables the words of the covenant, the ten commandments.

29 And it came to pass, when Moses came down from mount Sinai with the two tables of testimony in Moses' hand, when he came down from the mount, that Moses wist not that the skin of his face shone while he talked with him.

30 And when Aaron and all the children of Israel saw Moses, behold, the skin of his face shone; and they were afraid to come nigh him.

31 And Moses called unto them; and Aaron and all the rulers of the congregation returned unto him: and Moses talked with them.

32 And afterward all the children of Israel came nigh: and he gave them in commandment all that the LORD had spoken with him in mount Sinai.

33 And till Moses had done speaking with them, he put a vail on his face.

34 But when Moses went in before the LORD to speak with him, he took the vail off, until he came out. And he came out, and spake unto the children of Israel that which he was commanded.

35 And the children of Israel saw the face of Moses, that the skin of Moses' face shone: and Moses put the vail upon his face again, until he went in to speak with him.

The second example of Yahweh demonstrating the powers of the Supreme Being Archetype comes from the Book of Job: Satan suggests that the righteous man Job would not be so righteous if he were not so blessed. Yahweh allows Satan to test Job because he feels that Job will remain righteous and faithful no matter what ills befall him. Job loses everything—his family, his wealth, his flocks, his health—but never loses his faith. He does, however, question the reason for all the ills. Yahweh comes to Job in a whirlwind to demonstrate his powers and to implicate that no human could possibly understand God. Job is given a new family and has wealth and health restored to him as a reward for his faithfulness, and learns that it is best not to question the Supreme Being.

King James Version: Job Chapter 1

1 There was a man in the land of Uz, whose name was Job; and that man was perfect and upright, and one that feared God, and eschewed evil.

2 And there were born unto him seven sons and three daughters.

3 His substance also was seven thousand sheep, and three thousand camels, and five hundred yoke of oxen, and five hundred she asses, and a very great household; so that this man was the greatest of all the men of the east.

4 And his sons went and feasted in their houses, every one his day; and sent and called for their three sisters to eat and to drink with them.

5 And it was so, when the days of their feasting were gone about, that Job sent and sanctified them, and rose up early in the morning, and offered burnt offerings according to the number of them all: for Job said, It may be that my sons have sinned, and cursed God in their hearts. Thus did Job continually.

6 Now there was a day when the sons of God came to present themselves before the LORD, and Satan came also among them.

7 And the LORD said unto Satan, Whence comest thou? Then Satan answered the LORD, and said, From going to and fro in the earth, and from walking up and down in it.

8 And the LORD said unto Satan, Hast thou considered my servant Job, that there is none like him in the earth, a perfect and an upright man, one that feareth God, and escheweth evil?

9 Then Satan answered the LORD, and said, Doth Job fear God for nought?

10 Hast not thou made an hedge about him, and about his house, and about all that he hath on every side? thou hast blessed the work of his hands, and his substance is increased in the land.

11 But put forth thine hand now, and touch all that he hath, and he will curse thee to thy face.

12 And the LORD said unto Satan, Behold, all that he hath is in thy power; only upon himself put not forth thine hand. So Satan went forth from the presence of the LORD.

13 And there was a day when his sons and his daughters were eating and drinking wine in their eldest brother's house:

14 And there came a messenger unto Job, and said, The oxen were plowing, and the asses feeding beside them:

15 And the Sabeans fell upon them, and took them away; yea, they have slain the servants with the edge of the sword; and I only am escaped alone to tell thee.

16 While he was yet speaking, there came also another, and said, The fire of God is fallen from heaven, and hath burned up the sheep, and the servants, and consumed them; and I only am escaped alone to tell thee.

17 While he was yet speaking, there came also another, and said, The Chaldeans made out three bands, and fell upon the camels, and have carried them away, yea, and slain the servants with the edge of the sword; and I only am escaped alone to tell thee.

18 While he was yet speaking, there came also another, and said, Thy sons and thy daughters were eating and drinking wine in their eldest brother's house:

19 And, behold, there came a great wind from the wilderness, and smote the four corners of the house, and it fell upon the young men, and they are dead; and I only am escaped alone to tell thee.

20 Then Job arose, and rent his mantle, and shaved his head, and fell down upon the ground, and worshipped,

21 And said, Naked came I out of my mother's womb, and naked shall I return thither: the LORD gave, and the LORD hath taken away; blessed be the name of the LORD.

22 In all this Job sinned not, nor charged God foolishly.

Yahweh's answer to Job:

King James Version: Job Chapter 38

1 Then the LORD answered Job out of the whirlwind, and said,

2 Who is this that darkeneth counsel by words without knowledge?

3 Gird up now thy loins like a man; for I will demand of thee, and answer thou me.

4 Where wast thou when I laid the foundations of the earth? declare, if thou hast understanding.

5 Who hath laid the measures thereof, if thou knowest? or who hath stretched the line upon it?

6 Whereupon are the foundations thereof fastened? or who laid the corner stone thereof;

7 When the morning stars sang together, and all the sons of God shouted for joy?

8 Or who shut up the sea with doors, when it brake forth, as if it had issued out of the womb?

9 When I made the cloud the garment thereof, and thick darkness a swaddling-band for it,

10 And brake up for it my decreed place, and set bars and doors,

11 And said, Hitherto shalt thou come, but no further: and here shall thy proud waves be stayed?

12 Hast thou commanded the morning since thy days; and caused the dayspring to know his place;

13 That it might take hold of the ends of the earth, that the wicked might be shaken out of it?

14 It is turned as clay to the seal; and they stand as a garment.

15 And from the wicked their light is withholden, and the high arm shall be broken.

16 Hast thou entered into the springs of the sea? or hast thou walked in the search of the depth?

17 Have the gates of death been opened unto thee? or hast thou seen the doors of the shadow of death?

18 Hast thou perceived the breadth of the earth? declare if thou knowest it all.

19 Where is the way where light dwelleth? and as for darkness, where is the place thereof,

20 That thou shouldest take it to the bound thereof, and that thou shouldest know the paths to the house thereof?

21 Knowest thou it, because thou wast then born? or because the number of thy days is great?

22 Hast thou entered into the treasures of the snow? or hast thou seen the treasures of the hail,

23 Which I have reserved against the time of trouble, against the day of battle and war?

24 By what way is the light parted, which scattereth the east wind upon the earth?

25 Who hath divided a watercourse for the overflowing of waters, or a way for the lightning of thunder;

26 To cause it to rain on the earth, where no man is; on the wilderness, wherein there is no man;

27 To satisfy the desolate and waste ground; and to cause the bud of the tender herb to spring forth?

28 Hath the rain a father? or who hath begotten the drops of dew?

29 Out of whose womb came the ice? and the hoary frost of heaven, who hath gendered it?

30 The waters are hid as with a stone, and the face of the deep is frozen.

31 Canst thou bind the sweet influences of Pleiades, or loose the bands of Orion?

32 Canst thou bring forth Mazzaroth in his season? or canst thou guide Arcturus with his sons?

33 Knowest thou the ordinances of heaven? canst thou set the dominion thereof in the earth?

34 Canst thou lift up thy voice to the clouds, that abundance of waters may cover thee?

35 Canst thou send lightnings, that they may go and say unto thee, Here we are?

36 Who hath put wisdom in the inward parts? or who hath given understanding to the heart?

37 Who can number the clouds in wisdom? or who can stay the bottles of heaven,

38 When the dust groweth into hardness, and the clods cleave fast together?

39 Wilt thou hunt the prey for the lion? or fill the appetite of the young lions,

40 When they couch in their dens, and abide in the covert to lie in wait?

41 Who provideth for the raven his food? when his young ones cry unto God, they wander for lack of meat.

King James Version: Job Chapter 39

1 Knowest thou the time when the wild goats of the rock bring forth? or canst thou mark when the hinds do calve?

2 Canst thou number the months that they fulfil? or knowest thou the time when they bring forth?

3 They bow themselves, they bring forth their young ones, they cast out their sorrows.

4 Their young ones are in good liking, they grow up with corn; they go forth, and return not unto them.

5 Who hath sent out the wild ass free? or who hath loosed the bands of the wild ass?

6 Whose house I have made the wilderness, and the barren land his dwellings.

7 He scorneth the multitude of the city, neither regardeth he the crying of the driver.

8 The range of the mountains is his pasture, and he searcheth after every green thing.

9 Will the unicorn be willing to serve thee, or abide by thy crib?

10 Canst thou bind the unicorn with his band in the furrow? or will he harrow the valleys after thee?

11 Wilt thou trust him, because his strength is great? or wilt thou leave thy labour to him?

12 Wilt thou believe him, that he will bring home thy seed, and gather it into thy barn?

13 Gavest thou the goodly wings unto the peacocks? or wings and feathers unto the ostrich?

14 Which leaveth her eggs in the earth, and warmeth them in dust,

15 And forgetteth that the foot may crush them, or that the wild beast may break them.

16 She is hardened against her young ones, as though they were not her's: her labour is in vain without fear;

17 Because God hath deprived her of wisdom, neither hath he imparted to her understanding.

18 What time she lifteth up herself on high, she scorneth the horse and his rider.

19 Hast thou given the horse strength? hast thou clothed his neck with thunder?

20 Canst thou make him afraid as a grasshopper? the glory of his nostrils is terrible.

21 He paweth in the valley, and rejoiceth in his strength: he goeth on to meet the armed men.

22 He mocketh at fear, and is not affrighted; neither turneth he back from the sword.

23 The quiver rattleth against him, the glittering spear and the shield.

24 He swalloweth the ground with fierceness and rage: neither believeth he that it is the sound of the trumpet.

25 He saith among the trumpets, Ha, ha; and he smelleth the battle afar off, the thunder of the captains, and the shouting.

26 Doth the hawk fly by thy wisdom, and stretch her wings toward the south?

27 Doth the eagle mount up at thy command, and make her nest on high?

28 She dwelleth and abideth on the rock, upon the crag of the rock, and the strong place.

29 From thence she seeketh the prey, and her eyes behold afar off.

30 Her young ones also suck up blood: and where the slain are, there is she.

King James Version: Job Chapter 40

1 Moreover the LORD answered Job, and said,

2 Shall he that contendeth with the Almighty instruct him? he that reproveth God, let him answer it.

3 Then Job answered the LORD, and said,

4 Behold, I am vile; what shall I answer thee? I will lay mine hand upon my mouth.

5 Once have I spoken; but I will not answer: yea, twice; but I will proceed no further.

6 Then answered the LORD unto Job out of the whirlwind, and said,

7 Gird up thy loins now like a man: I will demand of thee, and declare thou unto me.

8 Wilt thou also disannul my judgment? wilt thou condemn me, that thou mayest be righteous?

9 Hast thou an arm like God? or canst thou thunder with a voice like him?

10 Deck thyself now with majesty and excellency; and array thyself with glory and beauty.

11 Cast abroad the rage of thy wrath: and behold every one that is proud, and abase him.

12 Look on every one that is proud, and bring him low; and tread down the wicked in their place.

13 Hide them in the dust together; and bind their faces in secret.

14 Then will I also confess unto thee that thine own right hand can save thee.

15 Behold now behemoth, which I made with thee; he eateth grass as an ox.

16 Lo now, his strength is in his loins, and his force is in the navel of his belly.

17 He moveth his tail like a cedar: the sinews of his stones are wrapped together.

18 His bones are as strong pieces of brass; his bones are like bars of iron.

19 He is the chief of the ways of God: he that made him can make his sword to approach unto him.

20 Surely the mountains bring him forth food, where all the beasts of the field play.

21 He lieth under the shady trees, in the covert of the reed, and fens.

22 The shady trees cover him with their shadow; the willows of the brook compass him about.

23 Behold, he drinketh up a river, and hasteth not: he trusteth that he can draw up Jordan into his mouth.

24 He taketh it with his eyes: his nose pierceth through snares.

King James Version: Job Chapter 41

1 Canst thou draw out leviathan with an hook? or his tongue with a cord which thou lettest down?

2 Canst thou put an hook into his nose? or bore his jaw through with a thorn?

3 Will he make many supplications unto thee? will he speak soft words unto thee?

4 Will he make a covenant with thee? wilt thou take him for a servant for ever?

5 Wilt thou play with him as with a bird? or wilt thou bind him for thy maidens?

6 Shall the companions make a banquet of him? shall they part him among the merchants?

7 Canst thou fill his skin with barbed irons? or his head with fish spears?

8 Lay thine hand upon him, remember the battle, do no more.

9 Behold, the hope of him is in vain: shall not one be cast down even at the sight of him?

10 None is so fierce that dare stir him up: who then is able to stand before me?

11 Who hath prevented me, that I should repay him? whatsoever is under the whole heaven is mine.

12 I will not conceal his parts, nor his power, nor his comely proportion.

13 Who can discover the face of his garment? or who can come to him with his double bridle?

14 Who can open the doors of his face? his teeth are terrible round about.

15 His scales are his pride, shut up together as with a close seal.

16 One is so near to another, that no air can come between them.

17 They are joined one to another, they stick together, that they cannot be sundered.

18 By his neesings a light doth shine, and his eyes are like the eyelids of the morning.

19 Out of his mouth go burning lamps, and sparks of fire leap out.

20 Out of his nostrils goeth smoke, as out of a seething pot or caldron.

21 His breath kindleth coals, and a flame goeth out of his mouth.

22 In his neck remaineth strength, and sorrow is turned into joy before him.

23 The flakes of his flesh are joined together: they are firm in themselves; they cannot be moved.

24 His heart is as firm as a stone; yea, as hard as a piece of the nether millstone.

25 When he raiseth up himself, the mighty are afraid: by reason of breakings they purify themselves.

26 The sword of him that layeth at him cannot hold: the spear, the dart, nor the habergeon.

27 He esteemeth iron as straw, and brass as rotten wood.

28 The arrow cannot make him flee: slingstones are turned with him into stubble.

29 Darts are counted as stubble: he laugheth at the shaking of a spear.

30 Sharp stones are under him: he spreadeth sharp pointed things upon the mire.

31 He maketh the deep to boil like a pot: he maketh the sea like a pot of ointment.

32 He maketh a path to shine after him; one would think the deep to be hoary.

33 Upon earth there is not his like, who is made without fear.

34 He beholdeth all high things: he is a king over all the children of pride.

King James Version: Job Chapter 42

1 Then Job answered the LORD, and said,

2 I know that thou canst do every thing, and that no thought can be withholden from thee.

3 Who is he that hideth counsel without knowledge? therefore have I uttered that I understood not; things too wonderful for me, which I knew not.

4 Hear, I beseech thee, and I will speak: I will demand of thee, and declare thou unto me.

5 I have heard of thee by the hearing of the ear: but now mine eye seeth thee.

6 Wherefore I abhor myself, and repent in dust and ashes.

7 And it was so, that after the LORD had spoken these words unto Job, the LORD said to Eliphaz the Temanite, My wrath is kindled against thee, and against thy two friends: for ye have not spoken of me the thing that is right, as my servant Job hath.

8 Therefore take unto you now seven bullocks and seven rams, and go to my servant Job, and offer up for yourselves a burnt offering; and my servant Job shall pray for you: for him will I accept: lest I deal with you after your folly, in that ye have not spoken of me the thing which is right, like my servant Job.

9 So Eliphaz the Temanite and Bildad the Shuhite and Zophar the Naamathite went, and did according as the LORD commanded them: the LORD also accepted Job.

10 And the LORD turned the captivity of Job, when he prayed for his friends: also the LORD gave Job twice as much as he had before.

11 Then came there unto him all his brethren, and all his sisters, and all they that had been of his acquaintance before, and did eat bread with him in his house: and they bemoaned him, and comforted him over all the evil that the LORD had brought upon him: every man also gave him a piece of money, and every one an earring of gold.

12 So the LORD blessed the latter end of Job more than his beginning: for he had fourteen thousand sheep, and six thousand camels, and a thousand yoke of oxen, and a thousand she asses.

13 He had also seven sons and three daughters.

14 And he called the name of the first, Jemima; and the name of the second, Kezia; and the name of the third, Kerenhappuch.

15 And in all the land were no women found so fair as the daughters of Job: and their father gave them inheritance among their brethren.

16 After this lived Job an hundred and forty years, and saw his sons, and his sons' sons, even four generations.

17 So Job died, being old and full of days.

■ ■ ■

Located on www.sacred-texts.com

Greek: Zeus

Zeus was the son of the Titan, Kronos, and his wife, Rhea. With the help of his siblings, the Hecatonchires and the Cyclopes, Zeus defeated the Titans and Kronos in battle, and defeated the Giants and the dragon, Typhon, that Gaia sent afterward. He was

Figure 4.1
© garanga/Shutterstock.com

armed with the lightning bolts made by the Cyclopes. He drew the lot for the Sky and became the third and final King of the Gods and Sky God in Greek Mythology. Zeus and his siblings, the Olympians, ruled from the tallest mountain in Greece, Mt. Olympos, where Zeus could keep an eye on the mortal world below.

Zeus was called the Father of Gods and Men by Homer and by Hesiod, two of the earliest Greek authors. While the two authors had slightly different takes on some of the Greek myths, they did agree on Zeus' status as the king of the gods. To illustrate his power and authority, here is a passage from Book IV of the *Iliad* in which Zeus (Jupiter/Jove) decides that Hera will be allowed to destroy Troy, but in return Zeus will be able to destroy a city that she loves.

The Iliad: BOOK IV

Now the gods were sitting with Jove in council upon the golden floor while Hebe went round pouring out nectar for them to drink, and as they pledged one another in their cups of gold they looked down upon the town of Troy. The son of Saturn then began to tease Juno, talking at her so as to provoke her. "Menelaus," said he, "has two good friends among the goddesses, Juno of Argos, and Minerva of Alalcomene, but they only sit still and look on, while Venus keeps ever by Alexandrus' side to defend him in any danger; indeed she has just rescued him when he made sure that it was all over with him—for the victory really did lie with Menelaus. We must consider what we shall do about all this; shall we set them fighting anew or make peace between them? If you will agree to this last Menelaus can take back Helen and the city of Priam may remain still inhabited."

Minerva and Juno muttered their discontent as they sat side by side hatching mischief for the Trojans. Minerva scowled at her father, for she was in a furious passion with him, and said nothing, but Juno could not contain herself. "Dread son of Saturn," said she, "what, pray, is the meaning of all this? Is my trouble, then, to go for nothing, and the sweat that I have sweated, to say nothing of my horses, while getting the people together against Priam and his children? Do as you will, but we other gods shall not all of us approve your counsel."

Jove was angry and answered, "My dear, what harm have Priam and his sons done you that you are so hotly bent on sacking the city of Ilius? Will nothing do for you but you must within their walls and eat Priam raw, with his sons and all the other Trojans to boot? Have it your own way then; for I would not have this matter become a bone of contention between us. I say further, and lay my saying to your heart, if ever I want to sack a city belonging to friends of yours, you must not try to stop me; you will have to let me do it, for I am giving in to you sorely against my will. Of all inhabited cities under the sun and stars of heaven, there was none that I so much respected as Ilius with Priam and his whole people. Equitable feasts were never wanting about my altar, nor the savour of burning fat, which is honour due to ourselves."

"My own three favourite cities," answered Juno, "are Argos, Sparta, and Mycenae. Sack them whenever you may be displeased with them. I shall not defend them and I shall not care. Even if I did, and tried to stay you, I should take nothing by it, for you are much stronger than I am, but I will not have my own work wasted. I too am a god and of the same race with yourself. I am Saturn's eldest daughter, and am honourable not on this ground only, but also because I am your wife, and you are king over the gods. Let it be a case, then, of give-and-take between us, and the rest of the gods will follow our lead. Tell Minerva to go and take part in the fight at once, and let her contrive that the Trojans shall be the first to break their oaths and set upon the Achaeans."

The sire of gods and men heeded her words, and said to Minerva, "Go at once into the Trojan and Achaean hosts, and contrive that the Trojans shall be the first to break their oaths and set upon the Achaeans."

■ ■ ■

The Iliad of Homer, translated by Samuel Butler, 1898. Located on www.sacred-texts.com

Zeus was a notorious philanderer, having numerous affairs behind Hera's back. He spread his seed far and wide and was truly the Father of Gods and Men. While this may sound immoral to modern ears, the Greeks took pride in his accomplishments because they demonstrated his fertility and thus his virility, both are often characteristics of a Supreme Being. In a scene from Book XIV of the *Iliad,* Hera attempts to distract Zeus from watching the battlefield where the Trojans are winning under his guidance in order for the Greek forces to rally, encouraged by Poseidon. Zeus has issued a command that the gods remain off the battlefield until his promise to Thetis (the mother of Achilles) that the Trojans win and the Greeks lose until the Greeks restore honor to Achilles is fulfilled. Hera is impatient to destroy Troy and doesn't care for his delay. However, when she appears in front of Zeus to seduce and distract him wearing the aphrodisiac belt of Aphrodite, Zeus first woos her by naming off a number of his former conquests in an attempt to persuade her that he loves her more right at this moment than any other goddess or human he has slept with.

> And Jove said, "Juno, you can choose some other time for paying your visit to Oceanus—for the present let us devote ourselves to love and to the enjoyment of one another. Never yet have I been so overpowered by passion neither for goddess nor mortal woman as I am at this moment for yourself—not even when I was in love with the wife of Ixion who bore me Pirithous, peer of gods in counsel, nor yet with Danae the daintily-ancled daughter of Acrisius, who bore me the famed hero Perseus. Then there was the daughter of Phoenix, who bore me Minos and Rhadamanthus: there was Semele, and Alcmena in Thebes by whom I begot my lion-hearted son Hercules, while Semele became mother to Bacchus the comforter of mankind. There was queen Ceres again, and lovely Leto, and yourself—but with none of these was I ever so much enamoured as I now am with you." (Iliad, XIV)

After their love making, Zeus falls asleep and Poseidon creeps onto the battlefield to rally the Greeks who begin to fight off the Trojans from their ships. When Zeus awakens in Book XV and sees what Hera and Poseidon have done by interfering with his plans, he issues stern commands and reminds them of his power as King of the Gods.

The Iliad: BOOK XV

BUT when their flight had taken them past the trench and the set stakes, and many had fallen by the hands of the Danaans, the Trojans made a halt on reaching their chariots, routed and pale with fear. Jove now woke on the crests of Ida, where he was lying with golden-throned Juno by his side, and starting to his feet he saw the Trojans and Achaeans, the one thrown into confusion, and the others driving them pell-mell before them with King Neptune in their midst. He saw Hector lying on the ground with his comrades gathered round him, gasping for breath, wandering in mind and vomiting blood, for it was not the feeblest of the Achaeans who struck him.

The sire of gods and men had pity on him, and looked fiercely on Juno. "I see, Juno," said he, "you mischief-making trickster, that your cunning has stayed Hector from fighting and has caused the rout of his host. I am in half a mind to thrash you, in which case you will be the first to reap the fruits of your scurvy knavery. Do you not remember how once upon a time I had you hanged? I fastened two anvils on to your feet, and bound your hands in a chain of gold which none might break, and you hung in mid-air among the clouds. All the gods in Olympos were in a fury, but they could not reach you to set you free; when I caught any one of them I gripped him and hurled him from the heavenly threshold till he came fainting down to earth; yet even this did not relieve my mind from the incessant anxiety which I felt about noble Hercules whom you and Boreas had spitefully conveyed beyond the seas to Cos, after suborning the tempests; but I rescued him, and notwithstanding all his mighty labours I brought him back again to Argos. I would remind you of this that you may learn to leave off being so deceitful, and discover how much you are likely to gain by the embraces out of which you have come here to trick me."

Juno trembled as he spoke, and said, "May heaven above and earth below be my witnesses, with the waters of the river Styx—and this is the most solemn oath that a blessed god can take—nay, I swear also by your own almighty head and by our bridal bed—things over which I could never possibly perjure myself—that Neptune is not punishing Hector and the Trojans and helping the Achaeans through any doing of mine; it is all of his own mere motion because he was sorry to see the Achaeans hard pressed at their ships: if I were advising him, I should tell him to do as you bid him."

The sire of gods and men smiled and answered, "If you, Juno, were always to support me when we sit in council of the gods, Neptune, like it or no, would soon come round to your and my way of thinking. If, then, you are speaking the truth and mean what you say, go among the rank and file of the gods, and tell Iris and Apollo lord of the bow, that I want them—Iris, that she may go to the Achaean host and tell Neptune to leave off fighting and go home, and Apollo, that he may send Hector again into battle and give him fresh strength; he will thus forget his present sufferings, and drive the Achaeans back in confusion till they fall among the ships of Achilles son of Peleus. Achilles will then send his comrade Patroclus into battle, and Hector will kill him in front of Ilius after he has slain many warriors, and among them my own noble son Sarpedon. Achilles will kill Hector to avenge Patroclus, and from that time I will bring it about that the Achaeans shall persistently drive the Trojans back till they fulfil the counsels of Minerva and take Ilius. But I will not stay my anger, nor permit any god to help the Danaans till I have accomplished the desire of the son of Peleus, according to the promise I made by bowing my head on the day when Thetis touched my knees and besought me to give him honour."

■ ■ ■

The Iliad of Homer, translated by Samuel Butler, 1898. Located on www.sacred-texts.com

Another famous example of Zeus' power comes in the story of Prometheus. In this story, Prometheus thinks to outwit the newly crowned Zeus in the division of the sacrificial offerings from man. Zeus does not like the trick that Prometheus plays, and retaliates by forbidding Prometheus to bring mankind fire. Prometheus brings fire in spite of his foreknowledge, which allows him to see the future and know that Zeus will punish him as well as mortal men for the fire theft. Here is the excerpt from Hesiod's *Theogony* that explains the theft and Zeus' punishment of Prometheus.

© Hoika Mikhail/Shutterstock.com

(ll. 507–543) Now Iapetus took to wife the neat-ankled maid Clymene, daughter of Ocean, and went up with her into one bed. And she bare him a stout-hearted son, Atlas: also she bare very glorious Menoetius and clever Prometheus, full of various wiles, and scatter-brained Epimetheus who from the first was a mischief to men who eat bread; for it was he who first took of Zeus the woman, the maiden whom he had formed. But Menoetius was outrageous, and far-seeing Zeus struck him with a lurid thunderbolt and sent him down to Erebus because of his mad presumption and exceeding pride. And Atlas through hard constraint upholds the wide heaven with unwearying head and arms, standing at the borders of the earth before the clear-voiced Hesperides; for this lot wise Zeus assigned to him. And ready-witted Prometheus he bound with inextricable bonds, cruel chains, and drove a shaft through his middle, and set on him a long-winged eagle, which used to eat his immortal liver; but by night the liver grew as much again everyway as the long-winged bird devoured in the whole day. That bird Heracles, the valiant son of shapely-ankled Alcmene, slew; and delivered the son of Iapetus from the cruel plague, and released him from his affliction—not without the will of Olympian Zeus who reigns on high, that the glory of Heracles the Theban-born might be yet greater than it was before over the plenteous earth. This, then, he regarded, and honoured his famous son; though he was angry, he ceased from the wrath which he had before because Prometheus matched himself in wit with the almighty son of Cronos. For when the gods and mortal men had a dispute at Mecone, even then Prometheus was forward to cut up a great ox and set portions before them, trying to befool the mind of Zeus. Before the rest he set flesh and inner parts thick with fat upon the hide, covering them with an ox paunch; but for Zeus he put the white bones dressed up with cunning art and covered with shining fat. Then the father of men and of gods said to him:

(ll. 543–544) 'Son of Iapetus, most glorious of all lords, good sir, how unfairly you have divided the portions!'

(ll. 545–547) So said Zeus whose wisdom is everlasting, rebuking him. But wily Prometheus answered him, smiling softly and not forgetting his cunning trick:

(ll. 548–558) 'Zeus, most glorious and greatest of the eternal gods, take which ever of these portions your heart within you bids.' So he said, thinking trickery. But Zeus, whose wisdom is everlasting, saw and failed not to perceive the trick, and in his heart he thought mischief against mortal men which also was to be fulfilled. With both hands he took up the white fat and was angry at heart, and wrath came to his spirit when he saw the white ox-bones craftily tricked out: and because of this the tribes of men upon earth burn white bones to the deathless gods upon fragrant altars. But Zeus who drives the clouds was greatly vexed and said to him:

(ll. 559–560) 'Son of Iapetus, clever above all! So, sir, you have not yet forgotten your cunning arts!'

(ll. 561–584) So spake Zeus in anger, whose wisdom is everlasting; and from that time he was always mindful of the trick, and would not give the power of unwearying fire to the Melian race of mortal men who live on the earth. But the noble son of Iapetus outwitted him and stole the far-seen gleam of unwearying fire in a hollow fennel stalk. And Zeus who thunders on high was stung in spirit, and his dear heart was angered when he saw amongst men the far-seen ray of fire. Forthwith he made an evil thing for men as the price of fire; for the very famous Limping God formed of earth the likeness of a shy maiden as the son of Cronos willed. And the goddess bright-eyed Athene girded and clothed her with silvery raiment, and down from her head she spread with her hands a broidered veil, a wonder to see; and she, Pallas Athene, put about her head lovely garlands, flowers of new-grown herbs. Also she put upon her head a crown of gold which the very famous Limping God made himself and worked with his own hands as a favour to Zeus his father. On it was much curious work, wonderful to see; for of the many creatures which the land and sea rear up, he put most upon it, wonderful things, like living beings with voices: and great beauty shone out from it.

(ll. 585–589) But when he had made the beautiful evil to be the price for the blessing, he brought her out, delighting in the finery which the bright-eyed daughter of a mighty father had given her, to the place where the other gods and men were. And wonder took hold of the deathless gods and mortal men when they saw that which was sheer guile, not to be withstood by men.

(ll. 590–612) For from her is the race of women and female kind: of her is the deadly race and tribe of women who live amongst mortal men to their great trouble, no helpmeets in hateful poverty, but only in wealth. And as in thatched hives bees feed the drones whose nature is to do mischief—by day and throughout the day until the sun goes down the bees are busy and lay the white combs, while the drones stay at home in the covered skeps and reap the toil of others into their own bellies—even so Zeus who thunders on high made women to be an evil to mortal men, with a nature to do evil. And he gave them a second evil to be the price for the good they had: whoever avoids marriage and the sorrows that women cause, and will not wed, reaches deadly old age without anyone to tend his years, and though he at least has no lack of livelihood while he lives, yet, when he is dead, his kinsfolk divide his possessions amongst them. And as for the man who chooses the lot of marriage and takes a good wife suited to his mind, evil continually contends with good; for whoever happens to have mischievous children, lives always with unceasing grief in his spirit and heart within him; and this evil cannot be healed.

(ll. 613–616) So it is not possible to deceive or go beyond the will of Zeus; for not even the son of Iapetus, kindly Prometheus, escaped his heavy anger, but of necessity strong bands confined him, although he knew many a wile.

■ ■ ■

The Theogony of Hesiod translated by Hugh G. Evelyn-White, 1914. Located on www.sacred-texts.com

India: Brahman

Brahman in the form of Vishnu incarnates in the form of Krishna and reveals himself as the ultimate reality to Arjuna (Arguna) from the *Bhagavad-Gita,* a chapter from the epic poem *The Mahábhárata,* that has formed the basis of Hindu thought. The

Figure 4.2
© saiko3p, 2010. Used under license from Shutterstock, Inc.

Bhagavad-Gita is divided into chapters also. It is Chapter 11 that we focus on here, where Arguna, the disciple of Krishna, asks to see Krishna in his divine form as Vishnu and ultimately as Brahman, the absolute reality. Krishna obliges by opening Arguna's third eye, the spiritual eye in the center of the forehead between the eyebrows.

For Hindus, the ultimate reality is Brahman. Brahman is everything and no thing, because to define Brahman as some thing limits Brahman and Brahman does not have any limitations. The fact that Brahman does not have a personality, which would limit Brahman, made Brahman a bit hard for the average person to relate to. Therefore, a trinity of male gods developed in ancient India who had distinct personalities and came to represent the power of Brahman. These three gods were Brahma, the Creator god; Vishnu, the Preserver god; and Shiva, the Destroyer god. Of the three, Vishnu is the most likely to take on animal or human form to intervene in the world. In the story of the *Mahábhárata*, Vishnu is born into human form as a prince, Krishna.

Krishna gains a reputation as a wise counselor and eventually attracts some of the descendents of Bharata as his followers, the most famous of which is Arguna. *The Mahábhárata* is too long an epic poem to do justice to its story here (it is over 90,000 stanzas long) so suffice it to say that on the day of a great battle Arguna loses confidence when he sees his relatives drawn up on the opposing side of the field. Not able to fight his family, he asks Krishna for the proper way to fulfill his *dharma* (duty) as a warrior. Krishna reveals the proper way to fulfill dharma under many different circumstances, which reassured Arguna that what he was doing was right so long as he did it without attachment to outcome or ego.

CHAPTER XI.

Arguna said:

In consequence of the excellent and mysterious words concerning the relation of the supreme and individual soul, which you have spoken for my welfare, this delusion of mine is gone away. O you whose eyes are like lotus leaves! I have heard from you at large about the production and dissolution of things, and also about your inexhaustible greatness. O highest lord! what you have said about yourself is so. I wish, O best of beings! to see your divine form. If, O lord! you think that it is possible for me to look upon it, then, O lord of the possessors of mystic power 1! show your inexhaustible form to me.

The Deity said:

In hundreds and in thousands see my forms, O son of Prithâ! various, divine, and of various colours and shapes. See the Âdityas, Vasus, Rudras, the two Asvins, and Maruts likewise. And O descendant of Bharata! see wonders, in numbers, unseen before. Within my body, O Gudâkesa! see to-day the whole universe, including (everything) movable and immovable, (all) in one, and whatever else you wish to see. But you will not be able to see me with merely this eye of yours. I give you an eye divine. (Now) see my divine power.

Sañgaya said

Having spoken thus, O king! Hari, the great

p. 93

lord of the possessors of mystic power, then showed to the son of Prithä his supreme divine form, having many mouths and eyes, having (within it) many wonderful sights, having many celestial ornaments, having many celestial weapons held erect, wearing celestial flowers and vestments, having an anointment of celestial perfumes, full of every wonder, the infinite deity with faces in all directions 1. If in the heavens, the lustre of a thousand suns burst forth all at once, that would be like the lustre of that mighty one. There the son of Pându then observed in the body of the god of gods the whole universe (all) in one, and divided into numerous 2 (divisions). Then Dhanañgaya filled with amazement, and with hair standing on end, bowed his head before the god, and spoke with joined hands.

Arguna said:

O god! I see within your body the gods, as also all the groups of various beings; and the lord Brahman seated on (his) lotus seat, and all the sages and celestial snakes. I see you, who are of countless forms, possessed of many arms, stomachs, mouths, and eyes on all sides. And, O lord of the universe! O you of all forms! I do not see your end or middle or beginning. I see you bearing a coronet and a mace and a discus—a mass of glory, brilliant on all sides, difficult to look at, having on

p. 94

all sides the effulgence of a blazing fire or sun, and indefinable. You are indestructible, the supreme one to be known. You are the highest support[1] of this universe. You are the inexhaustible protector of everlasting piety. I believe you to be the eternal being. I see you void of beginning, middle, end—of infinite power, of unnumbered arms, having the sun and moon for eyes, having a mouth like a blazing fire, and heating the universe with your radiance. For this space between heaven and earth and all the quarters are pervaded by you alone. Looking at this wonderful and terrible form of yours, O high-souled one! the three worlds are affrighted. For here these groups of gods are entering into you. Some being afraid are praying with joined hands, and the groups of great sages and Siddhas are saying 'Welfare[2]!' and praising you with abundant (hymns) of praise. The Rudras, and Ádityas, the Vasus, the Sâdhyas, the Visvas, the two Asvins, the Maruts, and the Ushmapas, and the groups of Gandharvas, Yakshas, demons, and Siddhas are all looking at you amazed. Seeing your mighty form, with many mouths and eyes, with many arms, thighs, and feet, with many stomachs, and fearful with many jaws, all people, and I likewise, are much alarmed, O you of mighty arms! Seeing you, O Vishnu! touching the skies, radiant, possessed of many hues, with a gaping mouth, and with large blazing eyes, I am much alarmed in my inmost self, and feel no courage, no tranquillity.

p. 95

[paragraph continues] And seeing your mouths terrible by the jaws, and resembling the fire of destruction, I cannot recognise the (various) directions, I feel no comfort. Be gracious, O lord of gods! who pervadest the universe. And all these sons of Dhritarâsh*t*ra, together with all the bands of kings, and Bhîshma and Dro*n*a, and this charioteer's son[1] likewise, together with our principal warriors also, are rapidly entering your mouths, fearful and horrific[2] by (reason of your) jaws. And some with their heads smashed are seen (to be) stuck in the spaces between the teeth. As the many rapid currents of a river's waters run towards the sea alone, so do these heroes of the human world enter your mouths blazing all round. As butterflies, with increased velocity, enter a blazing fire to their destruction, so too do these people enter your mouths with increased velocity (only) to their destruction. Swallowing all these people, you are licking them over and over again from all sides, with your blazing mouths. Your fierce splendours, O Vish*n*u! filling the whole universe with (their) effulgence, are heating it. Tell me who you are in this fierce form. Salutations be to thee, O chief of the gods! Be gracious. I wish to know you, the primeval, one, for I do not understand your actions.

The Deity said:

I am death, the destroyer of the worlds, fully developed, and I am now active about the overthrow

p. 96

of the worlds. Even without you, the warriors standing in the adverse hosts, shall all cease to be. Therefore, be up, obtain glory, and vanquishing (your) foes, enjoy a prosperous kingdom. All these have been already killed by me. Be only the instrument, O Savyasâ*k*in[1]! Dro*n*a, and Bhîshma, and *G*ayadratha, and Kar*n*a, and likewise other valiant warriors also, whom I have killed, do you kill. Be not alarmed. Do fight. And in the battle you will conquer your foes.

Sañgaya said:

Hearing these words of Kesava, the wearer of the coronet[2], trembling, and with joined hands, bowed down; and sorely afraid, and with throat choked up, he again spoke to Kri*sh*na after saluting him.

Ar*g*una said:

It is quite proper, O H*ri*shîke*s*a! that the universe is delighted and charmed by your renown, that the demons run away affrighted in all directions, and that all the assemblages of Siddhas bow down, (to you). And why, O high-souled one! should they not bow down to you (who are) greater than Brahman, and first cause? O infinite lord of gods! O you pervading the universe! you are the indestructible, that which is, that which is not, and what is beyond them[3]. You are the primal

p. 97

god, the ancient being, you are the highest support of this universe[1]. You are that which has knowledge, that which is the object of knowledge, you are the highest goal. By you is this universe pervaded., O you of infinite forms! You are the wind, Yama, fire, Varu*n*a, the moon, you Pra*g*âpati, and the great grandsire[2]. Obeisance be to thee a thousand times, and again and again obeisance to thee! In front and from behind obeisance to thee! Obeisance be to thee from all sides, O you who are all! You are of infinite power, of unmeasured glory; you pervade all, and therefore you are all! Whatever I have said contemptuously,—for instance, 'O Krishna!' 'O Yâdava!' 'O friend!'—thinking you to be (my) friend, and not knowing your greatness (as shown in) this (universal form), or through friendliness, or incautiously; and whatever disrespect I have shown you for purposes of merriment, on (occasions of) play, sleep, dinner, or sitting (together), whether alone or in the presence (of friends),—for all that, O undegraded one! I ask pardon of you who are indefinable[3]. You are the father of the world-movable and immovable,—you its great and venerable master; there is none equal to you, whence can there be one greater, O you whose power is unparalleled in all the three worlds? Therefore I bow and prostrate myself, and would propitiate you, the praiseworthy lord. Be pleased,

p. 98

[paragraph continues] O god! to pardon (my guilt) as a father (that of his) son, a friend (that of his) friend, or a husband (that of his) beloved. I am delighted at seeing what I had never seen before, and my heart is also alarmed by fear. Show me that same form, O god! Be gracious, O lord of gods! O you pervading the universe! I wish to see you bearing the coronet and the mace, with the discus in hand, just the same (as before)[1]. O you of thousand arms! O you of all forms! assume that same four-handed form.

The Deity said:

O Arguna! being pleased (with you), I have by my own mystic power shown you this supreme form, full of glory, universal, infinite, primeval, and which has not been seen before by any one else but you, O you hero among the Kauravas! I cannot be seen in this form by any one but you, (even) by (the help of) the study of the Vedas, or of[2] sacrifices, nor by gifts, nor by actions, nor by fierce penances. Be not alarmed, be not perplexed, at seeing this form of mine, fearful like this. Free from fear and with delighted heart, see now again that same form of mine.

Sañgaya said:

Having thus spoken to Arguna, Vâsudeva again showed his own form, and the high-souled one becoming again of a mild form, comforted him who had been affrighted.

p. 99

Arguna said:

O Ganardana! seeing this mild, human form of yours, I am new in my right mind, and have come to my normal state.

The Deity said:

Even the gods are always desiring to see this form of mine, which it is difficult to get a sight of, and which you have seen. I cannot be seen, as you have seen me, by (means of) the Vedas, not by penance, not by gift, nor yet by sacrifice. But, O Arguna! by devotion to me exclusively, I can in this form be truly known, seen, and assimilated 1 with, O terror of your foes! He who performs acts for (propitiating) me, to whom I am the highest (object), who is my devotee, who is free from attachment, and who has no enmity towards any being, he, O son of Pându! comes to me.

Footnotes

92:1 Madhusûdana takes power to mean capacity of becoming small or great, of obtaining what is wanted, &c.; the so-called eight Bhûtis.

93:1 Cf. p. 90 supra. Sankara explains it as meaning 'pervading everything.' The expression occurs in the Nrisimha-tâpinî-upanishad, p. 50, where it is said, 'as, without organs, it sees, hears, goes, takes from all sides and pervades everything, therefore it has faces on all sides.'

93:2 Gods, manes, men, and so forth.

94:1 The words are the same as at p. 97 infra, where see the note.

94:2 Seeing signs of some great cataclysm, they say, 'May it be well with the universe,' and then proceed to pray to you.

95:1 I. e. Karna, who was really the eldest brother of the Pândavas, but having been immediately on birth abandoned by Kuntî, was brought up by a charioteer. Karna was told of his, true origin by Bhîshma on his deathbed, and advised to join the Pândavas, but he declined.

95:2 By reason of the ruggedness and distortion of face.

96:1 Arguna, as he could shoot with his left hand as well as the right.—Srîdhara.

96:2 Arguna, who had this coronet given him by Indra.—Madhusûdana.

96:3 The commentators interpret this to mean the perceptible, the unperceived, and the higher principle. Cf. p. 84 supra, and also pp. 103, 113 infra and notes there.

97:1 See p. 94 supra. Here the commentators say the words mean 'that in which the universe is placed at deluge-time.'

97:2 Professor Tiele mentions great-grandfather as a name for the Creator among Kaffirs (History of Religion, p. 18). Cf. p. 83 supra.

97:3 I. e. of whom it is impossible to ascertain whether he is such or such. Cf. p. 94 supra.

98:1 This is the ordinary form of Krishna.

98:2 This is the original construction. One suspects that sacrifices and study of the Vedas are meant. Cf. the speech of Krishna on the next page.

Persian: Ahura-Mazda

From the Persian religion, Zoroasterianism, comes the Supreme Being Ahura-Mazda or Ormazd, the ultimate reality and source of all goodness and truth. Zoroasterianism is a dualistic religion, meaning it has two opposing forces: an ultimate God of Goodness, Ahura-Mazda, who is opposed by the Prince of Demons, Ahriman. The

Ahura Mazda

© NNNMMM/Shutterstock.com

foundational sacred text of the Zoroasterians was the *Avesta,* which exists primarily in fragments called the *Zend Avesta.* Other writings developed that further explained the religion and the nature of the battle between the forces of the Good God and the forces of the Lie. Here is an excerpt from one of the Pahlavi texts. (Ahura-Mazda is spelled Aûharmazd in this translation and Ahriman is spelled Aharman.)

▓ ▓ ▓

Pahlavi Texts, Part I (SBE05), translated by E. W. West, 1880. Located on www.sacred-texts.com

p. 3

BUNDAHIS.
CHAPTER I.

0. In the name of the creator Aûharmazd.

1. The Zand-âkâs ('Zand-knowing or tradition-informed[1]), which is first about Aûharmazd's original creation and the antagonism of the evil spirit[2] *and* afterwards about the nature of the creatures from the original creation till the end, which is the future existence (tanû-i pasînŏ). 2. As *revealed* by the religion of the Mazdayasnians, so it is declared that Aûharmazd is supreme in omniscience and goodness,

p. 4

and unrivalled 1 in splendour; the region of light is the place of Aûharmazd, which they call 'endless light,' and the omniscience *and* goodness of the unrivalled Aûharmazd is what they call 'revelation 2.' 3. Revelation is the explanation of both *spirits* together; one is he who is independent of unlimited time 3, because Aûharmazd and the region, religion, and time of Aûharmazd were and are and ever will be; *while* Aharman[4] in darkness, with backward understanding and desire for destruction, was *in* the abyss, and 'it is *he* who *will* not be; and the place of that destruction, and also of that darkness, is what they call the 'endlessly dark.' 4. And between them was empty space, *that* is, what they call 'air,' in which is now *their* meeting.

5. Both are limited and unlimited spirits, for the supreme is that which they call endless light, and the abyss that which is endlessly dark, so that between them is a void, and one is not connected with

p. 5

the other; and, again, both spirits are limited as to their own selves. 6. And, secondly, on account of the omniscience of Aûharmazd, both things are in the creation of Aûharmazd, the finite and the infinite; for this they know is that which is in the covenant of both spirits. 7. And, again, the complete sovereignty of the creatures of

Aûharmazd is in the future existence, and that also is unlimited for ever and everlasting; and the creatures of Aharman will perish at the time when[1] the future existence occurs, and that also is eternity.

8. Aûharmazd, through omniscience, knew that Aharman exists, *and* whatever he schemes he infuses with malice and greediness till the end; *and* because He accomplishes the end by many means, He also produced spiritually the creatures which were necessary for those means, *and* they remained three thousand years in a spiritual *state,* so that they were unthinking[2] and unmoving, with intangible bodies.

9. The evil spirit, on account of backward knowledge, was not aware of the existence of Aûharmazd; and, afterwards, he arose from the abyss, and came in unto the light which he saw. 10. Desirous of destroying, and because of *his* malicious nature, he
    p. 6
    rushed in to destroy that light of Aûharmazd unassailed by fiends, and he saw its bravery and glory were greater than his own; *so* he fled back to the gloomy darkness, and formed many demons and fiends; *and* the creatures of the destroyer arose for violence.

11. Aûharmazd, by whom the creatures of the evil spirit were seen, creatures terrible, corrupt, and bad, also considered them not commendable (bûrzisnîk). 12. Afterwards, the evil spirit saw the creatures of Aûharmazd; they appeared many creatures of delight (vâyah), enquiring creatures, and they seemed to him commendable, and he commended the creatures and creation of Aûharmazd.

13. Then Aûharmazd, with a knowledge[1] of which way the end of the matter *would be,* went to meet the evil spirit, and proposed peace to him, *and* spoke thus: 'Evil spirit! bring assistance unto my creatures, and offer praise! so that, in reward for it, ye (you and your creatures) may become immortal and undecaying, hungerless and thirstless.'

14. And the evil spirit shouted thus[2]: 'I *will* not depart, I *will* not provide assistance for thy creatures, I *will* not offer praise among thy creatures, and I am not of the same opinion with thee as to good things. I *will* destroy thy creatures for ever and everlasting; moreover, I *will* force all thy creatures into disaffection to thee and affection for myself.' 15. And the explanation thereof is this, that the evil spirit reflected in this manner, that
    p. 7
    [paragraph continues] Aûharmazd was helpless as regarded him 1, therefore He proffers peace; and he did not agree, but bore on even into conflict with Him.

16. And Aûharmazd spoke thus: 'You are not omniscient and almighty, O evil spirit! so that it is not possible for thee to destroy me, and it is not possible for thee to force my creatures so that they *will* not return to my possession.'

17. Then Aûharmazd, through omniscience, knew that: If I do not grant a period of contest, then it *will* be possible for him to act *so* that he *may* be able to cause the seduction of my creatures to himself. As even now there are many of the intermixture of mankind who practise wrong more than right. 18. And Aûharmazd spoke to the

evil spirit thus: 'Appoint a period! so that the intermingling of the conflict may be for nine thousand years.' For he knew that by, appointing this period the evil spirit *would* be undone.

19. Then the evil spirit, unobservant and through ignorance, was content with that agreement; just like two men quarrelling together, who propose a time thus: Let us appoint such-and-such a day for a fight.

20. Aûharmazd also knew this, through omniscience, that within these nine thousand years, *for* three thousand years everything proceeds *by* the will of Aûharmazd, three thousand years *there is* an intermingling of the wills of Aûharmazd and Aharman, and the last three thousand years the evil spirit is disabled, and they keep the adversary away 2 from the creatures.

p. 8

21. Afterwards, Aûharmazd recited the Ahunavar thus: Yathâ ahû vairyô ('as a heavenly lord is to be chosen'), &c.[1] once, *and* uttered the twenty-one words[2]; He also exhibited to the evil spirit His own triumph in the end, and the impotence of the evil spirit, the annihilation of the demons, and the resurrection *and* undisturbed future existence of the creatures for ever and everlasting. 22. And the evil spirit, who perceived his own impotence and the annihilation of the demons, became confounded, and fell back to the gloomy darkness; even so as is declared in revelation, that, when one of its (the Ahunavar's) three *parts* was uttered, the evil spirit contracted *his* body through fear, and when two parts of it were uttered he fell upon *his* knees, and when all of it was uttered he became confounded

p. 9

and impotent as to the harm he caused the creatures of Aûharmazd, *and* he remained three thousand years in confusion[1].

23. Aûharmazd created *his* creatures in the confusion of Aharman; first he produced Vohûman ('good thought'), by whom the progress of the creatures of Aûharmazd was advanced.

24. The evil spirit first created[2] Mîtôkht ('falsehood'), and then Akôman ('evil thought').

25. The first of Aûharmazd's creatures of the world *was* the sky, and his good thought (Vohûman), by good procedure[3], produced the light of the world, along with which was the good religion of the Mazdayasnians; this *was* because the renovation (frashakard)[4], which happens to the creatures *was* known to him. 26. Afterwards *arose* Ardavahist,

p. 10

and then Shatvaîrô, and then Spendarmad, and then Horvadad, and then Amerôdad[1].

27. From the dark world of Aharman *were* Akôman and Andar, and then Sôvar, and then Nâkahêd, and then Tâîrêv and Zâîrîk[2].

28. Of Aûharmazd's creatures of the world, the first *was* the sky; the second, water; the third, earth; the fourth, plants; the fifth, animals; the sixth, mankind.

Footnotes

3:1 The Pâzand and most of the modern Pahlavi manuscripts have, 'From the Zand-âkâs,' but the word min, 'from,' does not occur in the old manuscript K20, and is a modern addition to M6. From this opening sentence it would appear that the author of the work gave it the name Zand-âkâs.

3:2 The Avesta Angra-mainyu, the spirit who causes adversity or anxiety (see Darmesteter's Ormazd et Ahriman, pp. 92–95); the Pahlavi name is, most probably, merely a corrupt transliteration of the Avesta form, and may be read Ganrâk-maînôk, as the Avesta Spenta-mainyu, the spirit who causes prosperity, has become Spênâk-maînôk in Pahlavi. This latter spirit is represented by Aûharmazd himself in the Bundahis. The Pahlavi word for 'spirit,' which is read madônad by the Parsis, and has been pronounced mînavad by some scholars and mînôî by others, is probably a corruption of maînôk, as its Sasanian form was minô. If it were not for the extra medial letter in ganrâk, and for the obvious partial transliteration of spênâk, it would be preferable to read ganâk, 'smiting,' and to derive it from a supposed verb gandan, 'to smite' (Av. ghna), as proposed by most Zendists. A Parsi would probably suggest gandan, 'to stink.'

4:1 Reading aham-kaî, 'without a fellow-sovereign, peerless, unrivalled, independent.' This rare word occurs three times in §§ 2, 3, and some Pâzand writers suggest the meaning 'everlasting' (by means of the Persian gloss hamîsah), which is plausible enough, but hâmakî would be an extraordinary mode of writing the very common word hamâî, 'ever.'

4:2 The word dînô (properly dênô), Av. daêna, being traceable to a root dî, 'to see,' must originally have meant 'a vision' (see Haug's Essays on the Religion of the Parsis, 2nd ed. p. 152, note 2), whence the term has been transferred to 'religion' and all religious observances, rules, and writings; so it may be translated either by 'religion' or by 'revelation.'

4:3 This appears to be the meaning, but the construction of § 3 is altogether rather obscure, and suggestive of omissions in the text.

4:4 The usual name of the evil spirit; it is probably an older corruption of Angra-mainyu than Ganrâk-maînôk, and a less technical term. Its Sasanian form was Aharmanî.

5:1 Substituting amat, 'when,' for mûn, 'which,' two Huzvâris forms which are frequently confounded by Pahlavi copyists because their Pâzand equivalents, ka and ke, are nearly alike.

5:2 Reading aminîdâr in accordance with M6, which has amînîdâr in Chap. XXXIV, 1, where the same phrase occurs. Windischmann and Justi read amûîtâr, 'uninjured, invulnerable,' in both places. This sentence appears to refer to a preparatory creation of embryonic and immaterial existences, the prototypes, fravashis, spiritual counterparts, or guardian angels of the spiritual and material creatures afterwards produced.

6:1 The Huz. khavîtûnast stands for the Pâz. dânist with the meaning, here, of 'what is known, knowledge,' as in Persian.

6:2 Literally, 'And it was shouted by him, the evil spirit, thus:' the usual idiom when the nominative follows the verb.

7:1 The words dên val stand for dên valman.

7:2 That is, 'the adversary is kept away.' In Pahlavi the third p. 8 person plural is the indefinite person, as in English. These 9000 years are in addition to the 3000 mentioned in § 8, as appears more clearly in Chap. XXXIV, 1.

8:1 This is the most sacred formula of the Parsis, which they have to recite frequently, not only during the performance of their ceremonies, but also in connection with most of their ordinary duties and habits. It is neither a prayer, nor a creed, but a declaratory formula in metre, consisting of one stanza of three lines, containing twenty-one Avesta words, as follows:—

> Yathâ ahû vairyô, athâ ratus, ashâd kîd hakâ,
>
> Vanghœus dazdâ mananghô, skyaothnanãm anghœus mazdâi,
>
> Khshathremkâ ahurâi â, yim dregubyô dadad vâstârem.

[paragraph continues] And it may be translated in the following manner: 'As a heavenly lord is to be chosen, so is an earthly master (spiritual guide), for the sake of righteousness, *to be* a giver of the good thoughts of the actions of life towards Mazda; and the dominion is for the lord (Ahura) whom he (Mazda) has given as a protector for the poor' (see Haug's Essays on the Religion of the Parsis, 2nd ed. pp. 125, 141).

8:2 The word mârik must mean 'word' here, but in some other places it seems to mean 'syllable' or 'accented syllable.'

9:1 This is the first third of the 9000 years appointed in §§ 18, 20, and the second 3000 years mentioned in Chap. XXXIV, 1.

9:2 It is usual to consider dâdan (Huz. yehabûntan), when traceable to Av. dâ = Sans. dhâ, as meaning 'to create,' but it can hardly be proved that it means to create out of nothing, any more than any other of the Avesta verbs which it is sometimes convenient to translate by 'create.' Before basing any argument upon the use of this word it will, therefore, be safer to substitute the word 'produce' in all cases.

9:3 Or it may be translated, 'and from it Vohûman, by good procedure,' &c. The position here ascribed to Vohûman, or the good thought of Aûharmazd, bears some resemblance to that of the Word in John i. 1–5, but with this essential difference, that Vohûman is merely a creature of Aûharmazd, not identified with him; for the latter idea would be considered, by a Parsi, as rather inconsistent with strict monotheism. The 'light of the world' now created must be distinguished from the 'endless light' already existing with Aûharmazd in § 2.

9:4 The word frashakard, 'what is made durable, perpetuation,' is applied to the renovation of the universe which is to take place about the time of the resurrection, as a preparation for eternity.

10:1 These five, with Vohûman and Aûharmazd in his angelic capacity, constitute the seven Ameshaspends, 'undying causers of prosperity, immortal benefactors,' or archangels, who have, charge of the whole material creation, They are personifications of old Avesta phrases, such as Vohû-manô, 'good thought;' Asha-vahista, 'perfect rectitude;' Khshathra-vairya, 'desirable dominion;' Spenta-ârmaiti, 'bountiful devotion;' Haurvatâd, 'completeness or health;' and Ameretâd, 'immortality.'

10:2 These six demons are the opponents of the six archangels respectively (see Chap. XXX, 29); their names in the Avesta are, Akem-manô, 'evil thought;' Indra, Sauru, Naunghaithya, Tauru, Zairika (see Vendîdâd X, 17, 18 Sp., and XIX, 43 W.), which have been compared with the Vedic god Indra, Sarva (a name of Siva), the Nâsatyas, and Sans. tura, 'diseased,' and garas, 'decay,' respectively. For further details regarding them, see Chap. XXVIII, 7–13.

Catholic: The Trinity

Belief in the trinity of God, the Father; God, the Son; and God, the Holy Spirit became an official part of the Catholic faith at the Council of Nicea in 325 CE. Until that time, early Christians were not unified in their various beliefs. Groups of Christians existed independently from each other and with separate books of what eventually came together as the Christian Bible. The Roman Emperor, Constantine the Great, tired of the fighting amongst the many bishops and archbishops of the newly legalized Christian faith, ordered them to get together and decide what their exact beliefs would be. The Athanasian Creed, which equates Jesus with God, won out over the Arian belief, which proposed that Jesus was human but divinely inspired. Since 325 CE, the Athanasian Creed has been the foundation for the Catholic belief as well as other Christian sects in its form as the

© jorisvo/Shutterstock.com

Nicene Creed. Jesus and God and the Holy Spirit are one and that One is Supreme. (Protestant branches of Christianity did not come into official existence until after Martin Luther began the Protestant Reformation in 1517 CE. From 325 CE–1517 CE, Catholicism was the only official form of Christianity.)

Athanasian Creed

1. Whosoever will be saved, before all things it is necessary that he hold the catholic faith;
2. Which faith except every one do keep whole and undefiled, without doubt he shall perish everlastingly.
3. And the catholic faith is this: That we worship one God in Trinity, and Trinity in Unity;
4. Neither confounding the persons nor dividing the substance.
5. For there is one person of the Father, another of the Son, and another of the Holy Spirit.
6. But the Godhead of the Father, of the Son, and of the Holy Spirit is all one, the glory equal, the majesty coeternal.
7. Such as the Father is, such is the Son, and such is the Holy Spirit.
8. The Father uncreated, the Son uncreated, and the Holy Spirit uncreated.
9. The Father incomprehensible, the Son incomprehensible, and the Holy Spirit incomprehensible.
10. The Father eternal, the Son eternal, and the Holy Spirit eternal.
11. And yet they are not three eternals but one eternal.
12. As also there are not three uncreated nor three incomprehensible, but one uncreated and one incomprehensible.
13. So likewise the Father is almighty, the Son almighty, and the Holy Spirit almighty.
14. And yet they are not three almighties, but one almighty.
15. So the Father is God, the Son is God, and the Holy Spirit is God;
16. And yet they are not three Gods, but one God.
17. So likewise the Father is Lord, the Son Lord, and the Holy Spirit Lord;
18. And yet they are not three Lords but one Lord.
19. For like as we are compelled by the Christian verity to acknowledge every Person by himself to be God and Lord;
20. So are we forbidden by the catholic religion to say; There are three Gods or three Lords.
21. The Father is made of none, neither created nor begotten.
22. The Son is of the Father alone; not made nor created, but begotten.
23. The Holy Spirit is of the Father and of the Son; neither made, nor created, nor begotten, but proceeding.
24. So there is one Father, not three Fathers; one Son, not three Sons; one Holy

Spirit, not three Holy Spirits.

25. And in this Trinity none is afore or after another; none is greater or less than another.
26. But the whole three persons are coeternal, and coequal.
27. So that in all things, as aforesaid, the Unity in Trinity and the Trinity in Unity is to be worshipped.
28. He therefore that will be saved must thus think of the Trinity.
29. Furthermore it is necessary to everlasting salvation that he also believe rightly the incarnation of our Lord Jesus Christ.
30. For the right faith is that we believe and confess that our Lord Jesus Christ, the Son of God, is God and man.
31. God of the substance of the Father, begotten before the worlds; and man of substance of His mother, born in the world.
32. Perfect God and perfect man, of a reasonable soul and human flesh subsisting.
33. Equal to the Father as touching His Godhead, and inferior to the Father as touching His manhood.
34. Who, although He is God and man, yet He is not two, but one Christ.
35. One, not by conversion of the Godhead into flesh, but by taking of that manhood into God.
36. One altogether, not by confusion of substance, but by unity of person.
37. For as the reasonable soul and flesh is one man, so God and man is one Christ;
38. Who suffered for our salvation, descended into hell, rose again the third day from the dead;
39. He ascended into heaven, He sits on the right hand of the Father, God, Almighty;
40. From thence He shall come to judge the quick and the dead.
41. At whose coming all men shall rise again with their bodies;
42. and shall give account of their own works.
43. And they that have done good shall go into life everlasting and they that have done evil into everlasting fire.
44. This is the catholic faith, which except a man believe faithfully he cannot be saved.

African: Yoruban gods Olorun and Obatala

In the Yoruba myths from African, the chief god is Olorun. He is the sky god and is associated with rain, thunder, and lightning. However, the god of thunder actually uses the lightning bolts rather than Olorun, who is the "Owner of the Sky." The sky is considered tangible, an actual material place, not just a spiritual place, which Olorun owns. From the distant vault of the sky, Olorun can look down upon the earth, but as

ochosi Babalu-aye Obatala Elegua Bumba Shango

anansi Olorun oya abassi Yemaya ogun

© Charis Estelle/Shutterstock.com

the actual king of the gods, he doesn't have to. He can relax on his throne or in his palace at his leisure. The real work of ruling the world and making sure things run correctly falls upon the other gods of the Yoruba pantheon, which means that there are not a lot of myths concerning the Yoruban Supreme Being. He is there in the background, enjoying the perks of being king of the gods, but not taking an active role in governing the world. Ellis reports, "Since he is too lazy or too indifferent to exercise any control over earthly affairs, man on his side does not waste time in endeavouring to propitiate him, but reserves his worship and sacrifice for more active agents. Hence Olorun has no priests, symbols, images, or temples, . . ." (www.sacred-texts.com). If times are tough and none of the other gods seem to be helping, a person in great need might call on the Supreme Being, but this is not common or usual. Olorun may have been appealed to more in earlier times.

While Olorun may be the Supreme Being of the Yoruba people, Obatala is the god who is actually the most important. The following comes from A. B. Ellis' *Yoruba-Speaking Peoples of the Slave Coast of West Africa*, 1894.

(2) OBATALA.

Obatala is the chief god of the Yorubas. The name means "Lord of the White Cloth" (*Oba-ti-ala*.), and is explained by the fact that white is the colour sacred to Obatala, whose temples, images, and paraphernalia are always painted white, and whose followers wear white cloths. Another derivation is Oba-ti-ala, "Lord of Visions," and this gains some probability from the fact that Obatala has the epithets of Orisha *oj'enia*, "The Orisha who enters man," and Alabalese (*Al-ba-ni-ase*),[1] "He who predicts the future," because he inspires the oracles and priests, and unveils futurity by means of visions. "Lord of the White Cloth," however, is the translation most commonly adopted, and appears to be the correct one. The god is always represented as wearing a white cloth.

Obatala, say the priests, was made by Olorun, who then handed over to him the management of the firmament and the world, and himself retired to rest. Obatala is thus also a sky-god, but is a more anthropomorphic conception than Olorun, and performs functions which are not in the least connected with the firmament. According to a myth, which is, however, contradicted by another, Obatala made the first man and woman out of clay, on which account he has the title of *Alamorere*, "Owner of the best clay;" and because he kneaded the clay himself he is called Orisha *kpokpo*, "The Orisha who kneads clay" (*kpo*, to knead or temper clay). Though this point is disputed by some natives, all are agreed that Obatala forms the child in the mother's womb, and women who desire to become mothers address their prayers to him; while albinoism and congenital deformities are regarded as his handiwork, done either to punish [. . .] some neglect towards him on the part of the parents, or to remind his worshippers of his power.

Obatala is also styled "Protector of the Town Gates," and in this capacity is represented as mounted on a horse, and armed with a spear. On the panels of the temple doors rude carvings are frequently seen of a horseman with a spear, surrounded by a leopard, tortoise, fish, and serpent. Another epithet of Obatala is *Obatala gbingbiniki*, "The enormous Obatala." His special offerings are edible snails.

Amongst the Ewe-speaking Peoples at Porto Novo, Obatala determines the guilt or innocence of accused persons by means of an oracle termed *Onshe* or *Onishe* (messenger, ambassador). It consists of a hollow cylinder of wood, about 3½ feet in length and 2 feet in diameter, one end of which is covered with draperies and the other closed with shells of the edible snail. This cylinder is placed on the head of the accused, who kneels on the ground, holding it firmly on his head with a hand at each side. The god, being then invoked by the priests, causes the cylinder to rock backwards and forwards, and finally to fall to the ground. If it should fall forward the accused is innocent, if backward guilty. The priests say that Obatala, or a subordinate spirit to whom he deputes the duty, strikes the accused, so as to make the cylinder fall in the required direction; but sceptics and native Christians say that a child is concealed in the cylinder and overbalances it in front or behind, according to instructions given beforehand by the priests. They add that when a child has served for a year or two and grown too big for the cylinder he is put to death, in order that the secret may be preserved; and is succeeded by another, who, in his turn, undergoes the same fate-but all this is mere conjecture.

[1. Al-oni (one who has); ba (to overtake); ni (to have); ase (a coming to pass), "One who overtakes the coming to pass."] found on www.sacred-texts.com

Muslim: Allah

Islam is a monotheistic religion that developed in the sixth century CE. Allah is the only god of Islam and quite the supreme god. He is the creator, law-giver, and judge. The following excerpt from the English translation of the Qur'an is by Yusuf Ali and emphasizes the qualities of this Supreme Being.

Sūra XXXII
Sajda, or Adoration.

In the name of God, Most Gracious,
Most Merciful.

1. A. L. M.

2. (This is) the revelation
Of the Book in which
There is no doubt,—
From the Lord of the Worlds.

3. Or do they say,
"He has forged it"?
Nay, it is the Truth
From thy Lord, that thou
Mayest admonish a people
To whom no warner Has come before thee:
In order that they
May receive guidance.

4. It is God Who has
Created the heavens
And the earth, and all
Between them, in six Days,
And is firmly established
On the Throne (of authority):

Ye have none, besides Him,
To protect or intercede (for you):
Will ye not then
Receive admonition?

5. He rules (all) affairs
From the heavens
To the earth: in the end
Will (all affairs) go up
To Him, on a Day,
The space whereof will be
(As) a thousand years
Of your reckoning.

6. Such is He, the Knower
Of all things, hidden
And open, the Exalted
(In power), the Merciful;—

7. He Who has made
Everything which He has created
Most Good: He began
The creation of man
With (nothing more than) clay,

8. And made his progeny
From a quintessence
Of the nature of
A fluid despised:

9. But He fashioned him
In due proportion, and breathed
Into him something of
His spirit. And He gave
You (the faculties of) hearing
And sight and feeling
(And understanding):
Little thanks do ye give!

10. And they say: "What!
When we lie, hidden
And lost, in the earth,

Shall we indeed be
In a Creation renewed?
Nay, they deny the Meeting
With their Lord!"

11. Say: "The Angel of Death,
Put in charge of you,
Will (duly) take your souls:
Then shall ye be brought
Back to your Lord."

SECTION 2.

12. If only thou couldst see
When the guilty ones
Will bend low their heads
Before their Lord, (saying:)
"Our Lord! We have seen
And we have heard:
Now then send us back
(To the world): we will
Work righteousness: for we
Do indeed (now) believe."

13. If We had so willed, We could certainly have brought
Every soul its true guidance:
But the Word from Me
Will come true, "I will
Fill Hell with Jinns
And men all together."

14. "Taste ye then—for ye
Forgot the Meeting
Of this Day of yours
And We too will
Forget you—taste ye
The Penalty of Eternity
For your (evil) deeds!"

15. Only those believe
In Our Signs, who, when
They are recited to them,

Fall down in adoration,
And celebrate the praises
Of their Lord, nor are they
(Ever) puffed up with pride.

16. Their limbs do forsake
Their beds of sleep, the while
They call on their Lord,
In Fear and Hope:
And they spend (in charity)
Out of the sustenance which
We have bestowed on them.
17. Now no person knows
What delights of the eye
Are kept hidden (in reserve)
For them—as a reward
For their (good) Deeds.

18. Is then the man
Who believes no better
Than the man who is
Rebellious and wicked?
Not equal are they.

19. For those who believe
And do righteous deeds,
Are Gardens as hospitable
Homes, for their (good) deeds.

20. As to those who are
Rebellious and wicked, their abode
Will be the Fire: every time
They wish to get away
Therefrom, they will be forced
Thereinto, and it will be said
To them: "Taste ye
The Penalty of the Fire,
The which ye were wont
To reject as false."

21. And indeed We will make
Them taste of the Penalty
Of this (life) prior to

The supreme Penalty, in order
That they may (repent and) return.

22. And who does more wrong
Than one to whom are recited
The Signs of his Lord,
And who then turns away
Therefrom? Verily from those
Who transgress We shall exact
(Due) Retribution.

SECTION 3.

23. We did indeed aforetime
Give the Book to Moses:
Be not then in doubt
Of its reaching (thee):
And We made it
A guide to the Children
Of Israel.

24. And We appointed, from among
Them, Leaders, giving guidance
Under Our command, so long
As they persevered with patience
And continued to have faith
In Our Signs.

25. Verily thy Lord will judge
Between them on the Day
Of Judgment, in the matters
Wherein they differ
(among themselves)

26. Does it not teach them
A lesson, how many generations
We destroyed before them,
In whose dwellings they
(Now) go to and fro?
Verily in that are Signs:
Do they not then listen?

27. And do they not see
That We do drive Rain
To parched soil (bare
Of herbage), and produce therewith
Crops, providing food
For their cattle and themselves?
Have they not the vision?

28. They say: "When will
This Decision be, if ye
Are telling the truth?"
29. Say: "On the Day
Of Decision, no profit
Will it be to Unbelievers
If they (then) believe!
Nor Will they be granted
A respite."

30. So turn away from them,
And wait: they too
Are waiting.

■ ■ ■

The Holy Quran, translated by Yusuf Ali, 1934. Located on www.sacred-texts.com

In this chapter, we met powerful Sky Fathers, who rule from the Heavens above. They often wield the power of light, the fires of the Sun or lightning. They watch over the world below with all seeing eyes. They are the head of the family of gods if they are from a polytheistic tradition, and they have life and death control over all the gods, mortals, animals, and the world itself. Ideally, they rule with wisdom, and they have the power of the Paterfamilias, enforcing patriarchal values and upholding the role of kings and kingship among mortal men.

Study Questions for Chapter 4: Supreme Being Archetype

Supreme Being Archetype

1. List the characteristics of the Supreme Being Archetype.
2. What happens if a culture emphasizes only the good side of an archetype?

Mesopotamia: Marduk

1. Who is Marduk? Who are his parents?
2. What descriptions of Marduk are given in Tablet Four of the Enuma Elish that fit the Archetype of the Supreme Being?
3. What descriptions of Marduk are given in Tablet Seven of the Enuma Elish that fit the Archetype of the Supreme Being?

Hebrew: Yahweh

1. What kind of powers does Yahweh tell Moses that he has?
2. What descriptions of Yahweh, from the excerpt from Exodus, fit the characteristics of the Supreme Being Archetype?
3. What kind of powers does Yahweh tell Job he has?
4. What descriptions of Yahweh from the book of Job fit the characteristics of the Supreme Being Archetype?

Greek: Zeus

1. What kind of powers does Zeus display in the excerpt from Book IV of the *Iliad*?
2. What characteristics of the Supreme Being Archetype does Zeus display in the excerpts from Book 14 and Book 15 of the *Iliad*?
3. Who was Prometheus? Why did Zeus punish him?
4. How does the story of the punishment of Prometheus demonstrate Zeus' powers as an example of the Supreme Being Archetype?

Indian: Brahman

1. Who was Arguna (Arjuna)? What was his relationship to Krishna?
2. Who is Krishna?
3. How is Brahman unique among all of the Supreme Beings described in this chapter?
4. How does the description of what Arguna sees when Krishna reveals himself as Brahman demonstrate qualities of the Supreme Being Archetype?

Persian: Ahura-Mazda

1. What are the descriptions given concerning Aûharmazd (Ahura-Mazda) in the passage from the Pahlavi texts?
2. How do the descriptions in the Pahlavi texts line up with the characteristics of the Supreme Being Archetype?
3. Who is Aharman?

Catholic: The Trinity

1. What is the Trinity according to the Athanasian Creed?
2. What powers do each part of the Trinity have?
3. Do the powers of the Trinity coincide with the characteristics of the Supreme Being Archetype? Explain your answer.

Yoruban: Olorun and Obatala

1. Who is Olorun?
2. What powers does Olorun have?
3. Who is Obatala?
4. What powers does Obatala have?
5. How do Olorun and Obatala share the powers of the Supreme Being Archetype?
6. Why might the Yoruba conceive of two examples of the Supreme Being Archetype in their mythology?

Muslim: Allah

1. Who is Allah?
2. How is Allah described in Sūra XXXII of the Qur'an?
3. What part of the description of Allah matches the characteristics of the Supreme Being Archetype?

CHAPTER 5
THE GREAT GODDESS ARCHETYPE

The Great Goddess as an Archetype

Another brief word about archetypes: "It is an essential feature of the primordial archetype that it combines positive and negative attributes and groups of attributes. This union of opposites in the primordial archetype, its ambivalence, is characteristic of the original situation of the unconscious, which consciousness has not yet dissected into its antitheses. Early man experienced this paradoxical simultaneity of good and evil, friendly and terrible, in the godhead as a unity; while as consciousness developed, the good goddess and the bad goddess, for example, usually came to be worshiped as different beings" (Neumann, 12).

Characteristics of the Great Goddess Archetype

The Great Goddess Archetype is often associated with the Earth for like the Earth, she is the source of life and she nourishes life from her own body. She is the Mother of All, and the First Mother. Everything on the earth is her child and often all the gods come from her. Because she gives life she can also take it away. The Great Goddess has existed in images for thousands of years. "Images of giving birth, offering nourishment from the breast and receiving the dead back into the womb for rebirth occur in the Paleolithic as they do 10,000 years later in the Neolithic and 5,000 years after that in the Bronze and Iron ages [. . .]" (Baring and Cashford, 9). Her abilities to take life and restore life in some fashion are part of the archetype's inherent ambivalence.

The Great Goddess is associated with the life, death, and rebirth cycle, which often links her to the underworld or afterlife. Death is inseparable from life. No life exists without feeding on other life, thus bringing death. When a body is buried in the earth, it is like a seed planted in the ground waiting for the right combination of events to come to life. Thus the earth is often both the tomb and the womb of the Great Goddess. She is in charge of the mysteries of life and death and rebirth and knows what

119

transpires in the dark realms. As giver of life, she knows what it will take to wake the dormant seed buried in the earth, as well as the shade or soul in the land of the dead.

As the Great Mother, the Great Goddess is fertile and usually sexual. She gives birth to all life and nourishes and nurtures it. However, Great does not mean good in this context, but rather Great as in elemental. The Great Mother may turn out to be the neglectful or Terrible Mother that ends up smothering or devouring her young rather than nurturing them. Ceridwen from Celtic mythology is often referred to as the Great Sow because sows have the reputation of eating their young. At the same time, Ceridwen possesses the cauldron of rebirth. Whatever she places in the cauldron returns to life. Like the natural cycles such as the waning and waxing of the moon, the Goddess gives and she takes away and she gives again. Many times it is her own child or her lover whom she restores or attempts to restore to life, usually after a quest that may take her to the very realm of the dead to retrieve the lost loved one. Rebirth can take place in many forms and often represents a transformation of consciousness rather than a "return of the same" (Downing, 13). The moon is often the symbol of her association with this cycle of birth, death, and rebirth, but the moon is also the source of magic and dreams. The Great Goddess is often connected to both.

As the Maiden or Virgin, the Great Goddess represents youthfulness, the promise of fertility, and independence, the young crescent moon is her symbol and she is associated with spring and renewal. The Maiden may be a hunter or warrior and her weapons associate her with her death dealing aspect, while her youthfulness associates her with life.

As the Crone or Wise Woman, the Great Goddess may be the healer, sibyl, or sage warrior who teaches how to free the self (ego) from attachments in order to prepare for death.

Many times the Great Goddess appears in triple guise as maiden, mother, and crone, all three aspects appearing together and working together to make the totality of the Great Goddess. Her title is, quite frequently, Queen of Heaven and Earth.

The Great Goddess is omitted from the monotheisms for the most part, with the exception of the Virgin Mary, Mother of God and Queen of Heaven. Mary represents a purification of the archetype, a splitting away of the negative or ambiguous and ambivalent qualities so only the good, virginal maiden who is also a nurturing mother remains.

■ ■ ■

Baring, Anne and Jules Cashford. *The Myth of the Goddess: Evolution of an Image.* Arkana, London, 1991.

Downing, Christine. *The Goddess: Mythological Images of the Feminine.* New York, Author's Choice Press, 2007.

Neumann, Eric. *The Great Mother: An Analysis of the Archetype.* Trans. Ralph Manheim, Princeton University Press, Princeton, 1991.

Egypt: The Sky Goddess Nut

Nut was the Mother Sky of the Heliopolitan Creation myth from Egypt. She and her husband, Geb, Father Earth, had been so in love that they never let go of each other.

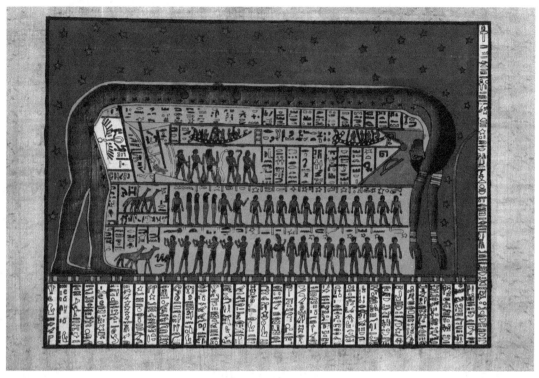

Figure 5.1
© Bernice Williams/Shutterstock.com

In order for creation to continue, their father, Shu, the god of atmosphere, separated the couple. He lifted Nut up so that only her toe tips and her fingertips touched the body of her husband, Geb. In Egyptian belief, Nut gave birth to the sun each morning and swallowed it each night. The sun was carried through the sky and the body of Nut in a boat or barque. Any of the gods who traveled through the sky had to pass through Nut's body. She embraced all things from above and was responsible not only for birth and death, but also rebirth.

19. IN PRAISE OF NUT, UTTERANCES 427–435

Utterance 429.

779a. To say by Geb: Nut, thou art become (spiritually) mighty:

779b. thou wast (already physically) mighty in the womb of thy mother, Tefnut, before thou wast born.

779c. Protect N. with life and well-being. He shall not die.

Utterance 430.

780a. To say: Mighty was, thy heart,

780b. when thou wast in the body of thy mother, in thy name of "Nut".

Utterance 431.

781a. (To say:) Thou art the daughter, who has gained (physical) power over her mother, who dawned as king of Lower Egypt.

781b. Make N. (spiritually) mighty in thy womb. He shall not die.

Utterance 432.

782a. To say: Great lady, who didst become heaven, thou didst become (physically) mighty,

782b. thou art become victorious, thou hast filled every place with thy beauty.

782c. The whole earth lies (lit. is) under thee; thou hast taken possession of it;

782d. thou encompassest the earth and all things (therein) in thine arms;

782e. mayest thou establish this N. in thee as an imperishable star.

Utterance 433.

783a. To say: I have fertilized thee as Geb, in thy name of "Heaven";

783b. I have united to thee the whole earth in every place.

Utterance 434.

784a. To say: High one over the earth, thou art above thy father Shu, who hast the mastery over him.

784b. He has loved thee in that he has set himself under thee; all things are thine.

785a. Thou hast taken each god to thyself with his boat;

785b. thou hast educated them as "She of a thousand souls,"

785c. so that they will not disappear from thee like stars.

785d. So let not N. leave thee, in thy name of "Far off one" (or, "High one").

Utterance 435.

786a. To say: I am Nut, "the Granary." I have proclaimed the name of Osiris N.,

786b. namely, "Horus, beloved of the two lands, N."; "King of Upper and Lower Egypt, N.";

786c. "*nb.ti,* beloved of the Corporation, N."; "falcon over gold, N.";

787a. "heir of Geb, his beloved N.", "beloved of all the gods, N.";

787b. given all life, stability, prosperity, health, joy like Rē', thou livest for ever.

21. SECOND SERIES IN PRAISE OF NUT, UTTERANCES 443–452.

Utterances 443.

823a. To say: Nut, two eyes are come forth from thy head.

823b. Thou hast taken possession of Horus and his Great-in-charms;

823c. thou hast taken possession of Set and his Great-in-charms.

823d. Nut, thou hast numbered thy children, in thy name of "*rp.t-*sedan-chair of Heliopolis."

823e. Thou shalt reclaim N. also for life; he shall not perish.

Utterances 444–445.

824a. To say: Nut, thou hast dawned as king of Lower Egypt, because thou hast gained power over the gods,

824b. together with their *kas,* together with their heritage,

824c. together with their food, together with all their possessions.

824d. Nut, him thou causest to endure, he will live.

824e. Nut, if thou livest, N. will live.

Utterance 446.

825a. To say: Osiris N., thy mother, Nut, has spread herself over thee,

825b. that she may hide thee from all evil things.

825c. Nut has guarded thee from all evil;

825d. thou art the greatest among her children.

Utterance 447.

826a. To say: He is gone who went to his *ka;* Osiris is gone to his *ka;* Set is gone to his *ka;*

826b. *Mḥnti-'irti* is gone to his *ka;* thou thyself art gone to thy *ka.*

827a. O N., he who comes, comes, thou shalt not be in need;

827b. thy mother comes, thou shalt not be in need; Nut, thou shalt not be in need;

827c. protectress of the great, thou shalt not be in need; protectress of the fearful, thou shalt not be in need.

828a. She protects thee, she prevents thy need, she gives back thy head to thee;

828b. she collects thy bones for thee;

828c. she brings thy heart into thy body for thee.

829a. Thou art (henceforth?) chief of those who were before thee;

829b. thou commandest those who will be after thee.

829c. Thou causest thy house to prosper after thee; thou protectest thy children from sorrow.

829d. Thy purity is the purity of the gods, who have gone to their *kas;*

829e. thy purity is the purity of the gods who have passed on, and so do not suffer hardship.

Utterance 450.

832a. To say: He is gone, who went to his *ka;* Osiris is gone to his *ka;* Set is gone to his *ka;*

832b. *Mḥnti-'irti* is gone to his *ka;* N. is gone to his *ka.*

833a. O N., thou art gone, that thou mayest live; thou art gone, that thou mayest not die;

833b. thou art gone, that thy spirit may be at the head of the spirits, that thou mayest be powerful at the head of the living;

833c. that thou mayest be mighty (a soul), and thou art mighty (a soul); that thou mayest be honoured, and thou art honoured.

834a. He who comes, comes; thou shalt not be in need.

834b. Thy mother comes to thee, thou shalt not be in need; Nut comes to thee, thou shalt not be in need;

834c. the protectress of the great comes to thee, thou shalt not be in need.
835a. She protects thee, she prevents thy need, she gives back thy head to thee;
835b. she assembles thy bones for thee, she unites thy limbs for thee;
835c. she brings thy heart into thy body for thee.
836a. Thou art (henceforth?) chief of those who were before thee;
836b. thou commandest those who were before thee;
836c. thou protectest thy children from sorrow.
836d. Thy purity is the purity of the gods,
836e. the lords of want, who have gone to their *kas*.

■ ■ ▨

The Pyramid Texts, Translation by Samuel A. B. Mercer, [1952, copyright not renewed] www.sacred-texts.com

Egypt: Isis

Isis was the daughter of Nut and Geb and the sister of Osiris, Seth, and Nephthys. She and Osiris were said to be in love in their mother's womb and were soon married after their birth from the sky goddess. Osiris was the first king of Egypt and with Isis at his side, taught the arts of civilization to the Egyptians. Isis was devoted to Osiris so that when his brother trapped him in a sarcophagus and threw it in the Nile, it was Isis who searched for him and eventually retrieved his corpse from Syria and sought to revive him. In the process, she determined to give birth to a son to inherit Osiris' throne: Horus, the avenger of his father. Isis wasn't able to revive Osiris fully because she needed more magic. In the end, Isis gained magic from Ra, the sun god, through trickery and was able to revive her husband, Osiris, who became the god of the afterlife. Isis was often portrayed with her sister Nephthys standing just behind Osiris' throne in the Duat, the Egyptian after life. Because of this myth, she was associated with the underworld, birth, death, and rebirth. Over time, Isis became one of the most loved and most powerful goddesses not only in Egypt, but also throughout much of the Roman world.

As a mother, Isis protected the infant Horus until he was old enough to fight his uncle, Seth, for the throne of Egypt. The two battled fiercely and the fighting became rather ugly. The elder gods were evenly split into two factions: one supported Horus and the other supported Seth. Isis did everything she could to ensure that Horus became Pharoah of Egypt. She disguised herself as a human widower and mother of a young son and attempted to seduce Seth into siding with her. When that failed, she took a more direct approach and shot Seth with a harpoon like weapon while he was in hippopota-mus form at the bottom of the Nile. Her aggressive attempts to support Horus, and her

Figure 5.2
© Liudmila Klymenko/Shutterstock.com

ambivalent love for her brother caused Horus to storm up out of the Nile and chop her head off. The gods gave Isis a cow's head until such a time as they could restore her own. Eventually peace was made among the gods and Horus and his mother resumed their normally happy relationship. The battles between Seth and Horus for the throne of Egypt continued until finally the gods asked Osiris who he wanted to succeed him, his brother or his son. Osiris supported his son and Seth, in recompense, was made guardian of Ra's sun boat as it traveled through the afterworld each night.

Isis was often portrayed as a seated figure with the child Horus on her lap or as a goddess with her outstretched wings hovering protectively over her son, the pharaoh's, shoulders. Isis was the throne itself that the pharaohs of Egypt sat upon. Thus the pharaoh sat in the lap of Isis just as Horus had done. She remained the guardian of the Egyptian throne and her hieroglyph meant throne.

Here is the story told by M. A. Murray of how Isis tricked Ra into giving her his secret name and thus increasing her magic in order for her to restore Osiris to life.

■ ■ ■

Ancient Egyptian Legends, by M. A. Murray, 1920. Located on www.sacred-texts.com

X
THE NAME OF RA

Now the Majesty of Ra was the creator of heaven and earth, of gods, men, and cattle, of fire, and the breath of life; and he ruled over gods and men. And Isis saw his might, the might that reached over heaven and earth, before which all gods and men bowed; and she longed in her heart for that power, that thereby she should be greater than the gods and have dominion over men.

There was but one way to obtain that power. By the knowledge of his own name did Ra rule, and none but himself knew that secret name. Whosoever could learn the secret, to that one—god or man—would belong the dominion over all the world, and even Ra himself must be in subjection. Jealously did Ra guard his secret, and kept it ever in his breast, lest it should be taken from him, and his power diminished.

Every morning Ra came forth in his glory at the head of his train from the horizon of the East, journeying across the sky, and in the evening they came to the horizon of the West, and the Majesty of Ra sank in his glory to lighten the thick darkness of the Duat. Many, many times had Ra made the journey, so many times that now he had waxed old. Very aged was Ra, and the saliva ran down from his mouth and fell upon the earth.

Then Isis took earth and mixed it with the saliva, and she kneaded the clay and moulded it, and formed it into the shape of a snake, the shape of the great hooded snake that is the emblem of all goddesses, the royal serpent which is upon the brow of the Kings of Egypt. No charms or magic spells did she use, for in the snake was the divine substance of Ra himself. She took the snake and laid it hidden in the path of Ra, the path on which he travelled in journeying from the eastern to the western horizon of heaven.

In the morning came Ra and his train in their glory journeying to the western horizon of heaven, where they enter the Duat and lighten the thick darkness. And the serpent shot out its pointed head which was shaped like a dart, and its fangs sank into the flesh of Ra, and the fire of its poison entered into the God, for the divine substance was in the serpent.

Ra cried aloud, and his cry rang through the heavens from the eastern to the western horizon; across the earth it rang, and gods and men alike heard the cry of Ra. And the gods who follow in his train said to him, "What aileth thee? What aileth thee?"

But Ra answered never a word, he trembled in all his limbs, and his teeth chattered, and naught did he say, for the poison spread over his body as Hapi spreads over the land, when the waters rise above their banks at the time of the overflowing of the river.

When he had become calm, he called to those who followed him and said, "Come to me, ye whom I created. I am hurt by a grievous thing. I feel it, though I see it not, neither is it the creation of my hands, and I know not who has made it. Never, never have I felt pain like this, never, never has there been an injury worse than this.

Who can hurt me? For none know my secret name, that name which was spoken by my father and by my mother, and hidden in me that none might work witchcraft upon me. I came forth to look upon the world which I had made, I passed across the Two Lands when something—I know not what—struck me. Is it fire? Is it water? I burn, I shiver, I tremble in all my limbs. Call to me the children of the gods, they who have skill in healing, they who have knowledge of magic, they whose power reaches to heaven."

Then came all the gods with weeping and mourning and lamentations; their power was of no avail against the serpent, for in it the divine substance was incorporated. With them came Isis the Healer, the Mistress of Magic, in whose mouth is the Breath of Life, whose words destroy disease and awake the dead.

She spoke to the Majesty of Ra and said. "What is this, O divine Father? what is this? Has a snake brought pain to thee? Has the creation of thy hand lifted up its head against thee? Lo, it shall be overthrown by the might of my magic, I will drive it out by means of thy glory."

Then the Majesty of Ra answered, "I passed along the appointed path, I crossed over the Two Lands, when a serpent that I saw not struck me with its fangs. Was it fire? Was it water? I am colder than water, I am hotter than fire, I tremble in all my limbs, and the sweat runs down my face as down the faces of men in the fierce heat of summer."

And Isis spoke again, and her voice was low and soothing, "Tell me thy Name, O divine Father, thy true Name, thy secret Name, for he only can live who is called by his name."

Then the Majesty of Ra answered, "I am the Maker of heaven and earth, I am the Establisher of the mountains, I am the Creator of the waters, I am the Maker of the secrets of the two Horizons, I am Light and I am Darkness, I am the Maker of Hours, the Creator of Days, I am the Opener of Festivals, I am the Maker of running streams, I am the Creator of living flame. I am Khepera in the morning, Ra at noontide, and Atmu in the evening."

But Isis held her peace; never a word did she speak, for she knew that Ra had told her the names that all men know; his true Name, his secret Name, was still hidden in his breast. And the power of the poison increased, and ran through his veins like burning flame.

After a silence she spoke again. "Thy Name, thy true Name, thy secret Name, was not among those. Tell me thy Name that the poison may be driven out, for only he whose name I know can be healed by the might of my magic." And the power of the poison increased, and the pain was as the pain of living fire.

Then the Majesty of Ra cried out and said, "Let Isis come with me, and let my Name pass from my breast to her breast."

And he hid himself from the gods that followed in his train. Empty was the Boat of the Sun, empty was the great throne of the God, for Ra had hidden himself from his Followers and from the creations of his hands.

When the Name came forth from the heart of Ra to pass to the heart of Isis, the goddess spoke to Ra and said, "Bind thyself with an oath, O Ra, that thou wilt give thy two eyes unto Horus." Now the two Eyes of Ra are the sun and the moon, and men call them the Eyes of Horus to this day.

Thus was the Name of Ra taken from him and given to Isis, and she, the great Enchantress, cried aloud the Word of Power, and the poison obeyed, and Ra was healed by the might of his Name.

And Isis, the great One, Mistress of the Gods, Mistress of magic, she is the skilful Healer, in her mouth is the Breath of Life, by her words she destroys pain, and by her power she awakes the dead.

In the Greco-Roman world, the cult of Isis spread and she became equated with most of the Greek and Roman goddesses as well as the near eastern goddesses such as Ishtar and Astarte. Apuleius, a Roman poet, perhaps summed up the Hellenistic Isis' powers the best, when his character, Lucius, who was turned into an ass by a witch, described the powers of Isis in the *Metamorphoses,* or *The Golden Ass.*

The Golden Ass of Apuleius, translated by Robert Graves
Pages 263–265

Lucius prayed to Isis for help and the goddess answered his prayer, appearing to him out of the sea and annoucing, "All the perfumes of Arabia floated into my nostrils as the Goddess deigned to address me: 'You see me here, Lucius, in answer to your prayer. I am Nature, the universal Mother, mistress of all the elements, primordial child of time, sovereign of all things spiritual, queen of the dead, queen also of the immortals, the single manifestation of all gods and goddesses that are. My nod governs the shining heights of Heaven, the wholesome sea-breezes, the lamentable silences of the world below. Though I am worshipped in many aspects, known by countless names, and propitiated with all manner of different rites, yet the whole round earth venerates me. The primeval Phrygians call me Pessinuntica, Mother of the gods; the Athenians, sprung from their own soil, call me Cecropian Artemis; for the islanders of Cyprus I am Paphian Aphrodite; for the archers of Crete I am Dictynna; for the trilingual Sicilians, Stygian Proserpine; and for the Eleusinians their ancient Mother of the Corn.

'Some know me as Juno, some as Bellona of the Battles; others as Hecate, others again as Rhamnubia, but both races of Aethiopians, whose lands the morning sun first shines upon, and the Egyptians who excel in ancient learning and worship me with ceremonies proper to my godhead, call me by my true name, namely, Queen Isis. I have come in pity of your plight, I have come to favour and aid you. Weep no more, lament no longer; the hour of deliverance, shone over by my watchful light, is at hand.'

Mesopotamia: Tiamat

Tiamat, who is the goddess of the salt waters in Mesopotamian mythology, is the first mother and ultimately the mother of all the gods in the Mesopotamian myth. She is a bit passive at the beginning of the creation story especially when her husband Apsu wants to destroy their offspring for making too much noise in the waters. Tiamat's protests are a bit weak. However, after Ea kills Apsu, Tiamat becomes the embodiment of the Terrible Mother and makes life miserable for the other gods in the water by breeding up a race of monsters with her second husband Kingu. Here are a few excerpts from the *Enuma Elish* that highlight Tiamat's characteristics.

THE FIRST TABLET
When in the height heaven was not named,
And the earth beneath did not yet bear a name,
And the primeval Apsu, who begat them,
And chaos, Tiamat, the mother of them both
Their waters were mingled together,
. . .
when Tiamat heard these words [concerning the noise of their offspring],
She raged and cried aloud . . .
She . . . grievously . . . ,
She uttered a curse, and unto Apsu she spake:
"What then shall we do?
Let their way be made difficult, and let us lie down again in peace."
. . .
They banded themselves together and at the side of Tiamat they advanced;
They were furious; they devised mischief without resting night and day.
They prepared for battle, fuming and raging;
They joined their forces and made war,
Ummu-Hubur [Tiamat] who formed all things,
Made in addition weapons invincible; she spawned monster-serpents,
Sharp of tooth, and merciless of fang;
With poison, instead of blood, she filled their bodies.
Fierce monster-vipers she clothed with terror,
With splendor she decked them, she made them of lofty stature.
Whoever beheld them, terror overcame him,
Their bodies reared up and none could withstand their attack.
She set up vipers and dragons, and the monster Lahamu,
And hurricanes, and raging hounds, and scorpion-men,
And mighty tempests, and fish-men, and rams;

They bore cruel weapons, without fear of the fight.
Her commands were mighty, none could resist them;
After this fashion, huge of stature, she made eleven [kinds of] monsters.
Among the gods who were her sons, inasmuch as he had given her support,
She exalted Kingu; in their midst she raised him to power.
To march before the forces, to lead the host,
To give the battle-signal, to advance to the attack,
To direct the battle, to control the fight,
Unto him she entrusted; in costly raiment she made him sit, saying:
I have uttered thy spell, in the assembly of the gods I have raised thee to power.
The dominion over all the gods have I entrusted unto him.
Be thou exalted, thou my chosen spouse,
May they magnify thy name over all of them the Anunnaki."
She gave him the Tablets of Destiny, on his breast she laid them, saying:
Thy command shall not be without avail, and the word of thy mouth shall be established."

. . .

THE SECOND TABLET

Tiamat made weighty her handiwork,
Evil she wrought against the gods her children.
To avenge Apsu, Tiamat planned evil, . . .

. . .

After winning the homage of the elder gods, Marduk challenges Tiamat to face him in single combat:

When Tiamat heard these words,
She was like one possessed, she lost her reason.
Tiamat uttered wild, piercing cries,
She trembled and shook to her very foundations.
She recited an incantation, she pronounced her spell,
And the gods of the battle cried out for their weapons.
Then advanced Tiamat and Marduk, the counselor of the gods;
To the fight they came on, to the battle they drew nigh.

During the battle, Marduk slays Tiamat by shooting an arrow down her throat and into her heart. After killing her, he splits her body into two parts, half of which he makes into the heavens and the other half the earth. Thus ends the rule of this particular terrible mother, whom the *Enuma Elish* describes as a "monster" at this point in the myth. From first mother to Terrible Mother, Tiamat fits the archetype of the Great Goddess.

■ ■ ■

Enuma Elish: The Epic of Creation, Translated by L. W. King from *The Seven Tablets of Creation,* 1902. Located on www.sacred-texts.com

Mesopotamia: Inanna

© Zvereva Yana/Shutterstock.com

Inanna is the Sumerian Queen of Heaven and Earth. She is the daughter of the moon god, Nanna, granddaughter of Enki, the god of Wisdom (Babylonia's Ea) and sister of the goddess of the Underworld, Ereshkigal. Inanna is often associated with the moon's cycle of waxing and waning, which associates her with life and death, increase and decrease, the upper world and the lower (underworld). She is also associated with the morning and evening star, which is known today as the planet Venus. Inanna gains many powers from her grandfather, Enki, in something that sounds a lot like a drinking contest to modern ears. The powers that Enki grants his granddaughter cover a wide range of abilities from procreation to strength in battle. Enki also grants his granddaughter the ability to enter and leave the underworld, which no one else seems to have. Death is normally final. In this particular case, Inanna's powers are to her good advantage and it is especially important that her grandfather know what her powers are. Here follows some excerpts of the Inanna myth.

In *Sumerian Mythology* located on www.sacred-texts.com, Samuel Kramer (1944, 1961) states:

Inanna, queen of heaven, and tutelary goddess of Erech, is anxious to increase the welfare and prosperity of her city, to make it the center of Sumerian civilization, and thus to exalt her own name and fame. She therefore decides to go to Eridu, the ancient and hoary seat of Sumerian culture where Enki, the Lord of Wisdom, who "knows the very heart of the gods," dwells in his watery abyss, the Abzu. For Enki has under his charge all the divine decrees that are fundamental to civilization. And if she can obtain them, by fair means or foul, and bring them to her beloved city Erech, its glory and her own will indeed be unsurpassed. As she approaches the Abzu of Eridu, Enki, no doubt taken in by her charms, calls his messenger Isimud and thus addresses him:

"Come, my messenger, Isimud, give ear to my instructions,
A word I will say to thee, take my word.
The maid, all alone, has directed her step to the Abzu,
Inanna, all alone, has directed her step to the Abzu,
Have the maid enter the Abzu of Eridu,
Have Inanna enter the Abzu of Eridu,
Give her to eat barley cake with butter,
Pour for her cold water that freshens the heart,
Give her to drink date-wine in the 'face of the lion,'
. . . for her . . . . make for her . . .,
At the pure table, the table of heaven,
Speak to Inanna words of greeting."

Isimud does exactly as bidden by his master, and Inanna and Enki sit down to feast and banquet. After their hearts had become happy with drink, Enki exclaims:

"O name of My power, O name of my power,
To the pure Inanna, my daughter, I shall present . . . .
Lordship, . . .-ship, godship, the tiara exalted and enduring, the throne of kingship."
Pure Inanna took them.

"O name of my power, O name of my power, To the pure Inanna, my daughter,
I shall present . . . . The exalted scepter, *staffs*, the exalted shrine, shepherdship,
kingship."

Pure Inanna took them.

He thus presents, several at a time, over one hundred divine decrees which are the basis of the culture pattern of Sumerian civilization. And when it is realized that this myth was inscribed as early as 2000 B. C. and that the concepts involved were no doubt current centuries earlier, it is no exaggeration to state that no other civilization, outside of the Egyptian, can at all compare in age and quality with that developed by the Sumerians. Among these divine decrees presented by Enki to Inanna are those referring to lordship, godship, the exalted and enduring crown, the throne of kingship, the exalted scepter, the exalted shrine, shepherdship, kingship, the numerous priestly offices, truth, descent into the nether world and ascent from it, the "standard," the flood, sexual intercourse and prostitution, the *legal* tongue and the *libellous* tongue, art, the holy cult chambers, the "hierodule of heaven," music, eldership, heroship and power, enmity, straightforwardness, the destruction of cities and lamentation, rejoicing of the heart, falsehood, the rebel land, goodness and justice, the craft of the carpenter, metal worker, scribe, smith, leather worker, mason, and basket weaver, wisdom and understanding, purification, fear and *outcry,* the kindling flame and the *consuming* flame, weariness, the shout of victory, counsel, the troubled heart, judgment and decision, exuberance, musical instruments.

Inanna is only too happy to accept the gifts offered her by the drunken Enki. She takes them, loads them on her "boat of heaven," and makes off for Erech with her precious cargo.

■ ■ ■

Sumerian Mythology, by Samuel Noah Kramer, 1944, 1961. Located on www.sacred-texts.com

After Inanna receives the gifts and the evening winds down, Enki falls asleep and Inanna slips out of the palace with all the Me tablets on which the various new powers were inscribed. She loads the Me tablets onto her boat and sets sail for her home city of Uruk. When Enki awakens the next morning, Inanna is gone, his palace looks a little empty from the lack of over a hundred Me tablets and he has a hazy memory of what has happened. His servant has to describe the events of the previous evening to Enki, who is not pleased with the news. He sends his armies out to retrieve the Me tablets from Inanna's ship but her ship is well defended and each time his army attacks, it is repelled by the defenders. Inanna makes it home safely and unloads the Me tablets respectfully greeted by her joyous people. When Enki learns of her care and respect for her new powers and her lack of abuse, he allows her to keep them.

Settled back into her life at Uruk, Inanna is now truly Queen of Heaven and Earth. She has procreative, life giving, nurturing powers, and war goddess, death-dealing, destructive powers.

Greece: Gaia

According to Hesiod's *Theogony*, Gaia is the first deity to emerge out of the void. She creates the features of the Earth by herself and marries her son, Ouranos, to continue the creation process. She is oppressed by Ouranos who will not allow her to give birth until Kronos separates them. Gaia's ambivalent nature is best demonstrated in her relationship with her grandson, Zeus, whom she raises in secrecy hidden from his father, Kronos. However, after Zeus and his siblings overthrow Kronos, Gaia sends the giants to attack them in anger that the Olympians had trapped some of the defeated Titans in the underworld. After the Olympians defeat the giants, Gaia sends a dragon, Typhon, to attack them in retaliation.

The Homeric Hymn to Mother Earth, translated by Evelyn-White, is in the public domain.

XXX. To Earth the Mother of All

(ll. 1–16) I will sing of well-founded Earth, mother of all, eldest of all beings. She feeds all creatures that are in the world, all that go upon the goodly land, and all that are in the paths of the seas, and all that fly: all these are fed of her store. Through you, O queen, men are blessed in their children and blessed in their harvests, and to you it belongs to give means of life to mortal men and to take it away. Happy is the man whom you delight to honour! He has all things abundantly: his fruitful land is laden with corn, his pastures are covered with cattle, and his house is filled with good things. Such men rule orderly in their cities of fair women: great riches and wealth follow them: their sons exult with ever-fresh delight, and their daughters in flower-laden bands play and skip merrily over the soft flowers of the field. Thus is it with those whom you honour O holy goddess, bountiful spirit.

(ll. 17–19) Hail, Mother of the gods, wife of starry Heaven; freely bestow upon me for this my song substance that cheers the heart! And now I will remember you and another song also.

Greece: Demeter

While strictly speaking, Demeter is not the earth itself, she does control the cycle of agriculture and is very involved with making the earth fruitful and productive. An Olympian, Demeter is more often found down on earth tending to the crops than up on Mt. Olympos with her siblings. Her preferred companion is her daughter, Persephone.

© Georgios Kollidas/Shutterstock.com

Out of the world's myths, the story of her bond with her daughter is one of the most compelling mother-daughter stories. Persephone fits the archetypal pattern of the Dying and Rising God Archetype, which will be covered in the next chapter.

Hymn to Demeter,
translated by Hugh G. Evelyn-White,
1914. Loeb Classical Library.
Located on www.sacred.texts.com

[Note: This Homeric Hymn, composed in approximately the seventh century BCE, served for centuries thereafter as the canonical hymn of the Eleusinian Mysteries. The text below was translated from the Greek by Hugh G. Evelyn-White and first published by the Loeb Classical Library in 1914. This text has been scanned and proof-read by Edward A. Beach, Department of Philosophy and Religious Studies, University of Wisconsin-Eau Claire.]

I begin to sing of rich-haired Demeter, awful goddess—of her and her trim-ankled daughter whom Aidoneus [Hades] rapt away, given to him by all-seeing Zeus the loud-thunderer. Apart from Demeter, lady of the golden sword and glorious fruits, she was playing with the deep-bosomed daughters of Oceanus and gathering flowers over a soft meadow, roses and crocuses and beautiful violets, irises also and hyacinths and the narcissus which Earth made to grow at the will of Zeus and to please the Host of Many, to be a snare for the bloom-like girl—a marvellous, radiant flower. It was a thing of awe whether for deathless gods or mortal men to see: from its root grew a hundred blooms and it smelled most sweetly, so that all wide heaven above and the whole earth and the sea's salt swell laughed for joy. And the girl was amazed and reached out with both hands to take the lovely toy; but the wide-pathed earth yawned there in the plain of Nysa, and the lord, Host of Many, with his immortal horses sprang out upon her— the Son of Cronos, He who has many names.[1]

He caught her up reluctant on his golden car and bare her away lamenting. Then she cried out shrilly with her voice, calling upon her father, the Son of Cronos, who is most high and excellent. But no one, either of the deathless gods or of mortal men, heard her voice, nor yet the olive-trees bearing rich fruit: only tenderhearted Hecate, bright-coiffed, the daughter of Persaeus, heard the girl from her cave, and the lord Helios, Hyperion's bright son, as she cried to her father, the Son of Cronos. But he was sitting aloof, apart from the gods, in his temple where many pray, and receiving sweet offerings from mortal men. So he, that Son of Cronos, of many names, who is Ruler of Many and Host of Many, was bearing her away by leave of Zeus on his immortal chariot—his own brother's child and all unwilling.

[**Line 33**] And so long as she, the goddess, yet beheld earth and starry heaven and the strong-flowing sea where fishes shoal, and the rays of the sun, and still hoped to see her dear mother and the tribes of the eternal gods, so long hope calmed her great heart for all her trouble. . . . and the heights of the mountains and the depths of the sea rang with her immortal voice: and her queenly mother heard her.

Bitter pain seized her heart, and she rent the covering upon her divine hair with her dear hands: her dark cloak she cast down from both her shoulders and sped, like a wild-bird, over the firm land and yielding sea, seeking her child. But no one would tell her the truth, neither god nor mortal man; and of the birds of omen none came with true news for her. Then for nine days queenly Deo wandered over the earth with flaming torches in her hands, so grieved that she never tasted ambrosia and the sweet draught of nectar, nor sprinkled her body with water. But when the tenth enlightening dawn had come, Hecate, with a torch in her hands, met her, and spoke to her and told her news:

"Queenly Demeter, bringer of seasons and giver of good gifts, what god of heaven or what mortal man has rapt away Persephone and pierced with sorrow your dear heart? For I heard her voice, yet saw not with my eyes who it was. But I tell you truly and shortly all I know."

[**Line 59**] So, then, said Hecate. And the daughter of rich-haired Rhea answered her not, but sped swiftly with her, holding flaming torches in her hands. So they came to Helios, who is watchman of both gods and men, and stood in front of his horses: and the bright goddess enquired of him: "Helios, do you at least regard me, goddess as I am, if ever by word or deed of mine I have cheered your heart and spirit. Through the fruitless air I heard the thrilling cry of my daughter whom I bare, sweet scion of my body and lovely in form, as of one seized violently; though with my eyes I saw nothing. But you—for with your beams you look down from the bright upper air over all the earth and sea—tell me truly of my dear child if you have seen her anywhere, what god or mortal man has violently seized her against her will and mine, and so made off."

So said she. And the Son of Hyperion answered her: "Queen Demeter, daughter of rich-haired Rhea, I will tell you the truth; for I greatly reverence and pity you in your grief for your trim-ankled daughter. None other of the deathless gods is to blame, but only cloud-gathering Zeus who gave her to Hades, her father's brother, to be called his buxom wife. And Hades seized her and took her loudly crying in his chariot down to his realm of mist and gloom. Yet, goddess, cease your loud lament and keep not vain anger unrelentingly: Aidoneus, the Ruler of Many, is no unfitting husband among the deathless gods for your child, being our own brother and born of the same stock: also, for honour, he has that third share which he received when division was made at the first and is appointed lord of those among whom he dwells."

So he spake, and called to his horses: and at his chiding they quickly whirled the swift chariot along, like long-winged birds.

[**Line 90**] But grief yet more terrible and savage came into the heart of Demeter, and thereafter she was so angered with the dark-clouded Son of Cronos that she avoided the gathering of the gods and high Olympos, and went to the towns and rich fields of men, disfiguring her form a long while. And no one of men or deep-bosomed women knew her when they saw her, until she came to the house of wise Celeus who then was lord of fragrant Eleusis. Vexed in her dear heart, she sat near the wayside by the Maiden Well, from which the women of the place were used to draw water, in a shady place over which grew an olive shrub. And she was like an ancient woman who is cut off from childbearing and the gifts of garland-loving Aphrodite, like the nurses of king's children who deal justice, or like the house-keepers in their echoing halls. There the daughters of Celeus, son of Eleusis, saw her, as they coming for easy-drawn water, to carry it in pitchers of bronze to their dear father's house: four were they and like goddesses in the flower of their girlhood, Callidice and Cleisidice and lovely Demo and Callithoe who was the eldest of them all. They knew her not—for the gods are not easily discerned by mortals—but startling near by her spoke winged words:

"Old mother, whence are you of folk born long ago? Why are you gone away from the city and do not draw near the houses? For there in the shady halls are women of just such age as you, and others younger; and they would welcome you both by word and by deed."

[**Line 118**] Thus they said. And she, that queen among goddesses answered them saying: "Hail, dear children, whosoever you are of woman-kind. I will tell you my story; for it is not unseemly that I should tell you truly what you ask. Doso is my name, for my stately mother gave it me. And now I am come from Crete over the sea's wide back—not willingly; but pirates brought me thence by force of strength against my liking. Afterwards they put in with their swift craft to Thoricus, and these the women landed on the shore in full throng and the men likewise, and they began to make ready a meal by the stern-cables of the ship. But my heart craved not pleasant food, and I fled secretly across the dark country and escaped my masters, that they should not take me unpurchased across the sea, there to win a price for me. And so I wandered and am come here: and I know not at all what land this is or what people are in it. But may all those who dwell on Olympos give you husbands and birth of children as parents desire, so you take pity on me, maidens, and show me this clearly that I may learn, dear children, to the house of what man and woman I may go, to work for them cheerfully at such tasks as belong to a woman of my age. Well could I nurse a new born child, holding him in my arms, or keep house, or spread my masters' bed in a recess of the well-built chamber, or teach the women their work."

So said the goddess. And straightway the unwed maiden Callidice, goodliest in form of the daughters of Celeus, answered her and said:

[Line 147] "Mother, what the gods send us, we mortals bear perforce, although we suffer; for they are much stronger than we. But now I will teach you clearly, telling you the names of men who have great power and honour here and are chief among the people, guarding our city's coif of towers by their wisdom and true judgements: there is wise Triptolemus and Dioclus and Polyxeinus and blameless Eumolpus and Dolichus and our own brave father. All these have wives who manage in the house, and no one of them, so soon as she had seen you, would dishonour you and turn you from the house, but they will welcome you; for indeed you are godlike. But if you will, stay here; and we will go to our father's house and tell Metaneira, our deep-bosomed mother, all this matter fully, that she may bid you rather come to our home than search after the houses of others. She has an only son, late-born, who is being nursed in our well-built house, a child of many prayers and welcome: if you could bring him up until he reached the full measure of youth, any one of womankind who should see you would straightway envy you, such gifts would our mother give for his upbringing."

So she spake: and the goddess bowed her head in assent. And they filled their shining vessels with water and carried them off rejoicing. Quickly they came to their father's great house and straightway told their mother according as they had heard and seen. Then she bade them go with all speed and invite the stranger to come for a measureless hire. As hinds or heifers in spring time, when sated with pasture, bound about a meadow, so they, holding up the folds of their lovely garments, darted down the hollow path, and their hair like a crocus flower streamed about their shoulders. And they found the good goddess near the wayside where they had left her before, and led her to the house of their dear father. And she walked behind, distressed in her dear heart, with her head veiled and wearing a dark cloak which waved about the slender feet of the goddess.

[Line 184] Soon they came to the house of heaven-nurtured Celeus and went through the portico to where their queenly mother sat by a pillar of the close-fitted roof, holding her son, a tender scion, in her bosom. And the girls ran to her. But the goddess walked to the threshold: and her head reached the roof and she filled the doorway with a heavenly radiance. Then awe and reverence and pale fear took hold of Metaneira, and she rose up from her couch before Demeter, and bade her be seated. But Demeter, bringer of seasons and giver of perfect gifts, would not sit upon the bright couch, but stayed silent with lovely eyes cast down until careful Iambe placed a jointed seat for her and threw over it a silvery fleece. Then she sat down and held her veil in her hands before her face. A long time she sat upon the stool[2] without speaking because of her sorrow, and greeted no one by word or by sign, but rested, never smiling, and tasting neither food nor drinks because she pined with longing for her deep-bosomed daughter, until careful Iambe—who pleased her moods in aftertime also—moved the holy lady with many a quip and jest to smile and laugh and cheer her heart. Then Metaneira filled a cup with sweet wine and offered it to her; but she refused it, for she said it was not lawful for her to drink red wine, but bade them mix meal and water with soft mint and give her to drink. And Metaneira mixed the draught and gave it to the goddess as she bade. So the great queen Deo received it to observe the sacrament.[3]

[**Line 212**] And of them all, well-girded Metaneira first began to speak: "Hail, lady! For I think you are not meanly but nobly born; truly dignity and grace are conspicuous upon your eyes as in the eyes of kings that deal justice. Yet we mortals bear per-force what the gods send us, though we be grieved; for a yoke is set upon our necks. But now, since you are come here, you shall have what I can bestow: and nurse me this child whom the gods gave me in my old age and beyond my hope, a son much prayed for. If you should bring him up until he reach the full measure of youth, any one of woman-kind that sees you will straightway envy you, so great reward would I give for his upbringing."

Then rich-haired Demeter answered her: "And to you, also, lady, all hail, and may the gods give you good! Gladly will I take the boy to my breast, as you bid me, and will nurse him. Never, I ween, through any heedlessness of his nurse shall witchcraft hurt him nor yet the Undercutter: for I know a charm far stronger than the Woodcutter, and I know an excellent safeguard against woeful witchcraft."[4]

When she had so spoken, she took the child in her fragrant bosom with her divine hands: and his mother was glad in her heart. So the goddess nursed in the palace Demophoon, wise Celeus' goodly son whom well-girded Metaneira bare. And the child grew like some immortal being, not fed with food nor nourished at the breast: for by day rich-crowned Demeter would anoint him with ambrosia as if he were the offspring of a god and breathe sweetly upon him as she held him in her bosom. But at night she would hide him like a brand in the heart of the fire, unknown to his dear parents. And it wrought great wonder in these that he grew beyond his age; for he was like the gods face to face. And she would have made him deathless and unaging, had not well-girded Metaneira in her heedlessness kept watch by night from her sweet-smelling chamber and spied. But she wailed and smote her two hips, because she feared for her son and was greatly distraught in her heart; so she lamented and uttered winged words:

[**Line 248**] "Demophoon, my son, the strange woman buries you deep in fire and works grief and bitter sorrow for me."

Thus she spoke, mourning. And the bright goddess, lovely-crowned Demeter, heard her, and was wroth with her. So with her divine hands she snatched from the fire the dear son whom Metaneira had born unhoped-for in the palace, and cast him from her to the ground; for she was terribly angry in her heart. Forthwith she said to well-girded Metaneira:

"Witless are you mortals and dull to foresee your lot, whether of good or evil, that comes upon you. For now in your heedlessness you have wrought folly past healing; for—be witness the oath of the gods, the relentless water of Styx—I would have made your dear son deathless and unaging all his days and would have bestowed on him ever-lasting honour, but now he can in no way escape death and the fates. Yet shall unfailing honour always rest upon him, because he lay upon my knees and slept in my arms. But, as the years move round and when he is in his prime, the sons of the Eleusinians shall ever wage war and dread strife with one another continually. Lo! I am that Demeter who has share of honour and is the greatest help and cause of joy to the undying gods and mortal men. But now, let all the people build me a great temple and an altar below it and beneath the city and its sheer wall upon a rising hillock above Callichorus. And I myself will teach my rites, that hereafter you may reverently perform them and so win the favour of my heart."

[**Line 275**] When she had so said, the goddess changed her stature and her looks, thrusting old age away from her: beauty spread round about her and a lovely fragrance was wafted from her sweet-smelling robes, and from the divine body of the goddess a light shone afar, while golden tresses spread down over her shoulders, so that the strong house was filled with brightness as with lightning. And so she went out from the palace.

And straightway Metaneira's knees were loosed and she remained speechless for a long while and did not remember to take up her late-born son from the ground. But his sisters heard his pitiful wailing and sprang down from their well-spread beds: one of them took up the child in her arms and laid him in her bosom, while another revived the fire, and a third rushed with soft feet to bring their mother from her fragrant chamber. And they gathered about the struggling child and washed him, embracing him lovingly; but he was not comforted, because nurses and handmaids much less skillful were holding him now.

All night long they sought to appease the glorious goddess, quaking with fear. But, as soon as dawn began to show, they told powerful Celeus all things without fail, as the lovely-crowned goddess Demeter charged them. So Celeus called the countless people to an assembly and bade them make a goodly temple for rich-haired Demeter and an altar upon the rising hillock. And they obeyed him right speedily and harkened to his voice, doing as he commanded. As for the child, he grew like an immortal being.

[**Line 301**] Now when they had finished building and had drawn back from their toil, they went every man to his house. But golden-haired Demeter sat there apart from all the blessed gods and stayed, wasting with yearning for her deep-bosomed daughter. Then she caused a most dreadful and cruel year for mankind over the all-nourishing earth: the ground would not make the seed sprout, for rich-crowned Demeter kept it hid. In the fields the oxen drew many a curved plough in vain, and much white barley was cast upon the land without avail. So she would have destroyed the whole race of man with cruel famine and have robbed them who dwell on Olympos of their glorious right of gifts and sacrifices, had not Zeus perceived and marked this in his heart. First he sent golden-winged Iris to call rich-haired Demeter, lovely in form. So he commanded. And she obeyed the dark-clouded Son of Cronos, and sped with swift feet across the space between. She came to the stronghold of fragrant Eleusis, and there finding dark-cloaked Demeter in her temple, spake to her and uttered winged words:

"Demeter, father Zeus, whose wisdom is everlasting, calls you to come join the tribes of the eternal gods: come therefore, and let not the message I bring from Zeus pass unobeyed."

Thus said Iris imploring her. But Demeter's heart was not moved. Then again the father sent forth all the blessed and eternal gods besides: and they came, one after the other, and kept calling her and offering many very beautiful gifts and whatever rights she might be pleased to choose among the deathless gods. Yet no one was able to persuade her mind and will, so wroth was she in her heart; but she stubbornly rejected all their words: for she vowed that she would never set foot on fragrant Olympos nor let fruit spring out of the ground, until she beheld with her eyes her own fair-faced daughter.

[**Line 334**] Now when all-seeing Zeus the loud-thunderer heard this, he sent the Slayer of Argus whose wand is of gold to Erebus, so that having won over Hades with soft words, he might lead forth chaste Persephone to the light from the misty gloom to join the gods, and that her mother might see her with her eyes and cease from her anger. And Hermes obeyed, and leaving the house of Olympos, straightway sprang down with speed to the hidden places of the earth. And he found the lord Hades in his house seated upon a couch, and his shy mate with him, much reluctant, because she yearned for her mother. But she was afar off, brooding on her fell design because of the deeds of the blessed gods. And the strong Slayer of Argus drew near and said:

"Dark-haired Hades, ruler over the departed, father Zeus bids me bring noble Persephone forth from Erebus unto the gods, that her mother may see her with her eyes and cease from her dread anger with the immortals; for now she plans an awful deed, to destroy the weakly tribes of earthborn men by keeping seed hidden beneath the earth, and so she makes an end of the honours of the undying gods. For she keeps fearful anger and does not consort with the gods, but sits aloof in her fragrant temple, dwelling in the rocky hold of Eleusis."

So he said. And Aidoneus, ruler over the dead, smiled grimly and obeyed the behest of Zeus the king. For he straightway urged wise Persephone, saying:

[**Line 360**] "Go now, Persephone, to your dark-robed mother, go, and feel kindly in your heart towards me: be not so exceedingly cast down; for I shall be no unfitting husband for you among the deathless gods, that am own brother to father Zeus. And while you are here, you shall rule all that lives and moves and shall have the greatest rights among the deathless gods: those who defraud you and do not appease your power with offerings, reverently performing rites and paying fit gifts, shall be punished for evermore."

When he said this, wise Persephone was filled with joy and hastily sprang up for gladness. But he on his part secretly gave her sweet pomegranate seed to eat, taking care for himself that she might not remain continually with grave, dark-robed Demeter. Then Aidoneus the Ruler of Many openly got ready his deathless horses beneath the golden chariots. And she mounted on the chariot and the strong Slayer of Argus took reins and whip in his dear hands and drove forth from the hall, the horses speeding readily. Swiftly they traversed their long course, and neither the sea nor river-waters nor grassy glens nor mountain-peaks checked the career of the immortal horses, but they clave the deep air above them as they went. And Hermes brought them to the place where rich-crowned Demeter was staying and checked them before her fragrant temple.

[Line 384] And when Demeter saw them, she rushed forth as does a Maenad down some thick-wooded mountain, while Persephone on the other side, when she saw her mother's sweet eyes, left the chariot and horses, and leaped down to run to her, and falling upon her neck, embraced her. But while Demeter was still holding her dear child in her arms, her heart suddenly misgave her for some snare, so that she feared greatly and ceased fondling her daughter and asked of her at once: "My child, tell me, surely you have not tasted any food while you were below? Speak out and hide nothing, but let us both know. For if you have not, you shall come back from loathly Hades and live with me and your father, the dark-clouded Son of Cronos and be honoured by all the deathless gods; but if you have tasted food, you must go back again beneath the secret places of the earth, there to dwell a third part of the seasons every year: yet for the two parts you shall be with me and the other deathless gods. But when the earth shall bloom with the fragrant flowers of spring in every kind, then from the realm of darkness and gloom thou shalt come up once more to be a wonder for gods and mortal men. And now tell me how he rapt you away to the realm of darkness and gloom, and by what trick did the strong Host of Many beguile you?"

[Line 405] Then beautiful Persephone answered her thus: "Mother, I will tell you all without error. When luck-bringing Hermes came, swift messenger from my father the Son of Cronos and the other Sons of Heaven, bidding me come back from Erebus that you might see me with your eyes and so cease from your anger and fearful wrath against the gods, I sprang up at once for joy; but he secretly put in my mouth sweet food, a pomegranate seed, and forced me to taste against my will. Also I will tell how he rapt me away by the deep plan of my father the Son of Cronos and carried me off beneath the depths of the earth, and will relate the whole matter as you ask. All we were playing in a lovely meadow, Leucippe and Phaeno and Electra and Ianthe, Melita also and Iache with Rhodea and Callirhoe and Melobosis and Tyche and Ocyrhoe, fair as a flower, Chryseis, Ianeira, Acaste and Admete and Rhodope and Pluto and charming Calypso; Styx too was there and Urania and lovely Galaxaura with Pallas who rouses battles and Artemis delighting in arrows.[5] We were playing and gathering sweet flowers in our hands, soft crocuses mingled with irises and hyacinths, and rose-blooms and lilies, marvellous to see, and the narcissus which the wide earth caused to grow yellow as a crocus. That I plucked in my joy; but the earth parted beneath, and there the strong lord, the Host of Many, sprang forth and in his golden chariot he bore me away, all unwilling, beneath the earth: then I cried with a shrill cry. All this is true, sore though it grieves me to tell the tale."

[**Line 434**] So did they then, with hearts at one, greatly cheer each the other's soul and spirit with many an embrace: their hearts had relief from their griefs while each took and gave back joyousness.

Then bright-coiffed Hecate came near to them, and often did she embrace the daughter of holy Demeter: and from that time the lady Hecate was minister and companion to Persephone.

And all-seeing Zeus sent a messenger to them, rich-haired Rhea, to bring dark-cloaked Demeter to join the families of the gods: and he promised to give her what rights she should choose among the deathless gods and agreed that her daughter should go down for the third part of the circling year to darkness and gloom, but for the two parts should live with her mother and the other deathless gods. Thus he commanded. And the goddess did not disobey the message of Zeus; swiftly she rushed down from the peaks of Olympos and came to the plain of Rharus, rich, fertile corn-land once, but then in nowise fruitful, for it lay idle and utterly leafless, because the white grain was hidden by design of trim-ankled Demeter. But afterwards, as spring-time waxed, it was soon to be waving with long ears of corn, and its rich furrows to be loaded with grain upon the ground, while others would already be bound in sheaves. There first she landed from the fruitless upper air: and glad were the goddesses to see each other and cheered in heart. Then bright-coiffed Rhea said to Demeter:

[**Line 459**] "Come, my daughter; for far-seeing Zeus the loud-thunderer calls you to join the families of the gods, and has promised to give you what rights you please among the deathless gods, and has agreed that for a third part of the circling year your daughter shall go down to darkness and gloom, but for the two parts shall be with you and the other deathless gods: so has he declared it shall be and has bowed his head in token. But come, my child, obey, and be not too angry unrelentingly with the dark-clouded Son of Cronos; but rather increase forthwith for men the fruit that gives them life."

So spake Rhea. And rich-crowned Demeter did not refuse but straightway made fruit to spring up from the rich lands, so that the whole wide earth was laden with leaves and flowers. Then she went, and to the kings who deal justice, Triptolemus and Diocles, the horse-driver, and to doughty Eumolpus and Celeus, leader of the people, she showed the conduct of her rites and taught them all her mysteries, to Triptolemus and Polyxeinus and Diocles also—awful mysteries which no one may in any way transgress or pry into or utter, for deep awe of the gods checks the voice. Happy is he among men upon earth who has seen these mysteries; but he who is uninitiate and who has no part in them, never has lot of like good things once he is dead, down in the darkness and gloom.

[**Line 483**] But when the bright goddess had taught them all, they went to Olympos to the gathering of the other gods. And there they dwell beside Zeus who delights in thunder, awful and reverend goddesses. Right blessed is he among men on earth whom they freely love: soon they do send Plutus as guest to his great house, Plutus who gives wealth to mortal men.

And now, queen of the land of sweet Eleusis and sea-girt Paros and rocky Antron, lady, giver of good gifts, bringer of seasons, queen Deo, be gracious, you and your daughter all beauteous Persephone, and for my song grant me heart-cheering substance. And now I will remember you and another song also.

Notes

[1] The Greeks feared to name Pluto directly and mentioned him by one of many descriptive titles, such as "Host of Many": compare the Christian use of *diabolos* or our "Evil One."

[2] Demeter chooses the lowlier seat, supposedly as being more suitable to her assumed condition, but really because in her sorrow she refuses all comforts.

[3] An act of communion—the drinking of the potion (*kykeon*) here described—was one of the most important pieces of ritual in the Eleusinian mysteries, as commemorating the sorrows of the goddess.

[4] Undercutter and Woodcutter are probably popular names (after the style of Hesiod's "Boneless One") for the worm thought to be the cause of teething and toothache.

[5] The list of names is taken—with five additions—from Hesiod, *Theogony* 349 ff.

Greece: Athena

Athena, the Greek virgin goddess of war, wisdom, and weaving, was born from her father Zeus' head after he swallowed his first consort, Metis, and ended up with a monumental headache. As she was born from her father's skull, Athena represents Zeus' wisdom, personified in goddess form. She asked for and received permission to remain a virgin, and never married or took any interest in men as lovers. She was, however, patroness to most of Greece's heroes, helping them succeed in their quests; whether it was Perseus in pursuit of Medusa or Odysseus trying to get home to Penelope, Athena was their guide and guardian.

Figure 5.3
© jaimaa, 2010. Used under license from Shutterstock, Inc.

When Athena was born she emerged from Zeus' skull dressed in armor and carrying a spear. She let out a battle cry as she emerged. She was the patron goddess of war and the protector of civilization. She was a much more rational and strategic war goddess than her half-brother, Ares, who was far more interested in pounding heads together than plotting out any strategies. Athena figured prominently in the *Iliad* as a supporter of the Greek army and in particular of the heroes Achilles and Odysseus, although she protected the Greeks at large and was an enemy of the Trojans.

Athena, while rational, had a temper. It was not a good idea to cross her or commit *hubris* against her. (Hubris was defined as excessive pride, but manifested in Greek myths as someone denying a god or goddess, comparing someone to a god or goddess, or challenging a god or goddess. None of these were advisable actions.) A good example of her temper and her desire to punish hubris was in the myth of Arachne, one of Athena's protégés. Athena as goddess of all women's household handicrafts, most notably, weaving, had taught Arachne to weave. The Greek girl became so confident in her abilities that she boasted she was better than her teacher. Athena appeared in her village disguised as an old woman and attempted to persuade Arachne to take back her hubristic words. Arachne refused, and went so far as to issue a challenge to the goddess. With that, Athena threw off her disguise and the two had a weaving contest. Although Arachne's work was indeed good she had the bad taste to weave the exploits of Zeus' love affairs into her tapestry while Athena chose to weave the exploits of the Olympians in the battles against the Titans and the Giants and Typhon. When the two were done with their work, Athena was furious with Arachne's work. She ripped the weaving from the loom, which she also broke into pieces. She used the pieces to beat Arachne until she heard the young woman's cries for mercy. At that point, Athena's fury abated and she transformed Arachne into the first spider so that she could continue to weave without challenging the goddess again.

■ ■ ■

The Homeric *Hymn to Pallas Athena*, translated by Evelyn-White, is in the public domain. Located on www.ancienthistory.about.com

XXVIII. To Athena (18 lines)

(ll. 1–16) I begin to sing of Pallas Athene, the glorious goddess, bright-eyed, inventive, unbending of heart, pure virgin, saviour of cities, courageous, Tritogeneia. From his awful head wise Zeus himself bare her arrayed in warlike arms of flashing gold, and awe seized all the gods as they gazed. But Athena sprang quickly from the immortal head and stood before Zeus who holds the aegis, shaking a sharp spear: great Olympos began to reel horribly at the might of the bright-eyed goddess, and earth round about cried fearfully, and the sea was moved and tossed with dark waves, while foam burst forth suddenly: the bright Son of Hyperion stopped his swift-footed horses a long while, until the maiden Pallas Athene had stripped the heavenly armour from her immortal shoulders. And wise Zeus was glad.

(ll. 17–18) And so hail to you, daughter of Zeus who holds the aegis! Now I will remember you and another song as well.

Greece: Artemis

Artemis, according to Hesiod's *Theogony*, was the daughter of Zeus by the titan Leto, and was twin to the sun god Apollo. Artemis was born first of the twins and helped her mother through the birth of Apollo, which lasted for days. Afterward, Artemis became goddess of childbirth, an unusual occupation for her as she also, according to Hesiod, asked to remain a virgin and was most associated with the hunt, wild animals, and the wilderness. Artemis originally came from outside of Greece and was incorporated into the Greek pantheon just as her brother Apollo was. In her origins, it is far more likely

Figure 5.4
© Jose Ignacio Soto, 2010. Used under license from
Shutterstock, Inc.

that Artemis was an earth goddess. She appeared as such in Phrygia, ancient Turkey, where there was a statue of her with many breasts or many sacrificed bull testicles, neither of which seems appropriate for a virgin goddess.

As goddess of the hunt, Artemis was an archer and was most often depicted with her bow and arrows. As goddess of the moon, she drove a golden chariot pulled by two horses across the sky, a job she shared with the older Greek moon goddess, Selene. Selene differed from Artemis in that she was not a virgin goddess and definitely took lovers. Artemis was highly protective of her chastity and would not allow any human males to see her even if they were her devotees such as the human hunter, Hippolytus, who was only allowed to hear the goddess' voice. One unfortunate human, Actaeon, inadvertently caught a glimpse of Artemis when she was bathing in a stream with her nymphs after a hot day of hunting. Actaeon had also been hunting, but had become separated from his party. Hot and thirsty, he heard the sound of water and moved toward it unaware that the goddess and her attendants were bathing nearby. When Actaeon approached the stream, he heard the noise of the nymphs as they scrambled to cover Artemis' body with their own. Angry that a human had intruded on her bath and seen her, Artemis cast water onto Actaeon, transforming him into a deer. As he stumbled through the wilderness looking for his friends, his own hunting dogs brought him to bay in a clearing where they ripped out his throat in front of his friends with none the wiser.

Artemis was not only fierce in protecting her chastity, along with Apollo, she was a fierce protector of her mother's honor. There was once a queen in the city of Thebes, Niobe by name, who was descended from the gods and had the good fortune to have seven sons and seven daughters. Niobe was jealous of her honors. When the citizens of Thebes held a celebration in honor of Leto, the mother of Artemis and Apollo, Niobe committed hubris by comparing herself with the goddess and saying that she was far better because she had been blessed with so many children. Leto heard Niobe and punished her hubris by sending Apollo and Artemis down to slay all of Niobe's children with their arrows. Apollo slew all of the sons of Niobe and Artemis slew all the daughters.

Jane Harrison, an author of the early twentieth century, in *Myths of Greece and Rome*, had this to say about the goddess Artemis:

Artemis is, of all the divine maidens, the most virginal. Perhaps because she is a Northerner she attains an austerity impossible to the warmer-blooded Southerners. While Athena refuses marriage, she is still, in very human fashion, foster-mother, guardian, and friend to many a hero. The relation of these early and husbandless matriarchal goddesses to the male figures who attend them is one altogether noble and womanly, though, perhaps, it is not what the modern mind regards as feminine. It is a relation that halts somewhere halfway between mother and lover, and has about it a touch of the patron-saint. These goddesses ask of the hero whom they choose to inspire and protect, not that he should love and adore, but that he should do great deeds. Such a relation is that of Hera to Jason, of Athena to Perseus, to Herakles, to Theseus. And, as the glory of the goddesses is in their heroes' high deeds, so their grace is his guerdon. With the coming of patriarchal conditions this high companionship ends; the women goddesses are sequestered to a servile domesticity, they become abject and amorous. By Artemis alone among the maidens this high companionship with heroes is all but renounced. She dwells apart in lonely mountains and wild, untouched forests. She is most of all the Lady-of-the-Wild-Things.

■ ■ ■

Myths of Greece and Rome, by Jane Harrison, 1928. Located on www.sacred-texts.com

To Artemis—Homeric *Hymns to Artemis*
IX. TO ARTEMIS

[1] Muse, sing of Artemis, sister of the Far-shooter, the virgin who delights in arrows, who was fostered with Apollo. She waters her horses from Meles deep in reeds, and swiftly drives her all-golden chariot through Smyrna to vine-clad Claros where Apollo, god of the silver bow, sits waiting for the far-shooting goddess who delights in arrows. And so hail to you, Artemis, in my song and to all goddesses as well. Of you first I sing and with you I begin; now that I have begun with you, I will turn to another song.

XXVII: To Artemis

(ll. 1–20) I sing of Artemis, whose shafts are of gold, who cheers on the hounds, the pure maiden, shooter of stags, who delights in archery, own sister to Apollo with the golden sword. Over the shadowy hills and windy peaks she draws her golden bow, rejoicing in the chase, and sends out grievous shafts. The tops of the high mountains tremble and the tangled wood echoes awesomely with the outcry of beasts: earthquakes and the sea also where fishes shoal. But the goddess with a bold heart turns every way destroying the race of wild beasts: and when she is satisfied and has cheered her heart, this huntress who delights in arrows slackens her supple bow and goes to the great house of her dear brother Phoebus Apollo, to the rich land of Delphi, there to order the lovely dance of the Muses and Graces. There she hangs up her curved bow and her arrows, and heads and leads the dances, gracefully arrayed, while all they utter their heavenly voice, singing how neat-ankled Leto bare children supreme among the immortals both in thought and in deed.

(ll. 21–22) Hail to you, children of Zeus and rich-haired Leto! And now I will remember you and another song also.

Artemis has an interesting blend of characteristics. She is associated with the moon and childbirth, both usually qualities associated with Great Mother goddesses. However, she is a virgin goddess, more associated with the crescent moon than the full moon. She is the protector of young children and mothers in labor. Girls on the threshold of puberty offered their childhood toys as a sacrifice to the goddess in her temple as part of the transition into adulthood and marriage. She is the huntress who prefers the wilderness and wild places uninhabited by man, yet she is also the protectress of the animals. It is my belief that when she was borrowed and included in the Olympian pantheon of gods, she was made a virgin goddess to limit her powers and make her fit into the patriarchal family hierarchy.

■ ■ ■

Homeric Hymns to Artemis, translated by Evelyn-White, is in the public domain. Located on www.ancienthistory.about.com

India: Devi

In Indian or Hindu myth, the ultimate reality is Brahman, all things and nothing. The feminine aspect of Brahman is called Devi, the Goddess, or sometimes Shakti, which means feminine energy. Interestingly, in India, the feminine energy is the active energy and the masculine energy is passive. None of the male gods can act in the world without their complementary female counterpart. Therefore, the Great Goddess takes many forms in Indian myths. Just as Brahman manifests as all the gods and goddesses, Devi manifests as all the various goddesses in India. She has nurturing, loving manifestations like Laxmi, fierce warrior manifestations like Durga, and dangerous, all consuming destructive manifestations like Kali.

Laxmi or Lakshmi, is the wife of Vishnu, and is the goddess of fertility and prosperity. She is associated with kings and elephants. There are almost always images of elephants near Lakshmi, as elephants are thought to bring the rain clouds (sky elephants) that bring the monsoon rains that fertilize the earth. Also, only royals can ride elephants. Lakshmi usually sits or stands on a lotus, the symbol of birth and rebirth, with one hand raised from which coins spill. As the wife of Vishnu, she represents the relationship of wife to husband in Hindu beliefs and is often shown massaging his feet as he lies on the back of the cosmic serpent Shesh, contemplating creation. Whenever Vishnu appears as his human avatars Rama or Krishna, Lakshmi takes on human form in order to reunite with him. Her avatars are Sita and Radha, respectively.

Figure 5.5
© AstroVed.com/Shutterstock.com

Durga represents the culmination of all the male gods' energy and is created to defeat a buffalo demon that none of the male gods can defeat. They determine that the buffalo demon can only be killed by a female so they pool all their energies to create Durga. Durga is most often depicted as seated on a lion or a tiger and holding weapons and one lotus blossom in all of her eight or twelve hands. She fights the demon in battle and defeats him. Even though she is very powerful and dangerous, she is also a loving mother who assists her worshippers.

The most truly dangerous and frightful looking of the Indian goddesses, particularly to western eyes, is the goddess Kali. Kali means Time and Kali the goddess is the embodiment of time. She gives birth to all things and she destroys all things, just as time does. She is most often depicted with blue black skin, the color of the infinite night sky, and long black hair; she may appear emaciated or skeletal, but her most distinguishing characteristics are the necklace of skulls or severed heads and the skirt made from severed limbs that she wears. She holds a trident much like her consort Shiva, and is found on the battlefield. In this regard, she has something in common with the Celtic battlefield goddess, the Morrigan.

Kali is often the spouse of Shiva, the lord of yoga and destruction. Both gods give their followers the ability to free themselves from attachments to the world and thus, prepare for enlightenment (moksha), and end of samasara (the wheel of life and death and rebirth), and union with Brahman. Kali is really scary to those who are attached to the world and fear death, otherwise she comes as a sweet mother releasing her children from the suffering that comes from attachment to the world.

© PremiumStock/Shutterstock.com

The Devî Gita
(Song of the Goddess)
Excerpt from *the Srimad Devî Bhagavatam*
translated by Swami Vijnanananda (Hari Prasanna Chatterji),
1921. Located on www.sacred-texts.com

An excerpt from Chapter XXXI. The Birth of Pârvatî in the House of Himâlayâs

The following excerpt describes the appearance of the Great Goddess (Devi) to the rest of the Hindu gods.

When the ninth Tithî came in the month of Chaitra on Friday, the Highest Light of the Supreme Force suddenly appeared in front of them. That Light was equal to Koti lightnings, of a red colour, and cool like the Koti Moons. Again the lustre was like the Koti Suns. The four Vedas personified, were chanting hymns all round Her. That mass of fire was above, below, on all sides, in the middle; nowhere it was obstructed. It had no beginning, nor end. It was of the form of a female with hands and feet and all the limbs. The appearance was not that of a male nor that of an hermophrodite. The Devas, dazzled by the brilliant lustre, first closed their eyes; but at the next moment, holding patience when they opened again their eyes, they found the Highest Light manifesting in the form of an exceedingly beautiful Divine Woman. Her youth was just blooming and Her rising breasts, plump and prominent, vying as it were, with a lotus bud, added to the beauty all around. Bracelets were on Her hands; armlets on Her four arms; necklace on Her neck; and the garland made of invaluable gems and jewels spread very bright lustre all arouud. Lovely ornaments on Her waist making tinkling sounds and beautiful anklets were on Her feet. The hairs of Her head, flowing between Her ears and cheek sparkled bright like the large black bees shining on the flower leaves of the blooning Ketakî flower. Her loins were nicely shaped and exquisitely lovely and the hairs on Her navel gave additional beauty. Her exquisitely lively lotus mouth rendered more lustrous and beautiful by the shining golden ear-ornaments, was filled with betel leaves mixed with camphor, etc.; on Her forehead there was the half crescent moon; Her eye-brows were extended and Her eyes looked bright and beautifully splendid like the red lotus; Her nose was elevated and Her lips very sweet. Her teeth were very beautiful like the opening buds of Kunda flowers; from Her neck was suspended a necklace of pearls; on Her head was the brilliant crown decked with diamonds and jewels; on Her ears, earrings were suspended like the lines on the Moon; Her hairs were ornamented with Mallikâ and Mâlatî flowers; Her forehead was pasted with Kâṣmîra Kunkuma drops; and Her three eyes gave unparalleled lustre to Her face. On Her one hand there was the noose and on Her other hand there was the goad; her two other hands made signs granting boons and dispelling fears; Her body shed lustre like the flowers of a Dârima tree. Her wearing is a red coloured cloth. All these added great beauty. Thus the Devas saw before them the Mother Goddess, the Incarnate of unpretended mercy, with a face ready to offer

Her Grace, the Mother of the Whole Universe, the Enchantreas of all, sweet-smiling, saluted by all the Devas, yielding all desires, and wearing a dress, indicative of all lovely feelings. The Devas bowed at once they saw Her; but they could not speak with their voice as it was choked with tears. Then holding their patience, with much difficulty, they began to praise and chant hymns to the World Mother with their eyes filled with tears of love and devotion and with their heads bent low.

44–54. The Devas said:—We bow down to Thee, the Devî and the Maha Devî, always obeisance to Thee! Thou art the Prakriti, and the Auspicious One; we always salute to Thee. O Mother! Thou art of a fiery colour (residing as a Red Flame in the heart of a Yogî) and burning with Asceticism and Wisdom (shedding lustre all around). Thou art specially shining everywhere as the Pure Chaitanya; worshipped by the Devas and all the Jîvas) for the rewards of their actions; We take refuge to Thee, the Durgâ, the Devî, we bow down to Thee, that can well make others cross the ocoan of Samsâra; so that Thou helpest us in crossing this terrible ocean of world. Mother! The Devas have created the words (*i.e.,* the words conveying ideas are uttered by the five Vâyus, Prâṇa, etc., which are called the Devas) which are of the nature of Vis'varûpu, pervading everywhere, like the Kâma Dhenu (the Heavenly Cow yielding all desires, riches, honor, food, etc.,) and by which the brutes (the gods) become egotistical, O Mother! Thou art that language to us; so Thou fulfillest our desires when we praise and eba at hymns to Thee. O Devî! Thou art the Night of Destruction at the end of the world; Thou art worshipped by Brahmâ; Thou art the Lakṣmi, the S'akti of Viṣṇu; Thou art the Mother of Skanda the S'aktî of S'iva; Thou art the S'aktî Sarasvatî of Brahmâ. Thou art Aditi, the Mother of the gods and Thou art Satî, the daughter of Dakṣa. Thus Thou art purifying the worlds in various forms and giving peace to all. We bow down to Thee. We know Thee to be the great Mahâ Lakṣmî; we meditate on Thee as of the nature of all the S'aktis as Bhaghavatî. O Mother! Illumine us so that we can meditate and know Thee. O Devî! Obeisance to Thee, the Virâṭ! Obeisance to Thee, the Sûtrâtmâ, the Hiraṇyagarbha; obeisance to Thee, the transformed into sixteen Vikritis (or transformations). Obeisance to Thee, of the natara of Brahma. We bow down with great devotion to Thee, the Goddess of the Universe, the Creatrix of Mâyic Avidyâ (the Nescience) under whose influence this world is mistaken as the rope as a garland is mistaken for a rope and again that mistake is corrected by whose Vidyâ.

We bow down to Thee who art indicated by both the letters Tat and Tvam in the sentence Tat Tvamasi (Thou art That), Tat indicating the Chit (Intelligence) of the nature of oneness and Tvam indicating the nature of Akhaṇda Brahma (beyond the Annamaya, Prâṇamaya, Manomaya, Vijnânamaya and the Ânandamaya—the five Kos'as, the Witness of the three states of wakefulness, dream, and deep sleep states) and indicating Thee. O Mother! Thou art of the nature of Praṇava Om; Thou art Hrîm; Thou art of the nature of various Mantras and Thou art merciful; we bow down again and again to Thy lotus Feet.

■ ■ ■

Verses 7 and 12 from the *Hymn to Kali,* by Arthur Avalon (Sir John George Woodroffe), 1922. Located on www.sacred-texts.com

VERSE 7

O MOTHER, even a dullard becomes a poet who meditates upon Thee raimented with space,[1] three-eyed[2] Creatrix[3] of the three worlds, whose waist[4] is beautiful with a girdle made of numbers of dead men's arms, and who on the breast of a corpse,[5] as Thy couch in the cremation-ground,[6] enjoyest Mahākāla.[7]

Footnotes

61:1 The Devī is naked, as is Śiva, for, like Him, She is clothed with space, and is the great void itself (Mahāśūnya).

61:2 *Triṇayanām.* The Three eyes are Sun, Moon and Fire (V). *Mahānirvāṇa-Tantra* says, 'Three eyes are attributed to *Kālikā* because She observes the whole world with such eyes as the Sun, the Moon, and so forth'. See as to the meaning of these three terms which do not merely denote these luminaries and elements, A. Avalon's 'Serpent Power' and Studies in *Mantra-Śāstra'*.

61:3 *Vidhātrim,* who provides Enjoyment and Liberation for all Jivas. (V).

61:4 *Nitaṁba,* literally, buttocks but the girdle goes all round. Kālī is represented as so girdled.

61:5 The corpse (*Śava*) represents *Śiva* (V) because He is inactive whilst his *Śakti* it is who does everything. *Śavahṛdi*—that is, on the breast of Śiva (*Viparītarati*). The Devī is given the dominant position in her union with Her consort, because She is *Kartri* (actress), and He is *Bhoktā* (unacting enjoyer). According to Sāṁkhya, *Puruṣa* is neither producer nor produced, but passive, and a looker-on upon the actions of *Prakṛti.* It is not the *Puruṣa* who is active in the creation of the world, but it is She who, in the light of His gaze, dances the world-dance. So Kubjikā-Tantra says: 'Not Brahmā, but Brahmāṇī, creates; it is Vaiṣṇavī, not Vishnu, who protects; Rudrāṇī, not Rudra, who takes all things back. Their husbands are like dead bodies.' For in respect of power they are dependent on their *Śakti.* As to the *Sādhana,* see Prāṇatoṣinī 622, *Viparitaratau japtvā nirvāṇapadavīṁ vrajet.* Two corpses are sometimes pictured, the lower being the eternally quiescent Śiva, and the upper being the Śiva united with Śakti in creation. Similarly the Devī is represented as reclining on a couch made of five corpses, which are the Mahāpreta (see Bhairavayāmala, Lalitā verse 174, etc). The

Mahāpretas, whose *Bīja* is *Hsau,* are Sadāśiva, Īśāna, Rudra, Viṣṇu, and Brahmā.
61:6 The site of certain forms of Tantrik *Sādhana,* such as *Śavāsana Muṇḍāsana,* etc.,
as to which the Phetkāriṇī-Tantra says that it is an excellent place for *Sādhana.* He who
makes japa a number of times on a corpse in a cremation-ground attains all manner
of success (*Siddhi*).'
61:7 Parama-Śiva.

VERSE 12

O MOTHER, Thou givest birth to and protectest the world, and at the time of dissolution dost withdraw to Thyself[1] the earth and all things; therefore Thou art Brahmā,
and the Lord of the three worlds, the Spouse of Śrī,[2] and Maheśa,[3] and all other
beings and things.[4] Ah Me! how, then, shall I praise Thy greatness?

Footnotes

72:1 It is commonly said that She destroys but not so. Devatā does not destroy (*Na devo
nāśakah*). Man does. She takes back what She has put forth.
72:2 *Viṣṇu,* husband of *Lakṣmi.*
72:3 *Śiva.* The *Trimūrti* is, in fact, Her manifestation.
72:4 *Prāyah sakalam api,* that is, all moving and unmoving things (Commentary, K. B.).
For the Devī is *Viśvarūpiṇī* in the form of the whole universe. She is the objective world,
'*jadātmikā*' (Lalitā, verse 90), as well as its Cause.

Gaelic Myth: The Morrigan

In Celtic tales there are many fierce warrior-like goddesses. Sometimes these goddesses live in the other world and are visited by mortal champions who desire training,
other times the goddesses appear in the mortal world to aid or tempt the heroes. One
of the most powerful and deadly of the warrior goddesses was the Morrigan. The following is a description of the Morrigan or Morrígú.

■ ■ ■

From *Celtic Myth and Legend* by Charles Squire, 1905. Located on www.sacred.texts.com

Morrigan

© NNNMMM/Shutterstock.com

THE GAELIC GODS AND THEIR STORIES
CHAPTER V
THE GODS OF THE GAELS

Of these warlike goddesses there were five—Fea, the "Hateful", Nemon, the "Venom-ous", Badb, the "Fury", Macha, a personification of "battle", and, over all of them, the Morrígú, or "Great Queen". This supreme war-goddess of the Gaels, who resembles a fiercer Herê, perhaps symbolized the moon, deemed by early races to have preceded the sun, and worshipped with magical and cruel rites. She is represented as going fully armed, and carrying two spears in her hand. As with Arês and Poseidon in the "Iliad", her battle-cry was as loud as that of ten thousand men. Wherever there was war, either among gods or men, she, the great queen, was present, either in her own shape or in her favourite disguise, that of a "hoodie" or carrion crow. An old poem shows her incit-ing a warrior:

"Over his head is shrieking
    A lean hag, quickly hopping
Over the points of the weapons and shields;
    She is the gray-haired Morrígú"

With her, Fea and Nemon, Badb and Macha also hovered over the fighters, inspiring them with the madness of battle. All of these were sometimes called by the name of "Badb".

■ ■ ■

Gods and Fighting Men, by Lady Gregory, 1904. Located on www.sacred-texts.com

Part I Book IV: The Morrígú

As to the Morrígú, the Great Queen, the Crow of Battle, where she lived after the coming of the Gael is not known, but before that time it was in Teamhair she lived. And she had a great cooking-spit there, that held three sorts of food on it at the one time: a piece of raw meat, and a piece of dressed meat, and a piece of butter. And the raw was dressed, and the dressed was not burned, and the butter did not melt, and the three together on the spit.

Nine men that were outlaws went to her one time and asked for a spit to be made for themselves. And they brought it away with them, and it had nine ribs in it, and every one of the outlaws would carry a rib in his hand wherever he would go, till they would all meet together at the close of day. And if they wanted the spit to be high, it could be raised to a man's height, and at another time it would not be more than the height of a fist over the fire, without breaking and without lessening.

And Mechi, the son the Morrígú had, was killed by Mac Cecht on Magh Mechi, that till that time had been called Magh Fertaige. Three hearts he had, and it is the way they were, they had the shapes of three serpents through them. And if Mechi had not met with his death, those serpents in him would have grown, and what they left alive in Ireland would have wasted away. And Mac Cecht burned the three hearts on Magh Luathad, the Plain of Ashes, and he threw the ashes into the stream; and the rushing water of the stream stopped and boiled up, and every creature in it died.

And the Morrígú used often to be meddling in Ireland in Cuchulain's time, stirring up wars and quarrels. It was she came and roused up Cuchulain one time when he was but a lad, and was near giving into some enchantment that was used against him. "There is not the making of a hero in you," she said to him, "and you lying there under the feet of shadows." And with that Cuchulain rose up and struck off the head of a shadow that was standing over him, with his hurling stick. And the time Conchubar was sending out Finched to rouse up the men of Ulster at the time of the war for the Bull of Cuafigne, he bade him to go to that terrible fury, the Morrígú, to get help for Cuchulain. And she had a dispute with Cuchulain one time he met her, and she bringing away a cow from the Hill of Cruachan; and another time she helped Taichinem, a Druid of the household of Conaire Mor, to bring away a bull his wife had set her mind on. And indeed she was much given to meddling with cattle, and one time she brought away a cow from Odras, that was of the household of the cow-chief of Connac Hua Cuined, and that was going after her husband with cattle. And the Morrígú brought the cow away with her to the Cave of Cruachan, and the Hill of the Sidhe. And Odras followed her there till sleep fell on her in the oak-wood of Falga; and the Morrígú awoke her and sang spells over her, and made of her a pool of water that went to the river that flows to the west of Slieve Buane.

And in the battle of Magh Rath, she fluttered over Congal Claen in the shape of a bird, till he did not know friend from foe. And after that again at the battle of Cluantarbh, she was flying over the bead of Murchadh, son of Brian; for she had many shapes, and it was in the shape of a crow she would sometimes fight her battles.

And if it was not the Morrígú, it was Badb that showed herself in the battle of Dunbolg, where the men of Ireland were fighting under Aedh, son of Niall; and Brigit was seen in the same battle on the side of the men of Leinster.

Africa: Odudua and Yemaja

Odudua is the Yoruba Mother Earth married to Obatala, the representative of the Heavens. They have a sacred union between them. Much like Isis, Odudua is usually depicted seated with a child nursing at her breast. Yemaja is the sea goddess of the Yoruba people. According to Ellis she has an unwelcome relationship with her son that leads to the birth of many waters and a lagoon plus many of the other gods.

■ ■ ■

Yoruba-Speaking Peoples of the Slave Coast of West Africa: Their Religion, Manners, Customs, Laws, Language, Etc. by A. B. Ellis, 1894. Located on December, 1999 from www.sacred-texts.com

ODUDUA.

Odudua, or Odua, who has the title of Iya agbe, the mother who receives, is the chief goddess of the Yorubas. The name means "Black One" (dit, to be black; dudit, black), and the [Africans] consider a smooth, glossy, black skin a great beauty, and far superior to one of the ordinary cigar-colour. She is always represented as a woman sitting down, and nursing a child.

Odudua is the wife of Obatala, but she was coeval with Olorun, and not made by him, as was her husband. Other natives, however, say that she came from Ife, the holy city, in common with most of the other gods, as described in a myth which we shall come to shortly. Odudua represents the earth, married to the anthropomorphic sky-god. Obatala and Odudua, or Heaven and Earth, resemble, say the priests, two large cut-calabashes, which, when once shut, can never be opened. This is symbolised in the temples by two whitened saucer-shaped calabashes, placed one covering the other; the upper one of which represents the concave firmament stretching over and meeting the earth, the lower one, at the horizon.

According to some priests, Obatala and Odudua represent one androgynous divinity; and they say that an image which is sufficiently common, of a human being with one arm and leg, and a tail terminating in a sphere, symbolises this. This notion, however, is not one commonly held, Obatala and Odudua being generally, and almost universally, regarded as two distinct persons. The phallus and yoni in juxtaposition are often seen carved on the doors of the temples both of Obatala and Odudua; but this does not seem to have any reference to androgyny, since they are also found similarly depicted in other places which are in no way connected with either of these deities.

According to a myth Odudua is blind. In the beginning of the world she and her husband Obatala were shut up in darkness in a large, closed calabash, Obatala being in the upper part and Odudua in the lower. The myth does not state how they came to be in this situation, but they remained there for many days, cramped, hungry, and uncomfortable. Then Odudua began complaining, blaming her husband for the confinement; and a violent quarrel ensued, in the course of which, in a frenzy of rage, Obatala tore out her eyes, because she would not bridle her tongue. In return she cursed him, saying "Naught shalt thou eat but snails," which is the reason why snails are now offered to Obatala. As the myth does not make Odudua recover her sight, she must be supposed to have remained sightless, but no native regards her as being blind.

Odudua is patroness of love, and many stories are told of her adventures and amours. Her chief temple is in Ado, the principal town of the state of the same name, situated about fifteen miles to the north of Badagry. The word *Ado* means a lewd person of either sex, and its selection for the name of this town is accounted for by the following legend. Odudua was once walking alone in the forest when she met a hunter, who was so handsome that the ardent temperament of the goddess at once took fire. The advances which she made to him were favourably received, and they forthwith mutually gratified their passion on the spot. After this, the goddess became still more enamoured, and, unable to tear herself away from her lover, she lived with him for some weeks in a hut, which they constructed of branches at the foot of a large silk-cotton tree. At the end of this time her passion had burnt out, and having become weary of the hunter, she left him; but before doing so she promised to protect him and all others who might come and dwell in the favoured spot where she had passed so many pleasant hours. In consequence many people came and settled there, and a town gradually grew up, which was named Ado, to commemorate the circumstances of its origin. A temple was built for the protecting goddess; and there, on her feast days, sacrifices of cattle and sheep are made, and women abandon themselves indiscriminately to the male worshippers in her honour.

© csp/Shutterstock.com

(4) AGANJU AND YEMAJA.

Before her amour with the hunter, Odudua bore to her husband, Obatala, a boy and a girl, named respectively Aganju and Yemaja. The name Aganju means uninhabited tract of country, wilderness, plain, or forest, and Yemaja, "Mother of fish" (*yeye,* mother; *eja,* fish). The offspring of the union of Heaven and Earth, that is, of Obatala and Odudua, may thus be said to represent Land and Water. Yemaja is the goddess of brooks and streams, and presides over ordeals by water. She is represented by a female figure, yellow in colour, wearing blue beads and a white cloth. The worship of Aganju seems to have fallen into disuse, or to have become merged in that of his mother; but there is said to be an open space in front of the king's residence in Oyo where the god was formerly worshipped, which is still called *Oju-Aganju*-"Front of Aga-nju."

Yemaja married her brother Aganju, and bore a son named Orungan. This name is compounded of orun, sky, and gan, from ga, to be high; and appears to mean "In the height of the sky." It seems to answer to the *khekheme,* or "Free-air Region" of the Ewe peoples; and, like it, to mean the apparent space between the sky and the earth. The offspring of Land and Water would thus be what we call Air.

Orungan fell in love with his mother, and as she refused to listen to his guilty passion, he one day took advantage of his father's absence, and ravished her. Immediately after the act, Yemaja sprang to her feet and fled from the place wringing her hands and lamenting; and was pursued by Orungan, who strove to console her by saying that no one should know of what had occurred, and declared that he could not live without her. He held out to her the alluring prospect of living with two husbands, one acknowledged, and the other in secret; but she rejected all his proposals with loathing, and continued to run away. Orungan, however, rapidly gained upon her, and was just stretching out his hand to seize her, when she fell backward to the ground. Then her body immediately began to swell in a fearful manner, two streams of water gushed from her breasts, and her abdomen burst open. The streams from Yemaja's breasts joined and formed a lagoon, and from her gaping body came the following:—(1) Dada (god of vegetables), (2) Shango (god of lightning), (3) Ogun (god of iron and war), (4) Olokun (god of the sea), (5) Olosa (goddess of the lagoon), (6) Oya (goddess of the river Niger), (7) Oshun (goddess of the river Oshun), (8) Oba (goddess of the river Oba), (9) Orisha Oko (god of agriculture), (10) Oshosi (god of hunters), (11) Oke (god of mountains), (12) Aje Shaluga (god of wealth), (13) Shankpanna (god of small-pox), (14) Orun (the sun), and (15) Oshu (the moon). To commemorate this event, a town which was given the name of Ife (distention, enlargement, or swelling up), was built on the spot where Yemaja's body burst open, and became the holy city of the Yoruba-speaking tribes. The place where her body fell used to be shown, and probably still is; but the town was destroyed in 1882, in the war between the Ifes on the one hand and the Ibadans and Modakekes on the other.

The myth of Yemaja thus accounts for the origin of several of the gods, by making them the grandchildren of Obatala and Odudua[. . .].

■ ■ ■

Yoruba-Speaking Peoples of the Slave Coast of West Africa: Their Religion, Manners, Customs, Laws, Language, Etc. by A. B. Ellis, 1894. Located on December, 1999 from www.sacred-texts.com

Scandinavia: Freya

In Scandinavia and Germanic Mythology, there are a few goddesses that qualify as Great Goddesses. These include Odin's wife, Frigg, the earth goddess and mother of Balder the Beautiful, and Freya (Freyja), the sister of Frey, the ruler of Vanaheim. Freya is one of the Vanir. She and her brother live with the Aesir as part of the truce they declared after years of warring with each other. Freya and her brother Frey live mostly in Asgard, but they keep homes in Vanaheim.

Freya is married to a god named Odur, although he disappears. Some think her husband may have been Odin. Freya is a goddess of sexuality and beauty, much like Aphrodite, but she is also a fierce warrior. She has an eye for golden things and unfortunately makes a disastrous decision to obtain a fabulously golden necklace that seems to cause the disappearance of her beloved husband. The following excerpt is from Chapter 6 of The Children of Odin by Padraic Colum, based on the Prose and Poetic Eddas. Padraic has made the story suitable for readers of all ages. In the original story, Freya does more than kiss the dwarves in order to obtain the necklace.

6. HOW FREYA GAINED HER NECKLACE AND HOW HER LOVED ONE WAS LOST TO HER

YES, Loki went through Asgard silent and with head bent, and the Dwellers in Asgard said one unto the other, "This will teach Loki to work no more mischief." They did not know that what Loki had done had sown the seeds of mischief and that these seeds were to sprout up and bring sorrow to the beautiful Vana Freya, to Freya whom the Giant wanted to carry off with the Sun and the Moon as payment for his building the wall around Asgard.

Freya had looked upon the wonders that Loki had brought into Asgard–the golden threads that were Sif's hair, and Frey's boar that shed light from its bristles as it flew. The gleam of these golden things dazzled her, and made her dream in the day time and the night time of the wonders that she herself might possess. And often she thought, "What wonderful things the Three Giant Women would give me if I could bring myself to go to them on their mountaintop."

Long ere this, when the wall around their City was not yet built, and when the Gods had set up only the court with their twelve seats and the Hall that was for Odin and the Hall that was for the Goddesses, there had come into Asgard Three Giant Women.

""They came after the Gods had set up a forge and had begun to work metal for their buildings. The metal they worked was pure gold. With gold they built Gladsheim, the Hall of Odin, and with gold they made all their dishes and household ware. Then was the Age of Gold, and the Gods did not grudge gold to anyone. Happy were the Gods then, and no shadow nor foreboding lay on Asgard.

But after the Three Giant Women came the Gods began to value gold and to hoard it. They played with it no more. And the happy innocence of their first days departed from them.

At last the Three were banished from Asgard. The Gods turned their thoughts from the hoarding of gold, and they built up their City, and they made themselves strong.

And now Freya, the lovely Vanir bride, thought upon the Giant Women and on the wonderful things of gold they had flashed through their hands. But not to Odur, her husband, did she speak her thoughts; for Odur, more than any of the other dwellers in Asgard, was wont to think on the days of happy innocence, before gold came to be hoarded and valued. Odur would not have Freya go near the mountaintop where the Three had their high seat.

But Freya did not cease to think upon them and upon the things of gold they had. "Why should Odur know I went to them?" she said to herself. "No one will tell him. And what difference will it make if I go to them and gain some lovely thing for myself? I shall not love Odur the less because I go my own way for once."

Then one day she left their palace, leaving Odur, her husband, playing with their little child Hnossa. She left the palace and went down to the Earth. There she stayed for a while, tending the flowers that were her charge. After a while she asked the Elves to tell her where the mountain was on which the Three Giant Women stayed.

The Elves were frightened and would not tell her, although she was queen over them. She left them and stole down into the caves of the Dwarfs. It was they who showed her the way to the seat of the Giant Women, but before they showed her the way they made her feel shame and misery.

"We will show you the way if you stay with us here," said one of the Dwarfs.

"For how long would you have me stay?" said Freya.

"Until the cocks in Svartheim crow," said the Dwarfs, closing round her. "We want to know what the company of one of the Vanir is like." "I will stay," Freya said.

Then one of the Dwarfs reached up and put his arms round her neck and kissed her with his ugly mouth. Freya tried to break away from them, but the Dwarfs held her. "You cannot go away from us now until the cocks of Svartheim crow," they said.

Then one and then another of the Dwarfs pressed up to her and kissed her. They made her sit down beside them on the heaps of skins they had. When she wept they screamed at her and beat her. One, when she would not kiss him on the mouth, bit her hands. So Freya stayed with the Dwarfs until the cocks of Svartheim crew.

They showed her the mountain on the top of which the Three banished from Asgard had their abode. The Giant Women sat overlooking the World of Men. "What would you have from us, wife of Odur?" one who was called Gulveig said to her.

"Alas! Now that I have found you I know that I should ask you for nought," Freya said.

"Speak, Vana," said the second of the Giant Women.

The third said nothing, but she held up in her hands a necklace of gold most curiously fashioned. "How bright it is!" Freya said. "There is shadow where you sit, women, but the necklace you hold makes brightness now. Oh, how I should joy to wear it!"

"It is the necklace Brisingamen," said the one who was called Gulveig.

"It is yours to wear, wife of Odur," said the one who held it in her hands.

Freya took the shining necklace and clasped it round her throat. She could not bring herself to thank the Giant Women, for she saw that there was evil in their eyes. She made reverence to them, however, and she went from the mountain on which they sat overlooking the World of Men.

In a while she looked down and saw Brisingamen and her misery went from her. It was the most beautiful thing ever made by hands. None of the Asyniur and none other of the Vanir possessed a thing so beautiful. It made her more and more lovely, and Odur, she thought, would forgive her when he saw how beautiful and how happy Brisingamen made her.

She rose up from amongst the flowers and took leave of the slight Elves and she made her way into Asgard. All who greeted her looked long and with wonder upon the necklace that she wore. And into the eyes of the Goddesses there came a look of longing when they saw Brisingamen.

But Freya hardly stopped to speak to anyone. As swiftly as she could she made her way to her own palace. She would show herself to Odur and win his forgiveness. She entered her shining palace and called to him. No answer came. Her child, the little Hnossa, was on the floor, playing. Her mother took her in her arms, but the child, when she looked on Brisingamen, turned away crying.

Freya left Hnossa down and searched again for Odur. He was not in any part of their palace. She went into the houses of all who dwelt in Asgard, asking for tidings of him. None knew where he had gone to. At last Freya went back to their palace and waited and waited for Odur to return. But Odur did not come. One came to her. It was a Goddess, Odin's wife, the queenly Frigga. "You are waiting for Odur, your husband," Frigga said. "Ah, let me tell you Odur will not come to you here. He went, when for the sake of a shining thing you did what would make him unhappy. Odur has gone from Asgard and no one knows where to search for him."

"I will seek him outside of Asgard," Freya said. She wept no more, but she took the little child Hnossa and put her in Frigga's arms. Then she mounted her car that was drawn by two cats, and journeyed down from Asgard to Midgard, the Earth, to search for Odur her husband.

Year in and year out, and over all the Earth, Freya went searching and calling for the lost Odur. She went as far as the bounds of the Earth, where she could look over to Jötunheim, where dwelt the Giant who would have carried her off with the Sun and the Moon as payment for the building of the wall around Asgard. But in no place, from the end of the Rainbow Bifröst, that stretched from Asgard to the Earth, to the boundary of Jötunheim, did she find a trace of her husband Odur.

At last she turned her car toward Bifröst, the Rainbow Bridge that stretched from Midgard, the Earth, to Asgard, the Dwelling of the Gods. Hemidall, the Watcher for the Gods, guarded the Rainbow Bridge. To him Freya went with a half hope fluttering in her heart.

"O Heimdall," she cried, "O Hemidall, Watcher for the Gods, speak and tell me if you know where Odur is."

"Odur is in every place where the searcher has not come; Odur is in every place that the searcher has left; those who seek him will never find Odur," said Heimdall, the Watcher for the Gods.

Then Freya stood on Bifröst and wept. Frigga, the queenly Goddess, heard the sound of her weeping, and came out of Asgard to comfort her.

"Ah, what comfort can. you give me, Frigga?" cried Freya. "What comfort can you give me when Odur will never be found by one who searches for him?"

"Behold how your daughter, the child Hnossa, has grown," said Frigga. Freya looked up and saw a beautiful maiden standing on Bifröst, the Rainbow Bridge. She was young, more youthful than any of the Vanir or the Asyniur, and her face and her for form were so lovely that all hearts became melted when they looked upon her.

And Freya was comforted in her loss. She followed Frigga across Bifröst, the Rainbow Bridge, and came once again into the City of the Gods. In her own palace in Asgard Freya dwelt with Hnossa, her child.

Still she wore round her neck Brisingamen, the necklace that lost her Odur. But now she wore it, not for its splendor, but as a sign of the wrong she had done. She weeps, and her tears become golden drops as they fall on the earth. And by poets who know her story she is called The Beautiful Lady in Tears.

from https://www.sacred-texts.com/neu/ice/coo/coo07.htm

The Great Goddess comes in a wide variety of forms, often as an Earth goddess and frequently as a mother. She is associated with life, death and rebirth, and often teaches the arts of agriculture to human beings. She is the giver of grain and she can also cause a bad harvest. She may appear as the wise woman, healer or prophetess, the fertile mother, or the warrior maiden. She changes like the moon changes and is associated with its cycle.

Study Questions for Chapter 5: The Great Goddess Archetype

Archetype

1. List the main characteristics of the Great Goddess Archetype.
2. What are the three main guises that the Great Goddess might wear?

Egyptian: Nut

1. Who is Nut?
2. What are some of the descriptions of Nut from *Utterances in Praise of Nut*?
3. Do these descriptions fit the characteristics of a Great Goddess Archetype? Explain.

Egyptian: Isis

1. Who is Isis?
2. How do Isis' relationships with her husband and son reflect Great Goddess Archetype qualities?
3. What characteristics of the Great Goddess Archetype are demonstrated by Isis in the myth of the Name of Ra?
4. What characteristics of the Great Goddess Archetype are included in the description Isis gives of herself in Apuleius' *The Golden Ass*?

Mesopotamian: Tiamat

1. Who is Tiamat?
2. What characteristics of the Great Goddess Archetype are evident in the descriptions of Tiamat from the excerpts from the First and Second Tablets of Creation?

Mesopotamian: Inanna

1. Who is Inanna?
2. What characteristics of the Great Goddess Archetype are evident in the descriptions of Inanna's powers given in the list of new powers bequeathed her by her grandfather Enki in the Mesopotamian myths?

Greek: Gaia

1. Who is Gaia?
2. What characteristics of the Great Goddess Archetype are evident in the descriptions of Gaia in the Homeric Hymn to Gaia?

Greek: Demeter

1. Who is Demeter?
2. How is she described in the Homeric *Hymn to Demeter?*
3. Does her description fit into the characteristics of the Great Goddess Archetype? Explain.

Greek: Athena

1. Who is Athena?
2. How is she described in the Homeric *Hymn to Pallas Athena?*
3. Does the description match the characteristics of the Great Goddess Archetype? Explain.

Greek: Artemis

1. Who is Artemis? Who is her twin?
2. How is Artemis described in the Homeric *Hymns to Artemis* and in Jane Harrison's *Myths of Greece and Rome* excerpts?
3. Do these descriptions match the characteristics of the Great Goddess Archetype? Explain.

Indian: Devi

1. Who is Devi?
2. What are some of the most common forms that Devi takes?
3. How well does the description of the birth of Parvati from the *Devi Gita* fit into the characteristics of the Great Goddess Archetype? Explain.
4. How is Kali described?
5. Does the description of Kali include the characteristics of Great Goddess Archetype? Explain why or why not.

Gaelic The Morrigan

1. Who is the Morrigan?
2. How well does the description of the Morrigan match the characteristics of the Great Goddess Archetype? Explain your answer.

African: Odudua and Yemaya

1. Who is Odudua?
2. How is Odudua described in the excerpt from the Yoruba people?
3. How well does Odudua fit into the Great Goddess Archetype? Explain.
4. Who is Yemaya?
5. How is Yemaya described in the excerpt from the Yoruba people?
6. How well does Yemaya fit into the Great Goddess Archetype? Explain.

Scandinavia: Freya

1. Who is Freya?
2. What is Freya's relationship to the Aesir and to Odin?
3. How does the story of Freya obtaining the golden necklace demonstrate some of the characteristics of the Great Goddess Archetype?

CHAPTER 6
THE DYING AND RISING GOD ARCHETYPE

Introduction to the Dying God Archetype

The god who dies and rises again was a common motif in the ancient Mediterranean and agricultural world. The Dying and Rising God is associated with the cycle of plants, often those planted as crops by humans. The Dying and Rising God is the seed planted in the earth (similar to a burial) that grows again in spring (rebirth) matures in the summer (marriage/union with the Great Mother) and is killed in the fall (harvest). In the northern hemisphere, the stages of the Dying and Rising God's life often

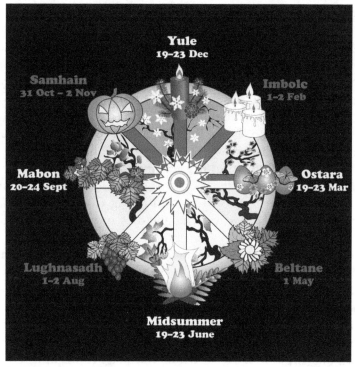

© Snowbelle/Shutterstock.com

correspond to the solstices and equinoxes as the sun has a direct impact on the growth of vegetation. Birth occurred on the Winter Solstice in December, rebirth was celebrated on the Spring Equinox in March, marriage and union with the great Mother was celebrated on the Summer Solstice in June, and the harvest or death of the god was celebrated at the Fall Equinox in September. In some areas the hot months of July and August were the deadly months as nothing could grow in the heat. In that case the solstices and equinoxes would represent a slightly different pattern for the Dying and Rising God's life, which is always less than a year. The god must die and experience some sort of rebirth, although it does not have to be a literal death. It could be symbolic. Any trip to the underworld is considered a symbolic death and a return from the underworld is a symbolic rebirth.

The Dying and Rising God is an archetype that is closely linked to the Great Goddess as Mother for the Dying and Rising God is usually the child of the Great Mother Goddess. The child, much like a plant, springs from the Mother Goddess (who is associated with the Earth), grows and matures like the plant grows and matures, and eventually dies or is killed, just as the plant life dies or is harvested. However, when the death of the god occurs it is followed by rebirth, whether literally or symbolically. The god's death and rebirth are closely tied to the vegetation or agricultural cycle of the region from which the myth of the god comes.

One of the characteristics that is sometimes hard to accept about the Dying and Rising God is that if the god is a male, he usually becomes the lover of the Great Mother Goddess when he matures, which means that incest often occurs within the myths. However, the god is a metaphor for the plant life that springs from the earth like a child from its mother. In the vegetation cycle, after the plants mature, seeds fall from the mature plant back onto the ground from which the plant came, ensuring more plants the following year. This image is conveyed metaphorically in the myths when the god matures and becomes the lover of his mother, impregnating her with his seed before he dies or is killed. Sometimes the god is castrated so that there is a literal scattering of his seed back onto the earth, fertilizing it so that new life may arise.

Because the Dying and Rising God is connected to the land, he may be sacrificed for the good of others whether to restore fertility to the land or end a drought or to appease an angry god, or to provide food for the people, especially if he is associated with a crop like corn or wheat. The Dying and Rising God may also act as the scapegoat, dying in place of another. Because the god dies and is reborn, his followers often have hope for a better afterlife.

Many of the Dying and Rising Gods had mystery religions associated with them that were not part of the mainstream religions, but something set apart and aside from them that offered a better afterlife or at least a sense of reconciliation with death. Some of the Hellenistic mystery religions include the Eleusinian Mysteries associated with Demeter and Persephone, the Orphic Mysteries associated with Dionysos, and the Mithraic Mysteries associated with Mithras, the son of the Persian Supreme Being Ahura-Mazda. Mithras was born of a virgin in a cave witnessed by magi (Perisan wise men) and shepherds. Mithras performed miracles as he grew and eventually gathered twelve disciples. He slew the bull of Ahriman that caused chaos in the land and a horrible drought, restoring the earth's fertility. After killing the bull, Mithras had a last supper with his disciples where they ate bread and drank wine. Then he ascended into Heaven in the chariot of the sun god where he awaits the final battle against Ahriman. Mithras will return to lead the forces of Good against the forces of Evil during that last battle.

Mithras' mystery religion was one of the greatest rivals to Christianity in the first centuries of the common era. Both religions, like most mystery religions, included initiation by baptism. Initiates were only allowed to discuss the religion with other initiates (thus the "mystery" designation). Mithras primarily appealed to Roman soldiers because he was a warrior as well as a savior. Only free born men were allowed to follow Mithras. Christianity had greater appeal because anyone could follow its dying and rising god, Jesus.

Egyptian: Osiris

The story of Isis and Osiris is one of the earliest love stories recorded. It is also a Dying and Rising God myth. The story of Isis' revival of Osiris from death became the basis of a mystery religion that the Romans adopted and spread throughout their empire. Because of this, Isis became one of the most popular goddesses in the Roman world. Osiris also rose in prominence in Egypt.

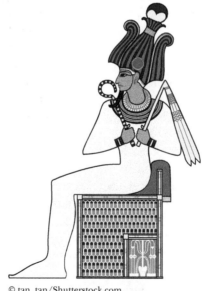

© tan_tan/Shutterstock.com

Isis and Osiris were born of Nut, Mother Sky, and Geb, Father Earth—along with their siblings, Seth, the god of the desert and chaos, and Nephthys, the goddess of dusk and dawn. Osiris and Isis were married as were Seth and Nephthys. Osiris became the first king of Egypt and was the god of fertility. Together with Isis, who was the goddess of magic and healing, he taught the people of Egypt the arts of agriculture and the making of wine and beer. The couple was dearly loved.

The couple's growing popularity bothered Seth who was jealous of his brother. Seth wanted to rule Egypt so he plotted to overthrow Osiris. Secretly, he had a sarcophagus made to Osiris' dimensions. He waited until there was a party going on amongst the gods and brought in the sarcophagus to be admired. Seth announced to the gods that anyone who could fit into the sarcophagus perfectly could have it as a gift. All the gods lined up to try it out, but it only fit Osiris. After Osiris was in the sarcophagus admiring the beautiful artwork detailing its interior, Seth signaled to his seventy-two accomplices who came rushing in with the lid and bound it to the sarcophagus with metal bands and threw the sarcophagus into the Nile River. The gods were stunned. Amidst the ensuing chaos, Seth claimed the throne of Egypt. Isis was left to search for her husband throughout the length and breadth of Egypt.

Isis sought the sarcophagus of her husband throughout Egypt asking everyone she met if they had seen it floating in the Nile. Eventually her travels took her to the mouth of the river where some children had seen the sarcophagus float out into the Mediterranean Sea heading east. Isis headed east in its wake. According to the story recorded by the Roman author, Plutarch, the sarcophagus ended up in Syria, where it washed ashore on the bank of a river. There, a tree grew up around it encompassing the sarcophagus in its trunk. The local king heard about the tree, which had gained a heavenly scent due to its divine occupant, and had it cut down and fashioned into a pillar for his palace. Isis heard the rumors of the fragrant pillar and disguising herself as a human woman, visited the king's palace and got a job as the nanny to the newborn prince.

At night, while the palace's occupants headed toward sleep, Isis would place the infant prince in the fireplace to burn away his mortal parts and make him immortal because she had come to love the little one. While the baby was occupied playing in the fire, Isis transformed herself into a swallow and flew mournfully around the pillar in which her husband was trapped. One night, the queen of Syria happened upon the scene when she came to check on her baby one last time before bed. She gave a scream when she saw her baby boy in the fire pit. Isis had to transform back into her goddess form to rescue the baby, and then explain who she was and what she had been attempting to do. Sadly, the queen had disrupted the spell and her son remained mortal. The king was moved by Isis' tale and gladly had the pillar taken down and split apart. Sure enough, inside the pillar was the sarcophagus of Osiris, which the king had loaded onto a barge in order for Isis to return with it to Egypt.

On the voyage home, Isis missed her husband so much that she took off the lid of the sarcophagus and used her magic to revive him long enough for one last embrace. The fruit of that union was their child, Horus, who was born after Isis reached the safety of the papyrus swamps along the Nile River in Egypt. When Isis went into labor she could not care for herself and the child as well as guard her husband's corpse. She left Osiris' body hidden among the papyrus plants along the banks of the Nile. Unfortunately, while she was occupied with tending to her son, Seth found the body of Osiris as he was hunting along the Nile. He was so enraged when he found the corpse of his brother that Seth cut the body of Osiris into fourteen pieces and scattered them up and down the length of Egypt. When poor Isis returned to look after Osiris' corpse, it was gone. She learned about the dismemberment of her husband and set out on a second quest to regain all his body parts and try to restore him to life.

When Isis searched for Osiris' dismembered body parts, she had the help of her sister Nephthys as well as Nephthys' son, Anubis, the god of mummification. Together, they searched the length of Egypt and at each location where they found a piece of the god, they left behind a copy of the body part and a command to build a temple to house the relic so that Osiris might not be forgotten. Eventually, they gathered thirteen of the fourteen missing pieces. The last piece, Osiris' genitalia, had fallen into the Nile where a fish had swallowed it. Thus the Nile became the source of fertility in Egypt. Isis had to fashion new genitals for Osiris out of either ivory or gold. However, she lacked the magic necessary to fully revive him. She needed more magic, thus she tricked Re. (The story of Isis tricking Re is told in the Great Goddess chapter.)

After Isis gained the necessary magic by deceiving Re into revealing to her his true name, she used that magic not only to restore Re to his full strength but also to revive her husband Osiris. However, Osiris was no longer a fertile god after his resurrection so he could no longer be king of Egypt. Instead he became the god of the afterlife, called the Duat. There, he sat in judgment over all the souls of the dead who made it to his hall, often times accompanied by his wife, Isis, and his sister, Nephthys. who stood behind his throne, while Anubis conducted the weighing of the soul's heart against the feather of Ma'at (Truth) before the throne, and Thoth, the god of wisdom, recorded the results in his book of life.

Back in Egypt a long drawn out battle for the throne of Egypt took place between Seth and Horus, the son of Isis and Osiris. After many contests between the two with the rest of the gods evenly split in their decision over who should take over for Osiris, someone finally suggested that the gods ask Osiris who he preferred to have rule after him. Osiris chose his son, Horus, as the next king of Egypt. Thus, the pharaohs of Egypt were often called the living Horus until they died, when they were referred to as Osiris. As Seth was a worthy candidate for the throne, Re made him guardian of the sun boat and it became Seth's job to protect Re and the sun boat as it moved through the afterlife each night and to fight off any of the demons that might attempt to stop the sun's reappearance the next morning, especially Apophis. And so the Egyptian gods obtained their places in the pantheon.

Mesopotamian: Dumuzi

Inanna's rise to power was told in the earlier chapter on the Great Goddess. This story focuses on her marriage to the shepherd god, Dumuzi, and her journey to the underworld. It comes from Mesopotamia, from Sumer, originally, and was later adopted by the Babylonians for their goddess Ishtar. There are several translations and not all of them agree on the exact reasons for what follows. My version is based mostly on Diane Wolkstein and Samuel Kramer's retellings, but told in my own words. The story is a little problematic, in that Inanna seems to be the prototype for the Dying and Rising God in this story even though she fits the characteristics of the Great Goddess much better. Dumuzi, her husband, and Dumuzi's sister, Geshtinanna, are the gods who cycle into and out of the underworld each year and are closer to the archetype of the Dying and Rising God. Each descent into the underworld is a symbolic death, and each return to earth is a symbolic rebirth.

After Inanna returned to Uruk carrying the Me that her grandfather Enki had given her, her parents encouraged her to seek out a husband. They proposed several suitors to her but seemed to favor the shepherd god, Dumuzi, the most. Inanna was more inclined toward the farmer god, but eventually listened to Dumuzi's courtship and apparently was inspired by it to choose him. Their wedding date was set and a big wedding was planned. Inanna seemed most eager to try out some of her new powers, especially those that related to the bedchamber. After the wedding was celebrated, Inanna and Dumuzi retired to their wedding chamber for over a month. At the end of that time, Dumuzi appeared to be worn out and pleaded with Inanna to let him go to the palace and rule as king. He said that he would treat her as his little sister and that his mother and father would treat her as his little sister. We are not entirely sure what Dumuzi meant. Sister may have been a generic kinship term used for all women, but regardless, it does not sound like a positive remark. Inanna let Dumuzi go to the palace to rule, which left her without much to do, and perhaps a little disappointed in the abrupt end to their love making. At this point Inanna took an interest in the underworld, which was ruled by her sister, the part-bestial goddess Ereshkigal.

The translations are not consistent in the reason for Inanna's descent to the underworld realm of Ereshkigal. Some of the translations say that Inanna went to help Ereshkigal through labor, others say that she went to witness the funeral rites for Ereshkigal's husband, the Bull of Heaven, who had been recently killed by the hero Gilgamesh and his friend Enkidu. One alternate translation implies that she went into the underworld to seize the power of her sister. In any case, she made a journey to the underworld, but first warned her servant, Ninshubar, that if she was not back in three days the servant should obtain help from the male gods of the pantheon. After enlisting the aid of her servant, Inanna dressed herself up in all her regalia, putting on her crown, her necklace of lapis lazuli, her chestplate, a belt with seven decrees, taking up the rod of queenship, etc. Then she went to the entrance to the underworld and knocked on the first gate.

When Inanna knocked on the gate, the guard, Neti, was very surprised. He was not certain what to do so he made Inanna wait while he descended to ask his mistress, Ereshkigal, what she desired. Ereshkigal was not pleased by Inanna's descent but allowed her to come down into the underworld on the condition that Neti treat her as anyone else who came to the land of the dead. When Neti returned to Inanna, he let her in the first gate, but removed her crown. When he did so, she asked him what he was doing and he responded that the ways of the underworld were perfect and that she should not question them. Neti proceeded to take Inanna down through the other six gates and at each gate he removed one item from her until finally she was stripped bare when she appeared before the throne of Ereshkigal.

Ereshkigal or the judges of the underworld, the Annunaki, killed Inanna after she appeared before Ereshkigal's throne. The translations do not all agree on why this happened, but all agreed that it occurred. Ereshkigal had Inanna's body hung on a hook from the wall where it rotted like a hank of meat for three days.

Back on the earth, at the entrance to the underworld, Inanna's faithful servant, Ninshubar, awaited her mistress. When Inanna did not return in three days time, Ninshubar approached the chief male gods, Enlil, Nanna, and Enki. Enlil and Nanna were not sympathetic stating that no one returned from the underworld, but father Enki recognized the importance of Inanna's return, especially after all the powers he had given her included the fertility of all the creatures on earth as well as the crops. It was imperative to return Inanna to her rightful place. He created two servants that could shape shift and fly as flies into the underworld carrying the Food and Water of Life. They were instructed to empathize with Ereshkigal who was suffering, whether from grief over her husband's death or through labor, we are not certain. Because no one appreciated Ereshkigal or showed her sympathy she responded favorably to the empathy of Enki's servants and rewarded them. When asked what reward they wanted for empathizing with the goddess, the servants told Ereshkigal that they would happily take the hank of rotting meat hanging from the hook on the wall. Ereshkigal gave them the corpse of Inanna, which they sprinkled with the Food and Water of Life given to them by Enki. Inanna revived. She was ready to leave the underworld, but Ereshkigal pointed out that no one left the underworld and the only way that Inanna could leave was to find someone to take her place in the underworld. Inanna agreed.

When Inanna departed the underworld demons or possibly rangers from the realm went with her and she was given the Eye of Death to wear. As Inanna moved through the seven gates that led to the earth's surface her items of power were restored to her so that she exited from the underworld as Queen of Heaven and Earth. She was greeted by her servants who wore sack cloth and had ashes in their hair and signs of mourning on their faces. When the demons asked if they could take one of the servants as Inanna's replacement, she said no. The demons were not allowed to take anyone who had mourned for her while she was in the underworld.

Eventually, the group made it all the way back to her city of Uruk, encountering on the way many people, all of which had mourned for Inanna. However, when they returned to her city and entered the throne room of the palace, her husband, Dumuzi, sat on the throne, apparently unmoved by Inanna's absence. There was not a tear or an ash or a piece of sack cloth in sight. When the demons asked if they could take Dumuzi away, Inanna said, "Take him!" Dumuzi was not eager to go into the underworld and hid as a sheep in his sheepfold, but the demons found him and dragged him unwilling into the underworld.

Time passed and Inanna resumed her rule over the city of Uruk. At some undisclosed point, Dumuzi's sister, Geshtinanna, appeared before Inanna's throne and begged for the return of her brother. She made an interesting offer; she offered to take Dumuzi's place in the underworld in order for him to return. Inanna was moved by Geshtinanna's compassion for her brother and agreed to let Dumuzi return; however, she felt it was not fair to send Geshtinanna, who had done nothing wrong at all, to the underworld permanently. Instead, she made a deal that Geshtinanna could take Dumuzi's place for half the year, but then she would return and Dumuzi would go back down to the underworld for the rest of the year. The two would cycle in and out of the underworld, spending half of each year with the goddess of the underworld and half of each year with Inanna on earth. Geshtinanna agreed and took Dumuzi's place and Dumuzi was reunited with Inanna in Uruk for half the year.

Greek: Orphic Version of Dionysos

One of the mystery religions from ancient Greece was the Orphic mysteries, named after a supposed prophet of the religion called Orpheus, who may or may not have been the Orpheus of Greek mythology. The mystery religion stresses the death and rebirth of Dionysos in ways that the mainstream story of his birth does not. Not a lot is known about the religion due to its secrecy and the need for baptism in it, but enough remains to piece together the rudiments of Dionysos' myth. It is a very unusual story for two reasons: 1–Zeus does not normally sleep with his daughters. Other female relatives are fine, but he usually refrains from seducing his offspring. 2–Persephone normally is childless as queen of the underworld, yet in the Orphic tradition she has a child. The second half of the myth that retells his near birth from the human Semele was the more commonly known story of Dionysos' birth.

After Persephone was married to Hades, Zeus realized how beautiful she was and decided to seduce her. He slipped into the underworld disguised as a serpent and approached her and impregnated her. Persephone gave birth to Dionysos-Zagreus, an adorable little god with curly horns like a ram's. Zeus was smitten with the child and brought him up to Mt. Olympos to live where he let Dionysos-Zagreus play on his throne, wear his crown and pretend to be king. This infuriated Hera who was deter-

Figure 6.1
© Eroshka/Shutterstock.com

mined to rid herself of the little god. In anger, Hera approached the Titans and riled them up against Dionysos-Zagreus by pointing out that if anyone should sit on Zeus' throne it should be one of them as elder gods and former rulers of the world. The Titans became so angry that they attacked Dionysos-Zagreus who attempted to escape by shape shifting into various animal forms. Unfortunately, the Titans surrounded and killed him by ripping him to pieces while he was in the form of a bull. Pomegranates sprang from wherever his blood spilled on the earth. After the Titans had ripped Dionysos-Zagreus apart, each Titan held the dripping pieces of bull's meat and decided to eat it. While they were thus occupied with their feast, Athena, the goddess of wisdom, rushed in and saved the heart of Dionysos-Zagreus, which she gave to Zeus.

Zeus was so enraged by the Titans' actions that he blasted them into ash with his lightning bolts. Looking at the pile of ash afterward, he decided to make something out of it and ordered that man be fashioned from the ash. The Orphics claimed that the corruptible part of humans came from the flesh of the Titans. The little sparks of Dionysos-Zagreus that were what remained in what the Titans had eaten became the humans' souls.

After the destruction of the Titans and the creation of humans, Zeus sought to recreate his favored son. He took the heart of Dionysos-Zagreus that Athena had rescued and either ground it into a potion and gave it to Semele, a mortal princess, to eat, or swallowed it himself before he slept with Semele. In either case, Semele became pregnant with Dionysos. When Hera found out, she was furious. She disguised herself as one of Semele's servants and questioned her about her pregnancy and the father of her child. She played on Semele's fears by asking Semele how she knew that the man who made love to her was really a god and not a human pretending to be one in order to sleep with her. Hera, in her disguise, pointed out that to claim Semele was sleeping with a god if she actually was not was a form of hubris. Semele did not want to commit hubris and asked for the servant's advice. How could she determine if her lover was really Zeus? The servant boldly claimed that Semele must ask Zeus for a gift. If he was really the king of the gods, he should reveal himself to her in all his glory just as he appeared to his wife Hera on Mt. Olympos.

The next time that Zeus came to visit Semele she followed her servant's advice and asked for a gift. Zeus said she could have whatever she wanted. She asked to see him in all his glory, but Zeus knew it would kill her and tried to persuade her to ask for something else. When she insisted, Zeus had to reveal himself. Knowing what would follow, he rescued the embryo of Dionysos from Semele's womb just before she was incinerated by Zeus' glory. He sewed the embryo into his thigh until the time when the baby was ready to be born. When that time occurred, Zeus cut the threads and out popped baby Dionysos, born from the thigh of Zeus. As he was born from a god, Dionysos became a god. If he had been born from Semele, he would have been mortal with some extraordinary ability, but due to Hera's interference he was a god again.

Because Hera did not like Dionysos, Zeus had him hidden away on the island of Nysa where he was protected by nymphs until he was old enough to travel. When he was old enough, the nymphs took him away from Greece, and thus Hera's ire, and traveled with him all the way to India and back. In the process, he grew up and he learned how to cultivate the grapevine. When he returned to Greece in triumph as an adult he brought with him the intoxicating beverage made from the fruit of the vine: wine. Those who accepted him as a god received the beverage as a gift and it led to sweet intoxication and ecstasy. Those who denied him as a god (hubris) received the beverage as a curse and it led to madness and often dismemberment.

Hera reconciled with the adult god and Dionysos was admitted into the pantheon of gods that ruled from Mt. Olympos, where he was the god of the grapevine, grapes, wine, and really the sap of all living things, which is blood in humans and animals and the green sap in plants.

Greek: Adonis

The story of Aphrodite and Adonis has its parallels not only to Persephone and Demeter's myth (told in the Great Goddess chapter) but also to the Inanna and Dumuzi myth told earlier in this chapter, and all its later variants including Ishtar and Tammuz and Astarte and Adonis' myths. Aphrodite and Adonis' myth is told by the Roman author Ovid, who was probably passing it along more in the form of entertaining literature than as a sacred story. Ovid tended to be a bit cynical in his retellings and the work in which he retells the Venus (Roman Aphrodite) and Adonis tale, the *Metamorphoses,* is primarily concerned with stories of shape-shifting and transformations rather than a connection to seasonal cycles or fertility rites. The following is the myth retold in my own words and strung together in a coherent whole although it exists in separate pieces from the ancient world.

The first version of the story of Aphrodite and Adonis says that there was a man named Cinyras in ancient Greece, whose wife committed hubris against the goddess by saying that their daughter, Myrrha, was lovelier than the goddess. Aphrodite punished the hubris by causing Myrrha to lust after her own father. The only way to assuage the desire that tormented her was to fulfill it with the help of her faithful nurse. Myrrha found a way to slip into her father's bed without his realization of her identity. Eventually she became pregnant and could not hide her state from her father. When he figured out how she had become pregnant, he was horrified. He sought to kill her in retaliation for the incest. Myrrha fled and as she fled she prayed to the gods to have mercy on her. They heard her prayer and transformed her into a myrrh tree. The tears she wept became the precious resin, myrrh, used as incense.

Even as a tree Myrrha remained pregnant. Months later, a crack appeared at the base of the tree, which grew wider and wider, until finally out popped a beautiful baby boy, Adonis. Adonis was discovered by the goddess, Aphrodite, who, recognizing his beauty, carefully placed him in a box and took him to her good friend Persephone in the underworld for safe keeping. When Adonis matured, Aphrodite returned to retrieve him, but Persephone did not want to let her surrogate son leave. The two goddesses quarreled until they asked Zeus to intercede. Zeus divided the year into thirds and gave one third of the year to Persephone to spend with Adonis and one third of the year to Aphrodite to spend with Adonis and one third of the year to Adonis to do with as he wished. Adonis, in turn, gave his one third of the year to Aphrodite.

Aphrodite and Adonis spent all their time together when he returned to the earth. Aphrodite neglected all her duties to spend time with him. They spent many hours engaged in one of his favorite activities, hunting. Adonis was a fearless hunter and for him, Aphrodite donned the hunting dress and carried a bow and arrows. After spending so much time with Adonis, Aphrodite eventually had to leave him to attend to her neglected duties. She warned him before she left to be wary of any animal that was not intimidated by him and to avoid hunting such an animal until she could return to his side. Adonis listened but did not heed the words of the goddess.

After Aphrodite left in her chariot pulled by swans, Adonis resumed hunting by himself. One day he came across a very large, very dangerous wild boar. Rather than remember the words of his lover about not hunting an animal not intimidated by him, all Adonis could think of was what a great trophy the larger than normal boar would make. Boars are not easily intimidated and in fact were known to charge hunters and chase them up trees or hamstring them if they got close enough. This boar was larger than normal. When Adonis injured, but did not kill it, with his spear or arrows, the boar lowered its head and charged the young hunter, rearing back with its cruel tusks to gouge Adonis' flesh. Instead of ripping apart his thigh, the boar castrated Adonis, scattering his blood and semen across the earth.

Aphrodite recognized that something was wrong with her lover. She jumped in her chariot and flew back to his side but she was too late. Adonis had bled to death. The goddess mourned over his body, weeping and beating her breast and scratching at her face. She swore that every year on the anniversary of his death, there would be a commemorative celebration of his life. Since she could not revive her lover, she transformed his scattered semen and blood into blood red flowers with delicate blooms called anemones.

Many times the myth of Adonis ends at this point, but some versions continue on with the aftermath of Adonis' death. Here it is as one coherent ending: After Adonis died his shade went to Hades where Persephone rejoiced to have him returned to her. Some say that she had conspired with the god, Ares, whose sacred animal was the wild boar. Others say that the two gods worked independently of each other. In either case, Adonis was in the underworld again. It took some time for Aphrodite to realize that her lover was reunited with Persephone. When she figured it out, she quarreled with Persephone again over who had the right to live with Adonis. Finally they appealed to Zeus and Zeus made the best decision possible this time. He split the year into two and said that Adonis would spend half the year with Persephone in the underworld and half the year with Aphrodite on the earth. With that final decision the goddesses had to be satisfied. Thus, Adonis is something more than human, but not quite a god, and perhaps connected with the seasons.

Phrygian: Cybele and Attis

The story of Cybele, the Great Mother Goddess from ancient Turkey (Phrygia) and her son/lover Attis has some striking parallels to the Adonis myth from Greece. It is a shorter myth and doesn't have the same resolution at the end that the Aphrodite and Adonis myth has. However, it has enough similarities that the Romans who borrowed the worship of Cybele and brought it to Rome often confused the two myths and put Attis with Venus (their Aphrodite) and Adonis with Cybele. Here is my retelling of the myth:

In Phrygia, Cybele, the Great Mother Goddess took on the human form of Nana to walk among her people on earth. One day, Nana sat underneath a pine tree and a pine cone dropped into her lap impregnating her. She gave birth to a beautiful baby

© Madrugada Verde/Shutterstock.com

boy named Attis. Cybele did not stay on earth in her human form, but left the baby with others to raise and resumed her goddess aspect. In time Attis grew up and became a priest of Cybele. His devotion to the goddess attracted her attention and she took him as her lover. She spent all her time with him and neglected all of her other responsibilities. Those responsibilities eventually caught up with her and she had to leave Attis for a while. She asked him to promise to remain loyal to her, and he swore that he would.

Unfortunately, Cybele was gone for a very long time and Attis grew lonely. He began an affair with one of the priestesses of Cybele. Cybele realized that he had broken his word to her and sent a frenzy of worship on him as punishment. In his frenzied worship, Attis decided to prove his love and loyalty to the goddess not just by cutting his flesh as many did to offer their blood to the earth, but by castrating himself. The castration killed Attis. He bled to death. Cybele rushed to save him but it was too late. She mourned over his body, weeping and beating on her breast and swore that every year there would be a commemorative celebration of his life. Wherever his blood and semen scattered she caused violets to spring up.

Much of what is known concerning this story comes from the Romans, who did not like to mutilate the human body, and were never comfortable with the worship of this goddess in their capitol city because all of Cybele's priests were eunuchs. No one knows if the priests of Cybele became eunuchs in honor of Attis, or if the myth of Attis developed to explain why the priests were eunuchs.

Greek: Persephone

This story was told in the earlier chapter on the Great Goddess.

© Marta Cobos/Shutterstock.com

African: Wanjiru

This tale comes from a collection of African tales edited by Susan Feldmann. It involves a woman as the sacrificial victim, who is killed in order to return the rains to the world. Here it is retold in my own words.

There once was a village in Africa that suffered year after year from a terrible drought. When they inquired of their Medicine Man what they should do, he told them they had to buy the maiden Wanjiru from her parents. Each person was required to bring a goat to offer in exchange for the maiden.

The next day when the people appeared in front of Wanjiru's parents with the goats, Wanjiru began to sink into the ground. The closer the people came with the goats the further Wanjiru sank into the earth. As she sank, she cried out that she was lost and her parents echoed those sentiments. As she sank more deeply into the earth her message increased to say she was lost, but much rain would come. Her family tried to rescue her, but as each person stepped up to grab her one of the villagers gave that person a goat. Rain began to fall and Wanjiru sank beneath the earth.

There was a young man who decided that he would seek Wanjiru wherever she had gone because he loved her and her people had sacrificed her to receive the rains. He found the spot where she had been sacrificed and stood on that spot until he too sunk beneath the earth. When he arrived below the earth, he found her disheveled and naked and picked her up and carried her back up the way he had come and told her that she had been sacrificed for the rains, and as the rains had come he was there to return her to the world.

When the young man had returned Wanjiru to the world he left her in the care of his mother, the only person he allowed to know that she was returned. He and his mother cared for Wanjiru and fed her and clothed her so that she no longer looked disheveled. The next day at a dance among her people, the young man brought Wanjiru but would not allow the villagers to greet her as they had sacrificed her for the rains and he reproached them for giving her up. Eventually the warrior allowed her family to greet her and he paid them the appropriate fee in order to marry her.

Norse: Balder

In Norse mythology, Odin, the king of the gods, goes through a shamanic experience that is retold in a fashion that sounds much like a Dying and Rising God's experiences. However, he doesn't really fit the archetype all that well. The closest figure from Norse myth to fit the Archetype was Balder, the son of Odin and his wife Frigg, the Earth goddess. He is slain by a god who was tricked by Loki and ends up in the underworld. He will return after the Norse Apocalypse to rule the new world that will be created.

Balder the Beautiful, the son of Odin and Frigg, was most beloved of the gods. When he experienced disturbing dreams associated with the underworld realm, the other gods became alarmed. His mother, Frigg, went around to every one of the nine realms and took oaths from every single thing that it would not harm her beloved son. After she had received all the oaths, the gods took great amusement from Balder's apparent invulnerability and passed the time in the hall of the gods by throwing darts at him made from the various substances that had sworn oaths to Mother Frigg. When the darts proved unable to hurt Balder, they took it in turn to throw more serious weapons like axes and knives. Still nothing harmed the golden haired god.

Observing all of this was the trickster god, Loki, who became jealous of the attention that Balder gained and envious of his invulnerability. Loki disguised himself as an old woman to speak with Frigg, and pretended horror at the games of the gods involving Balder. Frigg tried to assuage the old woman's worries by assuring her that nothing could harm Balder due to the oath she had taken from every single thing. Loki pried a little bit deeper and learned that the only thing Frigg had not required an oath from was a little, newly-born plant, called mistletoe. After learning this tidbit of news, Loki (still in disguise) slipped away to brew up a cunning and deceitful plot.

Loki fashioned darts from the mistletoe plant and rejoined the throng of gods playing their games with Balder. On the outskirts of the gods was the blind god, Hod, who could not play because of his blindness. He didn't know where to throw the missiles and darts and weapons since he could not see. Loki volunteered to help him join in the fun by guiding his hand. Hod wanted to play very much so he agreed. Unfortunately, the dart that Loki helped Hod throw was made of mistletoe and killed Balder.

Everyone knew that Loki was to blame but they could not act upon their anger in the hallowed halls of the gods. Loki fled the scene. The gods and goddesses mourned for Balder and Odin sent one of his sons to the underworld to inquire whether the goddess, Hel, would allow Balder to return to them. While the messenger traveled many days to the underworld, the rest of the gods prepared Balder's funeral. They laid him out and put him on his ship to set it afire and sail it out to sea. His wife, Nanna, died of grief after she saw her husband, Balder, lying on the deck of his ship. They laid her next to him. Finally they held the funeral and lit Balder's pyre, and he and his wife descended to Hel's realm.

Hel met with Odin's messenger and agreed that if every single thing in all the realms could be persuaded to weep for Balder, she would allow him to return, but she expressed doubt that every single thing would do so. On the messenger's way out of the underworld, he met the dead Balder and Nanna his wife, and they gave him words of greeting for the other gods. When the messenger returned to the gods, he told them Hel's requirement that every single thing must weep for Balder before Balder would be allowed to return. The gods sent out messengers to every single thing to weep for Balder and everything did, except for one old giantess who refused to weep no matter what persuasion was used. Because she refused, Balder could not return. All the gods suspected that the giantess was actually Loki in disguise, but Balder remained in the underworld until the end of Ragnorok, the Norse Apocalypse in which all the gods and the world itself were destroyed and a new world emerged. When it does, Balder will return with a few other gods who were in the underworld, to live in the New fair, green world.

Christian: Jesus

Although Jesus is not associated with fertility or sexuality, and he does not truly have a connection to the earth and the seasons, he still retains enough of the Dying and Rising God Archetype's characteristics to qualify as a Dying and Rising God, albeit a purified one, just as his mother, Mary, fits the archetype of the Great Mother in a purified form. As his story is fairly long and varies a bit from Gospel to Gospel, I have chosen to include the crucifixion and resurrection portions from the Gospel of Matthew only.

Figure 6.2
© jorisvo/Shutterstock.com

King James Version: Matthew Chapter 27

1 When the morning was come, all the chief priests and elders of the people took counsel against Jesus to put him to death:

2 And when they had bound him, they led him away, and delivered him to Pontius Pilate the governor.

3 Then Judas, which had betrayed him, when he saw that he was condemned, repented himself, and brought again the thirty pieces of silver to the chief priests and elders,

4 Saying, I have sinned in that I have betrayed the innocent blood. And they said, What is that to us? see thou to that.

5 And he cast down the pieces of silver in the temple, and departed, and went and hanged himself.

6 And the chief priests took the silver pieces, and said, It is not lawful for to put them into the treasury, because it is the price of blood.

7 And they took counsel, and bought with them the potter's field, to bury strangers in.

8 Wherefore that field was called, The field of blood, unto this day.

9 Then was fulfilled that which was spoken by Jeremy the prophet, saying, And they took the thirty pieces of silver, the price of him that was valued, whom they of the children of Israel did value;

10 And gave them for the potter's field, as the Lord appointed me.

11 And Jesus stood before the governor: and the governor asked him, saying, Art thou the King of the Jews? And Jesus said unto him, Thou sayest.

12 And when he was accused of the chief priests and elders, he answered nothing.

13 Then said Pilate unto him, Hearest thou not how many things they witness against thee?

14 And he answered him to never a word; insomuch that the governor marvelled greatly.

15 Now at that feast the governor was wont to release unto the people a prisoner, whom they would.

16 And they had then a notable prisoner, called Barabbas.

17 Therefore when they were gathered together, Pilate said unto them, Whom will ye that I release unto you? Barabbas, or Jesus which is called Christ?

18 For he knew that for envy they had delivered him.

19 When he was set down on the judgment seat, his wife sent unto him, saying, Have thou nothing to do with that just man: for I have suffered many things this day in a dream because of him.

20 But the chief priests and elders persuaded the multitude that they should ask Barabbas, and destroy Jesus.

21 The governor answered and said unto them, Whether of the twain will ye that I release unto you? They said, Barabbas.

22 Pilate saith unto them, What shall I do then with Jesus which is called Christ? They all say unto him, Let him be crucified.

23 And the governor said, Why, what evil hath he done? But they cried out the more, saying, Let him be crucified.

24 When Pilate saw that he could prevail nothing, but that rather a tumult was made, he took water, and washed his hands before the multitude, saying, I am innocent of the blood of this just person: see ye to it.

25 Then answered all the people, and said, His blood be on us, and on our children.

26 Then released he Barabbas unto them: and when he had scourged Jesus, he delivered him to be crucified.

27 Then the soldiers of the governor took Jesus into the common hall, and gathered unto him the whole band of soldiers.

28 And they stripped him, and put on him a scarlet robe.

29 And when they had platted a crown of thorns, they put it upon his head, and a reed in his right hand: and they bowed the knee before him, and mocked him, saying, Hail, King of the Jews!

30 And they spit upon him, and took the reed, and smote him on the head.

31 And after that they had mocked him, they took the robe off from him, and put his own raiment on him, and led him away to crucify him.

32 And as they came out, they found a man of Cyrene, Simon by name: him they compelled to bear his cross.

33 And when they were come unto a place called Golgotha, that is to say, a place of a skull,

34 They gave him vinegar to drink mingled with gall: and when he had tasted thereof, he would not drink.

35 And they crucified him, and parted his garments, casting lots: that it might be fulfilled which was spoken by the prophet, They parted my garments among them, and upon my vesture did they cast lots.

36 And sitting down they watched him there;

37 And set up over his head his accusation written, THIS IS JESUS THE KING OF THE JEWS.

38 Then were there two thieves crucified with him, one on the right hand, and another on the left.

39 And they that passed by reviled him, wagging their heads,

40 And saying, Thou that destroyest the temple, and buildest it in three days, save thyself. If thou be the Son of God, come down from the cross.

41 Likewise also the chief priests mocking him, with the scribes and elders, said,

42 He saved others; himself he cannot save. If he be the King of Israel, let him now come down from the cross, and we will believe him.

43 He trusted in God; let him deliver him now, if he will have him: for he said, I am the Son of God.

44 The thieves also, which were crucified with him, cast the same in his teeth.

45 Now from the sixth hour there was darkness over all the land unto the ninth hour.

46 And about the ninth hour Jesus cried with a loud voice, saying, Eli, Eli, lama sabachthani? that is to say, My God, my God, why hast thou forsaken me?

47 Some of them that stood there, when they heard that, said, This man calleth for Elias.

48 And straightway one of them ran, and took a spunge, and filled it with vinegar, and put it on a reed, and gave him to drink.

49 The rest said, Let be, let us see whether Elias will come to save him.

50 Jesus, when he had cried again with a loud voice, yielded up the ghost.

51 And, behold, the veil of the temple was rent in twain from the top to the bottom; and the earth did quake, and the rocks rent;

52 And the graves were opened; and many bodies of the saints which slept arose,

53 And came out of the graves after his resurrection, and went into the holy city, and appeared unto many.

54 Now when the centurion, and they that were with him, watching Jesus, saw the earthquake, and those things that were done, they feared greatly, saying, Truly this was the Son of God.

55 And many women were there beholding afar off, which followed Jesus from Galilee, ministering unto him:

56 Among which was Mary Magdalene, and Mary the mother of James and Joses, and the mother of Zebedees children.

57 When the even was come, there came a rich man of Arimathaea, named Joseph, who also himself was Jesus' disciple:

58 He went to Pilate, and begged the body of Jesus. Then Pilate commanded the body to be delivered.

59 And when Joseph had taken the body, he wrapped it in a clean linen cloth,

60 And laid it in his own new tomb, which he had hewn out in the rock: and he rolled a great stone to the door of the sepulchre, and departed.

61 And there was Mary Magdalene, and the other Mary, sitting over against the sepulchre.

62 Now the next day, that followed the day of the preparation, the chief priests and Pharisees came together unto Pilate,

63 Saying, Sir, we remember that that deceiver said, while he was yet alive, After three days I will rise again.

64 Command therefore that the sepulchre be made sure until the third day, lest his disciples come by night, and steal him away, and say unto the people, He is risen from the dead: so the last error shall be worse than the first.

65 Pilate said unto them, Ye have a watch: go your way, make it as sure as ye can.

66 So they went, and made the sepulchre sure, sealing the stone, and setting a watch.

King James Version: Matthew Chapter 28

1 In the end of the sabbath, as it began to dawn toward the first day of the week, came Mary Magdalene and the other Mary to see the sepulchre.

2 And, behold, there was a great earthquake: for the angel of the Lord descended from heaven, and came and rolled back the stone from the door, and sat upon it.

3 His countenance was like lightning, and his raiment white as snow:

4 And for fear of him the keepers did shake, and became as dead men.

5 And the angel answered and said unto the women, Fear not ye: for I know that ye seek Jesus, which was crucified.

6 He is not here: for he is risen, as he said. Come, see the place where the Lord lay.

7 And go quickly, and tell his disciples that he is risen from the dead; and, behold, he goeth before you into Galilee; there shall ye see him: lo, I have told you.

8 And they departed quickly from the sepulchre with fear and great joy; and did run to bring his disciples word.

9 And as they went to tell his disciples, behold, Jesus met them, saying, All hail. And they came and held him by the feet, and worshipped him.

10 Then said Jesus unto them, Be not afraid: go tell my brethren that they go into Galilee, and there shall they see me.

11 Now when they were going, behold, some of the watch came into the city, and shewed unto the chief priests all the things that were done.

12 And when they were assembled with the elders, and had taken counsel, they gave large money unto the soldiers,

13 Saying, Say ye, His disciples came by night, and stole him away while we slept.

14 And if this come to the governor's ears, we will persuade him, and secure you.

15 So they took the money, and did as they were taught: and this saying is commonly reported among the Jews until this day.

16 Then the eleven disciples went away into Galilee, into a mountain where Jesus had appointed them.

17 And when they saw him, they worshipped him: but some doubted.

18 And Jesus came and spake unto them, saying, All power is given unto me in heaven and in earth.

19 Go ye therefore, and teach all nations, baptizing them in the name of the Father, and of the Son, and of the Holy Ghost:

20 Teaching them to observe all things whatsoever I have commanded you: and, lo, I am with you alway, even unto the end of the world. Amen.

■ ■ ■

Located on Christianity: The Scriptures from www.sacred-texts.com

Study Questions for Chapter 6:
The Dying and Rising God Archetype

The Dying and Rising God Archetype

1. List the main characteristics of the Dying and Rising God Archetype.
2. What is an essential component of this type of myth?
3. How is the Dying and Rising God associated with the solstices and the equinoxes?

Egyptian: Osiris

1. Who was Osiris?
2. Who was Osiris' wife? Brother? Sister?
3. Why did Seth kill Osiris?
4. Where did Isis find Osiris' body?
5. How did Isis and Osiris create their son Horus?
6. What happened when Seth discovered the body of Osiris on the banks of the Nile?
7. How did Isis manage to revive Osiris?
8. What characteristics of the Dying and Rising God Archetype are present in the myth of Osiris?

Mesopotamian: Dumuzi

1. Who was Dumuzi?
2. Who was Dumuzi's wife?
3. Why was Dumuzi sent to the underworld?
4. Who is Ereshkigal?
5. What bargain was made between Geshtinanna and Inanna concerning Dumuzi?
6. What characteristics of the Dying and Rising God Archetype are evident in the myth of Dumuzi?

Greek: Orphic Version of Dionysos

1. Who was Dionysos-Zagreus?
2. Who were Dionysos-Zagreus' first parents?
3. Why did the Titans attack Dionysos-Zagreus?

4. What was created when Dionysos-Zagreus' blood fell on the ground as he was torn apart?
5. How did Zeus punish the Titans?
6. What did he make with the ashes?
7. How did Zeus recreate Dionysos-Zagreus?
8. What was Hera's reaction?
9. What was Dionysos' final birth?
10. What characteristics of the Dying and Rising God Archetype are evident in the myth of Dionysos as told by the Orphics?

Greek: Adonis

1. Who was Myrrha?
2. Why did the gods turn Myrrha into a tree?
3. Who found the baby Adonis?
4. Who raised the baby Adonis?
5. What happened when Aphrodite went to retrieve Adonis from the underworld?
6. What was Zeus' solution?
7. How did Adonis die?
8. What did Aphrodite do for him?
9. Where did Adonis end up?
10. Who may have killed Adonis?
11. What was Zeus' final decision about Adonis' life?
12. How does the story of Adonis fit into the archetype of the Dying and Rising God? Explain.

Phrygian: Attis

1. Who was Attis?
2. Who were Attis' parents?
3. What did Attis become when he grew up?
4. What happened when Cybele found out about his broken promise to her?
5. What did Cybele do for Attis?
6. What characteristics of the Dying and Rising God Archetype are present in the myth of Attis from Phrygia?

Greek: Persephone

1. Who is Persephone?
2. Who are her parents?
3. Who kidnaps and marries her?
4. What is Demeter's reaction to her daughter's marriage?
5. How does Zeus resolve the situation?
6. What characteristics of the Dying and Rising God Archetype are present in the myth of Persephone?

African: Wanjiru

1. Who is Wanjiru?
2. What happens to her in this myth?
3. Who searches for her after her disappearance?
4. What characteristics of the Dying and Rising God Archetype are present in the myth of Wanjiru?

Norse: Balder

1. Who is Balder?
2. Who are his parents?
3. How does Balder die?
4. When will he return?
5. What characteristics of the Dying and Rising God are present in the myth of Balder?

Christian: Jesus

1. Who is Jesus?
2. Who are his parents?
3. What happens to Jesus in this excerpt from the New Testament?
4. What characteristics of the Dying and Rising God Archetype are present in the myth of Jesus?
5. What characteristics of the Dying and Rising God Archetype are missing from the myth of Jesus?

CHAPTER 7
TRICKSTER ARCHETYPE

Introduction to the Trickster Archetype

The archetype of the Trickster is one of the most beloved archetypes, especially in America where many people are enamored of the Peter Pan type of young man who never seems to want to grow up. Tricksters are predominantly male figures. Although a few female tricksters have been found, the majority of tricksters are male. They are the clowns and pranksters and sometimes the fools of the mythological pantheons. They perform outrageous deeds often crossing boundaries and breaking taboos, or disrupting the normal order of things. Because of the chaos that follows them, not all Tricksters are welcome visitors. However, after the disruption is over, growth is often achieved. The Trickster is the one who shakes things up when they are in a rut and causes change, which many people do not like or want. Tricksters may cause the change because it amuses them, they may cause it accidentally, or they may cause it maliciously. Just as in the other archetypes, the Trickster archetype spans the whole range from good to evil, but the local expressions of the archetype will vary depending on how a particular culture views the Trickster and change.

Tricksters are usually associated with animal instincts—the need to consume, the need to procreate, and the need to master and control. Because of this association with bodily functions, Tricksters remind us, sometimes crudely, of the importance and perhaps even the wisdom and humor of our animal bodies. They may assume an animal form or they may pursue many romances to emphasize these connections. They may behave like a child or, in Freudian terms, let their Id control them, saying and/or doing things polite adults would never do. They are often notorious for their promiscuity. They take many lovers but don't often stick around afterwards. They are more the love them and leave them kinds of gods.

Tricksters love to play pranks, some of which may not be very nice while other tricks may turn out to be helpful to those involved. Sometimes the tricks backfire and the Trickster becomes the butt of the joke instead. Not only are Tricksters mischievous, they are also very clever and may be responsible for important inventions in their cultures, which make them cultural heroes as well as Tricksters. Some Native American Tricksters are fire thieves and bring fire down to earth for the animals and humans.

Tricksters serve their own interests first, and are amoral. Some tricksters tend to play more by the rules than others, such as Hermes, who, while deceitful, never seems to act maliciously—unlike the Norse Trickster, Loki, who seems to have a much more malicious nature.

Greek: Hermes

Hermes is the charming and playful Greek trickster whose tricks started on the very day that he was born.

Hermes was the son of Zeus by the nymph, Maia, who gave birth to Hermes in a cave in order to avoid discovery by Zeus' wife, Hera. Hermes was quite precocious. On the day that he was born, he looked like an infant but he had the full awareness of an adult god. Quickly becoming bored with the baby routine, Hermes decided to slip out of his bed and explore the cave behind his mother's back. When that became boring too, he decided to venture out into the world beyond the cave. When he exited the

Figure 7.1
© delcarmat/Shutterstock.com

cave, Hermes found a turtle and was delighted. He told the turtle that they would be friends forever then he killed it and scooped out its body to use its shell as a sounding board for the lyre, a musical instrument. After playing on the lyre for a bit, Hermes wandered away from the cave, exploring the hills and mountains and valleys.

Eventually Hermes came across a large herd of cattle that were sacred to the god Apollo. Hermes thought it would be greatly amusing to steal some of the herd. In one of the most humorous accounts of his theft, he made the cows walk backward out of the field and covered his own footprints by making the first pair of sandals. Hermes guided the cows to a field far away and there he sacrificed two cows to the Olympian gods. He built an altar and put the proper portions of the sacrificed cows upon it, one pile for each of the gods, including himself. He drank in the savor of the sacrifice. After the sacrifice had burned up, Hermes cleaned everything up and zipped back to the cave where he laid himself back down in his bed and pretended to be a mere infant again. Maia never knew that he had left.

Later that evening, Apollo paid a visit to Maia and her son, demanding to know what had become of his cattle. Maia had no idea what Apollo was talking about and pointed out that Hermes was only a little baby and could not have done what Apollo said. She told him to see for himself. When Apollo approached Hermes, Hermes played up the baby routine, grabbing his toes and cooing and making cute little baby noises. Apollo wasn't fooled. He demanded that Hermes return his cows at once. Hermes replied, "What's a cow? I'm just a little bitty baby who was born just today. I don't know what a cow is!" Apollo was not impressed. When Hermes would not confess to the theft, Apollo took him to see their father Zeus.

When the two gods arrived before Zeus, Apollo explained what had happened and Zeus asked to hear Hermes' side of the story. Hermes batted his lashes and asked his father, "What's a cow? I'm just a little bitty baby. I was just born today. I don't know what a cow is!" Zeus could barely control his amusement. He told Hermes, "Enough is enough, Hermes. Give your brother his cows back." Hermes responded, "Okay."

Hermes took Apollo down to earth where the cows had been penned. When they arrived, Apollo counted over the herd to make sure they were all there, but there were two missing. When he asked Hermes why two cows were missing from those that the young thief had stolen, Hermes said, "I sacrificed them to the fourteen Olympian gods." Apollo replied, "Fourteen Olympians? But there are only thirteen of us." Hermes spread his arms wide with a sort of ta-da gesture. Apollo groaned and put his head in his hands, he knew that he would have to put up with pranks from his younger sibling for a long time. He decided that he had better give the big brother speech and let Hermes know who was the elder of the two, and which of Apollo's possessions must be respected. Hermes dutifully listened, but stole Apollo's bow and arrows while his brother was giving his lecture. At an appropriate moment he pulled the bow and arrows out from behind his back and showed them to Apollo. Apollo was furious. Hermes, judging that he should not push his brother any further, pulled out his recent creation, the lyre, and played it for Apollo. Apollo was so enchanted by the music that he made a deal with Hermes. He promised to forgive Hermes' theft, and in fact even offered him the stolen cattle to keep, if Hermes would give the lyre to Apollo. Hermes agreed and the two became good friends.

Zeus was so pleased by his son's cleverness that he gave Hermes the job of messenger to the gods and gave him winged sandals and a hat so that he could travel much more swiftly bearing Zeus's messages throughout the world, including the seas and underworld. Hermes was also given a staff or wand with two serpents entwined around it called a caduceus, which showed that he spoke with Zeus' voice. It is the staff of an ancient herald. As a by product of this myth, Hermes also became the god of thieves and travelers as well as Zeus' messenger.

Yoruba: Eshu

© INTERFOTO/Alamy Stock Photo

Eshu is the popular West African Trickster of the Yoruba people. He came with the Africans when they were brought to the new world and appears in Voudoun as Legba. He is cunning and creative and the messenger of the gods. He also controls divination and crossroads and often is responsible for guiding or guarding the dead. The following overview comes from a nineteenth century work: *Yoruba-Speaking Peoples of the Slave Coast of West Africa,* by A. B. ELLIS, 1894.

(7) ELEGBA.

Elegba, or Elegbara (Elegba-Bara), often called Esbu, is the same phallic divinity who was described in the volume on the Ewe-speaking Peoples. The name Elegba seems to mean, "He who seizes"

(Eni-gba), and Bara is perhaps Oba-ra, "Lord of the rubbing" (Ra, to rub one thing against another). Eshu appears to be from shu, to emit, throw out, evacuate, The propensity to make mischief, which we noted as a minor characteristic of the Ewe Elegba, is much more prominent in the Yoruba god, who thus more nearly approaches a personification of evil. He is supposed always to carry a short knobbed club, which, originally intended to be a rude representation of the phallus, has, partly through want of skill on the part of the modellers of the images, and partly through the growing belief in Elegba's malevolence, come to be regarded as a weapon of offence. Because he bears this club he has the title of Agongo ogo. Ogo is the name of the knobbed club, and is most probably a euphemism for the phallus; it is derived from go, to hide in a bending or stooping posture. The derivation of agongo is less easy to determine, but it seems to be from gongo, tip, extremity.

The image of Elegba, who is always represented naked, seated with his bands on his knees, and with an immensely, disproportionate phallus, is found in front of almost every house, protected by a small hut roofed with palm-leaves. It is with reference to this that the proverb says: "As Eshw has a malicious disposition, his house is made for him in the street" (instead of indoors). The rude wooden representation of the phallus is planted in the earth by the side of the hut, and is seen in almost every public place; while at certain festivals it is paraded in great pomp, and pointed towards the young girls, who dance round it.

Elegba, in consequence of the bargain he made with Ifa, receives a share of every sacrifice offered to the other gods. His own proper sacrifices are, as among the Ewe tribes, cocks, dogs and he-goats, chosen on account of their amorous propensities; but on very important occasions a human victim is offered. In such a case, after the head has been struck off, the corpse is disembowelled, and the entrails placed in front of the image in a large calabash or wooden dish; after which the body is suspended from a tree, or, if no tree be at hand, from a scaffolding of poles. Turkeybuzzards are sacred to Elegba and are considered his messengers, no doubt because they devour the entrails and bodies of the sacrifices.

There is a noted temple Lo Elegba in a grove of palms near Wuru, a village situated about ten miles to the east of Badagry. The market of Wuru is under his protection, and each vendor throws a few cowries on the ground as a thank-offering. Once a year these cowries are swept up by the priests, and with the sum thus collected a slave is purchased to be sacrificed to the god. A slave is also sacrificed annually, towards the end of July, to Elegba in the town of Ondo, the capital of the state of the same name. Elegba's principal residence is said to be on a mountain named Igbeti, supposed to be situated near the Niger. Here he has a vast palace of brass, and a large number of attendants.

▪ ▪ ▪

Yoruba-Speaking Peoples of the Slave Coast of West Africa, by A. B. Ellis, 1894. Located on www.sacred-texts.com

There is a myth about Eshu that says that there used to be two farmers who were neighbors and very close friends. One evening after working in their fields all day the men came together to drink. During their drinking they swore an oath to be eternal friends and never let anything come between them. The god Eshu heard their prayer and decided to test their resolve as they had not honored him when they swore their oath.

The next day Eshu dressed in a magnificent robe and rode a gorgeous black stallion on the path between their two fields. On his head, Eshu wore a magnificent hat. It was quite stunning. The two men both paused in their work to admire the stranger on his gorgeous black stallion in his stunning hat. At the end of the day they went to refresh themselves with some drinks. As they drank, they discussed their day and naturally their talk turned to the handsome stranger with the stunning hat who had ridden between their fields on the black stallion earlier in the day. The two men compared notes and both agreed that the stranger had been a truly handsome man with an amazing outfit, although one of the friends claimed that the hat was black while the other friend said emphatically that it was red. Neither was willing to concede to the other and soon their argument became more heated and turned to blows.

When the two men, so recently sworn to eternal friendship, began fighting, the stranger appeared among the group and strolled over to where they were fighting and bade them stop. He told them that they were both correct and displayed his hat of two colors to them. Both men felt foolish for their angry words and blows. At that point, the stranger revealed himself as Eshu, the Trickster god, and demanded that from that day forward no oath would be made among men that did not take into account his power.

West Africa: Anansi

Anansi is a West African trickster figure who can appear as a man or a spider. He is very sly and cunning and loves to play pranks. Anansi came to control all the stories that had once belonged to the Sky God Nyame and since that time all stories are considered Anansi stories. Anansi acts as an intermediary between humans and the sky god, Nyame. He is often credited with creating humans and sometimes the stars, the sun and moon, and day and night. While he is a trickster he is also seen as a cultural hero in some tales where he is credited with teaching agriculture to humankind.

How All Stories became Anansi Stories

Spider went to the Sky God Nyame to purchase his stories, but the Sky God scoffed and asked how Anansi could possibly afford the stories of the sky god when even large cities could not afford them. Anansi was confident that he could buy the stories and asked what the price was. The Sky God said that price was a certain python, a fairy, a hornet, and a leopard. Anansi replied that he would obtain not only those four beings but he would throw in his own mother.

Anansi consulted with his wife about how to obtain the python and she advised him to cut some palm branches and some creepers. Anansi did so and walked along the stream muttering to himself, as if in an argument about something that was longer or shorter. The python heard Anansi's muttering and asked what he was arguing about and Anansi said that he and his wife were debating the length of the python, whether it was longer than the palm branch or not. The python agreed to be measured against the palm branch and before he knew what had happened Anansi wrapped the python up to the branch with the creepers and gave him to Nyame.

Next, Anansi went after the hornets. Again his wife gave him some good advice and told him to take a hollow gourd filled with water. Anansi did so and tricked the hornets into believing it was raining when he shook the water out from the gourd. He told them to take refuge inside the empty gourd, which they thankfully did, after which Anansi trapped them inside the gourd and gave it to the sky god, Nyame.

After that, Anansi went after the leopard by digging a hole in the ground and covering it over as a trap, following the advice of his wife. The leopard fell into the hole and when Anansi came to check on it the next day, he pretended to help the leopard out of the hole but actually knocked him unconscious and took the leopard to the sky god.

Finally, he trapped a fairy by making a doll and smearing it with sticky sap and placing mashed yam in the doll's hand. The fairy could not resist the food, but when she attempted to eat the yam, she stuck to the doll and Anansi caught her and took her to the sky god.

After Anansi trapped the fairy he escorted his mother up to the sky god's abode. The sky god received the fairy and Anansi's mother as the last of the bargain. Then the sky god summoned all the gods to bear witness that Anansi had done what no one else had been able to do; he had bought the sky god's stories.

Occasionally, Anansi's cleverness got the better of him. In one such story, Anansi visited many different animal friends, back in the day when the animals could talk to each other. At each friend's house he was invited to stay for a meal, but the food was not quite ready and Anansi did not want to have to help out with any chores. Instead, Anansi told each animal that he would string some of his web to the cooking pots and his legs. When the food was ready the animal could summon him by pulling on the web string. Each animal thought that this was a very good idea. Unfortunately for Anansi many of the meals were ready at the same time and each of the animals pulled on the web strings at the same moment, leaving him trapped in the middle of the web with his legs pulled on by the various animals. Thus, Anansi ended up with eight very long skinny legs.

Norse: Loki

One of the powerful gods in Norse mythology, Loki definitely fits the characteristics of the Trickster Archetype. He is a shape-shifter and can take many forms, both male and female. He plays pranks on the other gods, some of which are malicious. He is cunning and deceitful and crafty and clever. Eventually, his acts bring about the Norse Apocalypse: Ragnarok.

■ ■ ■

The Prose Edda of Snorri Sturlson, Translated by Arthur Gilchrist Brodeur, 1916. Located on www.sacred-texts.com

XXXIII. "Also numbered among the Æsir is he whom some call the mischief-monger of the Æsir, and the first father of falsehoods, and blemish of all gods and men: he is named Loki or Loptr, son of Fárbauti the giant; his mother was Laufey or Nál; his brothers are Bÿleistr and Helblindi. Loki is beautiful and comely to look upon, evil in spirit., very fickle in habit. He surpassed other men in that wisdom which is called 'sleight,' and had artifices for all occasions; he would ever bring the Æsir into great hardships, and then get them out with crafty counsel. His wife was called Sigyn, their son Nari or Narfi.*

Loki is responsible for many infamous deeds among the Aesir, but one of the most infamous is the death of Baldr, the beautiful son of Odin and Frigg.

The beginning of the story is this, that Baldr the Good dreamed great and perilous dreams touching his life. When he told these dreams to the Æsir, then they took counsel together: and this was their decision: to ask safety for Baldr from all kinds of dangers. And Frigg took oaths to this purport, that fire and water should spare Baldr, likewise iron and metal of all kinds, stones, earth, trees, sicknesses, beasts, birds, venom, serpents. And when that was done and made known, then it was a diversion of Baldr's and the Æsir, that he should stand up in the Thing,[1] and all the others should some shoot at him, some hew at him, some beat him with stones; but whatsoever was done hurt him not at all, and that seemed to them all a very worshipful thing.

"But when Loki Laufeyarson saw this, it pleased him ill that Baldr took no hurt. He went to Fensalir to Frigg, and made himself into the likeness of a woman. Then Frigg asked if that woman knew what the Æsir did at the Thing. She said that all were shooting at Baldr, and moreover, that he took no hurt. Then said Frigg: 'Neither weapons nor trees may hurt Baldr: I have taken oaths of them all.' Then the woman asked: 'Have all things taken oaths to spare Baldr?' and Frigg answered: 'There grows a tree-sprout alone westward of Valhall: it is called Mistletoe; I thought it too young to ask the oath of.' Then straightway the woman turned away; but Loki took Mistletoe and pulled it up and went to the Thing.

"Hödr stood outside the ring of men, because he was blind. Then spake Loki to him: 'Why dost thou not shoot at Baldr?' He answered: 'Because I see not where Baldr is; and for this also, that I am weaponless.' Then said Loki: 'Do thou also after the manner of other men, and show Baldr honor as the other men do. I will direct thee where he stands; shoot at him with this wand.' Hödr took Mistletoe and shot at Baldr, being guided by Loki: the shaft flew through Baldr, and he fell dead to the earth; and that was the greatest mischance that has ever befallen among gods and men.

"Then, when Baldr was fallen, words failed all the Æsir and their hands likewise to lay hold of him; each looked at the other, and all were of one mind as to him who had wrought the work, but none might take vengeance, so great a sanctuary was in that place. But when the Æsir tried to speak, then it befell first that weeping broke out, so that none might speak to the others with

words concerning his grief. But Odin bore that misfortune by so much the worst, as he had most perception of how great harm and loss for the Æsir were in the death of Baldr.

Balder's mother, Frigg, begged Hel, the goddess of the underworld, to release her son. Hel agreed on one condition: that every living thing must weep for Balder. Frigg sought out each and every being and asked that he or she weep for her son on the appointed day and hour; all agreed, all except one frost giantess, who most believe was Loki in disguise. Sadly, Hel refused to return Balder and he remained in the underworld until after the Norse apocalypse.

When Balder was not returned to them, the Aesir punished Loki. "*Now Loki was taken truceless, and was brought with them into a certain cave. Thereupon they took three flat stones, and set them on edge and drilled a hole in each stone. Then were taken Loki's sons, Vli and Nari or Narfi; the Æsir changed Váli into the form of a wolf, and he tore asunder Narfi his brother. And the Æsir took his entrails and bound Loki with them over the three stones: one stands under his shoulders, the second under his loins, the third under his boughs; and those bonds were turned to iron. Then Skadi took a venomous serpent and fastened it up over him, so that the venom should drip from the serpent into his face. But Sigyn, his wife, stands near him and holds a basin under the venom-drops; and when the basin is full, she goes and pours out the venom, but in the meantime the venom drips into his face. Then he writhes against it with such force that all the earth trembles: ye call that 'earthquakes.' There he lies in bonds till the Weird of the Gods.*"

[1. The Thing was the legislative assembly of Iceland; less specifically, a formal assembly held for judicial purposes or to settle questions of moment; an assembly of men.]

■ ▩ ▨

The Prose Edda of Snorri Sturlson, Translated by Arthur Gilchrist Brodeur, 1916. Located on www.sacred-texts.com

Not all of Loki's tricks were quite as malicious as the death of Balder. Some of his tricks actually backfired as when he cut off the beautiful golden hair of Sif, the wife of Thor. Thor caught him and made Loki promise to replace it with even more glorious hair. The only people who could help him achieve his goal were the dwarves. Loki talked them into making fine hair out of gold for Sif and while they were at it they made gifts for Odin and Freyr too. When Loki returned to the gods with the hair for Sif, she placed it on her head and it took root and grew just if it were her own hair.

Loki's pranks tended to grow progressively worse over time so that in the earlier stories about him he resembles other tricksters from around the world, especially Native American tricksters, but as time goes by, his pranks become more malicious and some might even describe them as evil, until with the death of Balder the gods lock him up until the Apocalypse.

Indian: Krishna

Krishna is a beloved figure from India where there are numerous stories of his child-hood, youthful adventures in which he is most Trickster like. He is the 8th incarnation of the Hindu god Vishnu.

Krishna was born to Vasudeva and Devaki, who were imprisoned by his uncle, Kansa, a demon who feared that his sister would give birth to a son that would kill him. In order to prevent the prophecy, Kansa kept his sister and her husband under guard in their palace. Each time she gave birth to a child, Kansa killed the baby. That was until Vishnu agreed to take on human form as Krishna to rid the world of Kansa and restore order to the world of men. When his mother gave birth to him, Krishna appeared in divine form and reassured them that all would be well. Then he cast a sleep over the palace so that no one would wake and had his birth father transport him out to the fields where the gopi kept watch over the cattle. There, Krishna was exchanged for the daughter of Nand and Yasoda and was raised in secrecy as a cow-herder by his adoptive parents while their little girl was raised in the palace by Krishna's birth parents. During his years in the fields, Krishna was quite a prankster. He pulled many pranks on his adoptive mother as well as on the female gopi, cow-herders, that he grew up with.

Figure 7.2
© stockshoppe/Shutterstock.com

Even as an infant Krishna possessed great strength as illustrated by the following two examples.

The following excerpts come from the *The Vishnu Purana*, translated by Horace Hayman Wilson, 1840.

Some time after they were settled at Gokula, the female fiend Pútaná, the child-killer, came thither by night, and finding the little Krishńa asleep, took him up, and gave him her breast to suck. Now whatever child is suckled in the night by Pútaná instantly dies; but Krishńa, laying hold of the breast with both hands, sucked it with such violence, that he drained it of the life; and the hideous Pútaná, roaring aloud, and giving way in every joint, fell on the ground expiring. The inhabitants of Vraja awoke in alarm at the cries of the fiend, ran to the spot, and beheld Pútaná lying on the earth, and Krishńa in her arms. Yaśodá snatching up Krishńa, waved over him a cow-tail brush to guard him from harm, whilst Nanda placed dried cow-dung powdered upon his head; he gave him also an amulet, saying at the same time, "May Hari, the lord of all beings without reserve, protect you; he from the lotus of whose navel the world was developed, and on the tip of whose tusks the globe was upraised from the waters. May that Keśava, who assumed the form of a boar, protect thee. May that Keśava, who, as the man-lion, rent with his sharp nails the bosom of his foe, ever protect thee. May that Keśava, who, appearing first as the dwarf, suddenly traversed in all his might, with three paces, the three regions of the universe, constantly defend thee. May Govinda guard thy head; Keśava thy neck; Vishńu thy belly; Janárddana thy legs and feet; the eternal and irresistible Náráyańa thy face, thine arms, thy mind, and faculties of sense. May all ghosts, goblins, and spirits malignant and unfriendly, ever fly thee, appalled by the bow, the discus, mace, and sword of Vishńu, and the echo of his shell. May Vaikuńtha guard thee in the cardinal points; and in the intermediate ones, Madhusúdana. May Rishikeśa defend thee in the sky, and Mahídhara upon earth." Having pronounced this prayer to avert all evil, Nanda put the child to sleep in his bed underneath the wagon. Beholding the vast carcass of Pútaná, the cowherds were filled with astonishment and terror.

On one occasion, whilst Madhusúdana was asleep underneath the waggon, he cried for the breast, and kicking up his feet he overturned the vehicle, and all the pots and pans were upset and broken. The cowherds and their wives, hearing the noise, came exclaiming, "Ah! ah!" and there they found the child sleeping on his back. "Who could have upset the waggon?" said the cowherds. "This child," replied some boys, who witnessed the circumstance; "we saw him," said they, "crying, and kicking the waggon with his feet, and so it was overturned: no one else had any thing to do with it." The cowherds were exceedingly astonished at this account; and Nanda, not knowing what to think, took up the boy; whilst Yaśodá offered worship to the broken pieces of pots and to the waggon, with curds, flowers, fruit, and unbruised grain.

■ ■ ■

The Vishnu Purana, translated by Horace Hayman Wilson, 1840. Located on www.sacred-texts.com

Krishna is affectionately known as the butter thief for his penchant as a child to steal the butter and anything else made from it from the homes of the cow-herders. In this excerpt he convinces the other children to help him and enjoys himself until he is caught. However, he escapes punishment by tricking the other children's mothers. When his own mother catches him eating dirt, he escapes punishment by showing her the universe inside of himself. (In this translation, which comes from the nineteenth century, the author spelled names a bit differently. Krishna is spelled as Krishnù and Yasoda, Krishna's adoptive mother, is spelled Jusodha, and his adoptive father, Nand, is spelled Nund.)

The Prem Sagur of Lallu Lal, translated by W. Hollings

When Shree Krishnù grew bigger, he one day took the cowherds' children with him to Bruj to steal butter.

They searched for it in empty houses, and Krishnù allowed them to steal whatever they found. They carried away the milk pails, which were set apart and covered up, belonging to all whom they found asleep in their houses. Wherever they found it suspended on strings, placing a board upon a stool, a wooden mortar upon the board, and making one of their companions stand upon the mortar, and getting upon his back, they took down the butter, ate some of it, stole some, and spilt some about: in this manner, they constantly committed theft in the houses of the cowherdesses. One day, they all took counsel together, and allowed Krishnù to come into the house. Having entered the house, as he was on the point of stealing the butter and curds, they laid hold of him, and said, "You have been in the habit of coming night and morning; where will you escape now, you butter thief?"

Having thus spoken, when all the cowherdesses in a body, taking Krishnù with them, were going to make a complaint to Jusodha regarding him, Krishnù practised this deception upon them, he made each mother take hold of her own child by the hand, and ran off himself, and again joined the sons of the cowherds. When the cowherdesses came to Nund's wife, they fell at her feet, and said, "If you will not be offended, we will inform you, what acts of tyranny Krishnù has committed—milk, curds, butter, buttermilk do not escape from his hand; in Bruj he commits such thefts, and roams about, thieving, morning and evening. Wherever he finds them laid bye, and covered up, he fearlessly takes them away, eats some, and allows his companions to steal. If any one points out the mark of curds on his mouth, he perversely says, that the same person placed it there. In this manner, he used to come constantly, and commit thefts; to-day, we have caught him, and brought him to show to you." Jusodha replied, "Friends! whose child have you laid hold of, and brought to me; since yesterday, my Krishnù has not gone out of the house? Is this the way you speak truth?" Hearing this, and perceiving that they had hold of their own children, they laughed and were ashamed of themselves. Upon this, Jusodha sent for Krishnù, and said to him, "Son! do not go to any one's house; whatever you wish to eat, eat at home."

Having heard this, Krishnù said, lisping, "Do not, mother, place any reliance on what they say. These false cowherdesses have spoken falsely, and have come roaring in pursuit of me. Sometimes, they make me lay hold of the milk-pails and calves; sometimes they make me perform the drudgery of the house; and having placed me at the door to watch, they go about their business, and then come and tell you stories." Hearing this, the cowherdesses looking at Krishnù, and smiling, went away.

One day after this, Krishnù and Bulram were playing with some companions in a court-yard, when Krishnù ate some dirt:—one of his companions went and told Jusodha, who came running towards him in a passion, with a stick in her hand. Seeing his mother coming towards him in a very angry humour, wiping his mouth, he was frightened, and remained standing in the same spot. She, on coming up, asked him, "Why have you been eating mud?" Krishnù replied with fear and trembling, "Mother! who has told you this?" She said, "One of your companions has told me." Upon this, Mohun, being enraged, said to the companion, "When did I eat mud?" He replied in alarm, "Brother! I do not understand what you say—what answer shall I give?" When Krishnù began to explain to his companion, Jusodha went and laid hold of him. Upon this, Krishnù began to say, "Be not angry, mother! do human creatures ever eat mud?" She said, "I will not listen to your thoughtless speeches; if you really speak the truth, show me your mouth." When Shree Krishnù opened his mouth, the three worlds were seen inside it. Jusodha was then convinced, and she began to say to herself, "I am a great fool in looking upon the lord of the three worlds as my son."

When Krishna grows a bit older, he becomes the delight of all the female cow herders (gopi) and often summons them by playing his flute. They long for him and bathe in the river to purify themselves when he decides to play a prank on them. (Huri = Hari, Krishnu = Krishna, Shree = Shri, Parvutee = Parvati, Dewee = Devi, poojah = puja)

The Prem Sagur of Lallu Lal, translated by W. Hollings
CHAPTER XXIII

SHREE SHOOKDEO, the sage, said, on the departure of the surud season, the winter came, when there was very great cold and frost. At this time the women of Bruj said to one another, "By bathing in the month Aghun, the sins of every birth are obliterated, and the hopes of the mind are accomplished. I have heard so from old people." On hearing this, they all resolved to bathe in Aghun, that they might without doubt obtain Shree Krishnù. Having resolved upon this, and risen very early in the morning, the women of Bruj dressed and ornamented themselves, and went in a body to bathe in the Jumna. Having bathed and made an offering to the sun, of eight ingredients, coming out of the water, they made an earthen image of Parvutee. Putting sandal, rice, flowers and fruits upon it, placing before it perfumes, lamps and consecrated food, performing poojah with hands joined, and holding their heads, they beseeched Parvutee, saying "O Dewee! we constantly supplicate this boon from you, that Shree Krishnù may be our lord." In this manner the cowherdesses constantly bathed. Fasting all day, they ate coagulated milk and rice in the evening, and slept on the ground at night. With a view of quickly obtaining the fruit of their fasting, all the women of Bruj went one day to a very steep ghaut to bathe; and on arrival, having taken off their clothes, and placed them on the bank, they went naked into the water. They began sporting about, and singing the praises of Huri.

Shree Krishnù was also at this time pasturing cows, sitting under the shade of a fig tree. Having heard by chance the sound of their singing, he came silently to the spot, and having concealed himself began to look on. A sudden thought struck him, while he was looking on, and having stolen all their clothes, he climbed up a "kudum" tree, and placed them all in a bundle before him. In the meantime, the cowherdesses looking on the bank for their clothes could not find. them. Being alarmed, they got up and began searching all round, and saying to each other, "Not even a bird has come here; who can have taken away our clothes?" Just then a cowherdess saw Krishnù sitting hid on a "kudum" tree, with a crown on his head, a club in his hand, marked with saffron on the forehead, in a yellow silk dress, with a garland of flowers reaching to his feet, and preserving a strict silence, with a bundle of clothes before him. She called out, "Behold him! who has stolen our hearts and our clothes, seated on a "kudum" tree with our bundles." Hearing this, and seeing Krishnù, all the women were ashamed, sitting down in the water, joining their hands and bending their heads, they supplicated and entreated. Krishnù, saying "O compassionate to the poor! beloved destroyer of our griefs! O Mohan! please give us our clothes." Krishnù replied, "By the oath of Nund, I will not give them thus; come out of the water one by one, and you shall obtain your clothes."

The women of Bruj said angrily, "This is a pretty lesson you have learnt, in telling us to come out of the water naked. We will go and tell this to your father and brother, and they will come and lay hold of you as a thief. And we will mention it also to Nund and Jusodha, who will teach you better. We are ashamed at what you have done; you have put an end to all recognition (acquaintance) between us." On hearing this, Shree Krishnù Jee was enraged and said, "You shall not have the clothes until you come, and fetch them yourselves." The cowherdesses were

Figure 7.3
© reddees/Shutterstock.com

alarmed and said, "O kind to the poor! it is you, who constantly keep us in remembrance, and who are the guardian of our good name; how shall we fetch them? It is for your sake, that we have offered up our vows, and bathed in the month of Mungsir." Krishnù replied, "If you have bathed with sincerity on my account in the month of Aghun, lay aside all bashfulness and deceit, and come and take your clothes." When Shree Krishnù Chund had thus spoken, the cowherd-esses on reflection began to say to each other, "Let us go friend! let us mind what Krishnù says, because he knows all the secrets of our bodies and minds. Why should we be ashamed before him?" Having thus determined, acting according to what Shree Krishnù had said, and concealing their breasts and privities with their hands, all the women came out of the water, bowing their heads. When they stood opposite to Shree Krishnù on the bank, he said laughing, "Now put your hands together, and come forward, and I will give you your clothes." The cowherdesses said, "Darling of Nund! why do you deceive us, we are plain, simple women of Bruj. We have been tricked, and all our mind and memory are gone. Is this the game you have determined upon playing, Huri? Whenever we think of this, we shall be ashamed; now do something for us, O lord of Bruj!" When they had thus spoken, and put their hands together, Shree Krishnù Chund Jee giving them their clothes, and approaching them said, "Be not displeased at what has happened, because this is a lesson I have given you. The habitation of the god Varoonù is in water: for this reason, if any one goes naked into the water, his character is entirely destroyed. Having been delighted at beholding the affection of your mind, I have told you this secret, now go home, and return in the month of Kartik to dance the circular dance with me."

■ ■ ■

The Prem Sagur of Lallu Lal, translated by W. Hollings, 1848. Located on www.sacred-texts.com

Polynesian: Maui

Maui is a cultural hero and trickster god who is found not only in Hawaiian mythology but also in the myths of New Zealand and other Polynesian islands. Maui was famous for bringing fire to man, for creating the islands of Hawaii and for slowing the sun in its course across the sky. Here is one of Maui's tales in which he captures the sun to help out his mother and humankind.

Legends of Maui—A Demi-God of Polynesia and His Mother Hina, by W. D. Westervelt

As Rev. A. O. Forbes, a missionary among the Hawaiians, relates, Maui's mother was troubled very much by the heedless haste of the sun. She had many kapa-cloths to make, for this was the only kind of clothing known in Hawaii, except sometimes a woven mat or a long grass fringe worn as a skirt. This native cloth was made by pounding the fine bark of certain trees with wooden mallets until the fibres were beaten and ground into a wood pulp. Then she pounded the pulp into thin sheets from which the best sleeping mats and clothes could be fashioned. These kapa cloths had to be thoroughly dried, but the days were so short that by the time she had spread out the kapa the sun had heedlessly rushed across the sky and gone down into the under-world, and all the cloth had to be gathered up again and cared for until another day should come. There were other troubles. "The food could not be prepared and cooked in one day. Even an incantation to the gods could not be chanted through ere they were overtaken by darkness."

This was very discouraging and caused great suffering, as well as much unnecessary trouble and labor. Many complaints were made against the thoughtless sun.

Maui pitied his mother and determined to make the sun go slower that the days might be long enough to satisfy the needs of men. Therefore, he went over to the northwest of the island on which he lived. This was Mt. Iao, an extinct volcano, in which lies one of the most beautiful and picturesque valleys of the Hawaiian Islands. He climbed the ridges until he could see the course of the sun as it passed over the island. He saw that the sun came up the eastern side of Mt. Haleakala. He crossed over the plain between the two mountains and climbed to the top of Mt. Haleakala. There he watched the burning sun as it came up from Koolau and passed directly over the top of the mountain. The summit of Haleakala is a great extinct crater twenty miles in circumference, and nearly twenty-five hundred feet in depth. There are two tremendous gaps or chasms in the side of the crater wall, through which in days gone by the massive bowl poured forth its flowing lava. One of these was the Koolau, or eastern gap, in which Maui probably planned to catch the sun.

Mt. Hale-a-ka-la of the Hawaiian Islands means House-of-the-sun. "La," or "Ra," is the name of the sun throughout parts of Polynesia. Ra was the sun-god of ancient Egypt. Thus the antiquities of Polynesia and Egypt touch each other, and today no man knows the full reason thereof.

The Hawaiian legend says Maui was taunted by a man who ridiculed the idea that he could snare the sun, saying, "You will never catch the sun. You are only an idle nobody."

Maui replied, "When I conquer my enemy and my desire is attained, I will be your death."

After studying the path of the sun, Maui returned to his mother and told her that he would go and cut off the legs of the sun so that he could not run so fast.

His mother said: "Are you strong enough for this work?" He said, 'Yes." Then she gave him fifteen strands of well-twisted fiber and told him to go to his grandmother, who lived in the great crater of Haleakala, for the rest of the things in his conflict with the sun. She said: "You must climb the mountain to the place where a large wiliwili tree is standing. There you will find the place where the sun stops to eat cooked bananas prepared by your grandmother.

Stay there until a rooster crows three times; then watch your grandmother go out to make a fire and put on food. You had better take her bananas. She will look for them and find you and ask who you are. Tell her you belong to Hina."

When she had taught him all these things, he went up the mountain to Kaupo to the place Hina had directed. There was a large wiliwili tree. Here he waited for the rooster to crow. The name of that rooster was Kalauhele-moa. When the rooster had crowed three times, the grandmother came out with a bunch of bananas to cook for the sun. She took off the upper part of the bunch and laid it down. Maui immediately snatched it away. In a moment she turned to pick it up, but could not find it. She was angry and cried out: "Where are the bananas of the sun?" Then she took off another part of the bunch, and Maui stole that. Thus he did until all the bunch had been taken away. She was almost blind and could not detect him by sight, so she sniffed all around her until she detected the smell of a man. She asked—"Who are you? To whom do you belong?" Maui replied: "I belong to Hina." "Why have you come?" Maui told her, "I have come to kill the sun. He goes so fast that he never dries the tapa Hina has beaten out."

The old woman gave a magic stone for a battle axe and one more rope. She taught him how to catch the sun, saying: "Make a place to hide here by this large wiliwili tree. When the first leg of the sun comes up, catch it with your first rope, and so on until you have used all your ropes. Fasten them to the tree, then take the stone axe to strike the body of the sun."

Maui dug a hole among the roots of the tree and concealed himself. Soon the first ray of light-the first leg of the sun-came up along the mountain side. Maui threw his rope and caught it. One by one the legs of the sun came over the edge of the crater's rim and were caught. Only one long leg was still hanging down the side of the mountain. It was hard for the sun to move that leg. It shook and trembled and tried hard to come up. At last it crept over the edge and was caught by Maui with the rope given by his grandmother.

When the sun saw that his sixteen long legs were held fast in the ropes, he began to go back down the mountain side into the sea. Then Maui tied the ropes fast to the tree and pulled until the body of the sun came up again. Brave Maui caught his magic stone club or axe, and began to strike and wound the sun, until he cried: "Give me my life." Maui said: "If you live, you may be a traitor. Perhaps I had better kill you." But the sun begged for life. After they had conversed a while, they agreed that there should be a regular motion in the journey of the sun. There should be longer days, an yet half the time he might go quickly as in the winter time, but the other half he must move slowly as in summer. Thus men dwelling on the earth should be blessed.

There are many variations on Maui's theft of fire in the Polynesian Islands. Here is one version of that myth:

One legend of the Hervey Islands says that Maui and his brothers had been living on un-cooked food-but learned that their mother sometimes had delicious food which had been cooked. They learned also that fire was needed in order to cook their food. Then Alatii wanted fire and watched his mother.

Maui's mother was the guardian of the way to the invisible world. When she desired to pass from her home to the other world, she would open a black rock and pass inside. Thus she went to Hawaiki, the under-world. Maui planned to follow her, but first studied the forms of birds that he might assume the body of the strongest and most enduring. After a time he took the shape of a pigeon and, flying to the black rock, passed through the door and flew down the long dark passage-way.

After a time he found the god of fire living in a bunch of banyan sticks. He changed himself into the form of a man and demanded the secret of fire.

The fire god agreed to give Maui fire if he would permit himself to be tossed into the sky by the god's strong arms.

Maui agreed on condition that he should have the right to toss the fire god afterwards.

The fire-god felt certain that there would be only one exercise of strength—he felt that he had everything in his own hands—so readily agreed to the tossing contest. It was his intention to throw his opponent so high that when he fell, if he ever did fall, there would be no antagonist uncrushed.

He seized Maui in his strong arms and, swinging him back and forth, flung him upward-but the moment Maui left his hands he changed himself into a feather and floated softly to the ground.

Then the boy ran swiftly to the god and seized him by the legs and lifted him up. Then he began to increase in size and strength until he had lifted the fire god very high. Suddenly he tossed the god upward and caught him as he fell—again and again—until the bruised and dizzy god cried enough, and agreed to give the victor whatever he demanded.

Maui asked for the secret of fire producing. The god taught him how to rub the dry sticks of certain kinds of trees together, and, by friction, produce fire, and especially how fire could be produced by rubbing fire sticks in the fine dust of the banyan tree.

■ ■ ■

Legends of Maui—A Demi-God of Polynesia and His Mother Hina, by W. D. Westervelt, 1910. Located on www.sacred-texts.com

Native American: Coyote

Coyote is a popular trickster figure in the desert southwest. Coyote is a popular trickster figure in the desert southwest and in the Pacific northwest. He is quite clever but often rather foolish, and he often becomes the butt of his own jokes or the jokes of others. In fact, Coyote is such a popular figure in Native American mythology that he became the prototype for the beloved cartoon character, Wile E. Coyote. Much like his cartoon counterpart, Coyote can be particularly unsuccessful as a trickster, often becoming the butt of his pranks. In the following excerpt from the Atsugewi Creation myth, Coyote embodies many of the characteristics of the archetype. He seems to be ruled by his hunger, and is especially associated with bodily humor. He represents animal instincts, and he crosses boundaries. Coytote often acts foolishly, much like a clown. However, because his tricks may inadvertently help others, on a few occasions he may be viewed as a cultural hero, whose tricks help create the world or benefit humans.

Pueblo Indian Folk-Stories, By Charles Lummis
THE COYOTE AND THE BLACKBIRDS

In the beginning there was nothing but water. Coyote and Silver-Fox lived above in the sky, where there was a world like this one. Silver-Fox was anxious to make things, but Coyote was opposed to the plan. Finally, Silver-Fox got tired of Coyote's opposition, and sent him off one day to get wood. While he was gone, Silver-Fox took an arrow-flaker and made a hole through the upper world, and looked down on the sea below. When Coyote came back, Silver-Fox did not tell him about the hole he had made. Next day he sent Coyote off again for wood; and in his absence Silver-Fox thrust down the arrow-flaker, and found that it reached to the water, and down to the bottom even. So he descended; and as he came near the surface of the water, he made a small round island, on which he stayed. When Coyote returned, he could not find Silver-Fox, and, after hunting for a long time, began to feel remorse. Finally he found the hole, and peeped through, seeing Silver-Fox far below on the island. He called down that he was sorry he had acted as he had, and asked how to get down. Receiving no reply, he said that Silver-Fox ought not to treat him this way; and after a while the latter put up the arrow-flaker, and Coyote came down.

The island was very small, and there was not room enough for Coyote to stretch out. For some time they slept, and when they woke up, they were very hungry, as there was no food to be had. For five days things continued thus, Silver-Fox finally giving Coyote some sunflower seeds. This pleased him much, and he asked where they came from, but received no answer. After five more days more, Silver-Fox made the island a little larger, so that Coyote could have room to stretch out. At last he could be comfortable, and went fast asleep. At once Silver-Fox got up, dressed himself up finely, and smoked awhile, and then made a big sweat-house. When it was all done, he woke Coyote, and the latter was much surprised to find the house there. Silver-Fox then told Coyote to sweep out the house, spread grass down on the floor, and go to sleep again. He did so, and then Silver-Fox dressed up again, putting on a finely-beaded (?) shirt and leggings, and sang, and smoked some more. Then, going outside, he pushed with his foot, and stretched the earth out in all directions, first to the east, then to the north, then to the west, and last to the south. For five nights he repeated this performance, until the world became as large as it is to-day. Each day Silver-Fox told Coyote to run around the edge, and see how large it was getting. At first he was able to do this very quickly; but after the last time he grew old and gray before he got back. Then Silver-Fox made trees and springs, and fixed the world up nicely. He also made all kinds of animals merely by thinking them. These animals, however, were like people.

When the world was all made, Coyote asked what they were going to have for food, but Silver-Fox did not reply. Coyote then said that he thought there ought to be ten moons of winter in the year, to which Silver-Fox replied that there would not be enough food for so long a winter. Coyote declared it would be better not to have much food, that people could make soup out of dirt. To this he received no answer. Silver-Fox then said that it was not right that there should be ten moons, that two were enough, and that people could then eat sunflower seeds, roots, and berries. Coyote repeated what he had said before, and they argued about it for a long time. Finally Silver-Fox said, "You talk too much! I'm going to make four moons for the whole year. I won't talk about it any more. There are going to be two moons of winter, and one of spring, and one of autumn.

That's enough." They, Silver-Fox said, "When people get married, they will have children by taking a dentalium-shell and putting it between them, or a disk-bead: the One will make a boy, the other a girl." Coyote replied, "Hm! That's not the right way. It will be better for people to get married: they will not be satisfied any other way. People must live as man and wife: they ought not to do as you said." Silver-Fox did not want to argue the matter; and finally, after repeating what he said before, he yielded to Coyote, and said, "Let it be as you say."

Silver-Fox then went out to get some pine-nuts. He climbed a tree and shook the branches, and the nuts fell down already shelled and ready to eat. He filled a basket with them, and brought them in. Coyote had gone to get wood; and when he got back, Silver-Fox divided the pine-nuts, and gave him half. Silver-Fox ate only part of his, and put the rest away; but Coyote ate nearly all night, going out and defecating, and then returning and eating more, until he had finished them. Next morning Silver-Fox went out and looked for pines having large "witch-brooms" on them. When he found one, he would set fire to it, then walk away looking constantly on the ground, and a grouse would straightway fall out of the tree. Then he placed them in a basket, and brought them back to the house. Coyote wanted to begin eating at once, and helped him in with his load. As before, Coyote ate all his share up, whereas Silver-Fox kept most of his.

Next day Coyote asked Silver-Fox how he got his pine-nuts. He told him to go to a tree, scrape the brush away, climb up, and then shake the boughs with his foot. Coyote thought he could do this, so went out to try. He was successful, but, on coming down, ate up all the nuts. Then he went to another tree and attempted to repeat the process; but this time no nuts fell, and Coyote himself lost his footing, and was badly hurt by the fall. He came back to the house with his neck bent to one side, and in great pain. Silver-Fox knew all that had been going on, but said nothing. After a while Coyote told him what had happened.

The next day Coyote asked how the grouse had been secured, and Silver-Fox told him to set fire to the tree, and then sit with his back to the trunk, and not look up. So Coyote went off to get the grouse. He was successful in his attempt, but opened his eyes and looked up, and saw the grouse falling. When he had picked them all up, he cooked and ate them on the spot, and then went to another tree to repeat the process. This time, however, it was burning branches that fell, and they hit him and burned him badly. So he ran away back to the house, crying. Silver-Fox gave him some of his food, however.

In the morning Silver-Fox went out, and, going up to a cedar-tree, pulled off the boughs, which became a sort of camas (?). He brought back a great load of these; and when he got back, as before, Coyote ate all his share at once. He then asked how to get them, and was told to make a long hook and pull the limbs off, but to keep his eyes shut all the time. As in the other cases, Coyote was very successful the first time, and ate all the roots up. When he tried to repeat the plan, however, only big limbs came down, and hit him on the head.

By and by Silver-Fox went rabbit-hunting. He built a brush fence, and drove the rabbits into it, where they all piled up. Then he killed them with a club, and carried them to the house. Just as before, Coyote ate up all his share at once. Silver-Fox could not prevent Coyote from eating up all there was in the house, except by not letting him know when he was eating. He would put pine-nuts in a milkweed-stem, and pretend to be making cord, whereas in reality he was eating the nuts. Coyote soon suspected, and asked Silver-Fox to let him help make string. He agreed, but gave Coyote the stems without any nuts in them. Next night Coyote pretended to sleep, and so caught Silver-Fox putting the nuts in the stems. He jumped up and seized Silver-Fox; but the latter swallowed quickly, and when he opened his mouth there were no nuts there. He told Coyote that before people ate nuts, they would put them in a basket, and Coyote believed him. Silver-Fox then went out to get more milkweed, as he said; and while he was gone, Coyote took a large stone and struck the roof-beams, trying to find where Silver-Fox had hidden the nuts. Finally he found the right one, and the nuts began to pour down. He called out, "Stop! That is enough. I am a chief! That is enough." But the nuts kept falling, and by and by there was a huge pile there. Then Coyote said, "Let big baskets come!" and there they were there; and he gathered up the nuts, and put them in the baskets, and then ate and ate all the nuts he could. Then he brought in some wood, and was going to say that the nuts fell down when he threw in the wood, as he had hit the beam by accident. Just then Silver-Fox came in with a lot of milkweed, and began to make string. Coyote told him his story, and said that he had been scared when the nuts began to fall, that it was not right to put them in the roof-beams, but in baskets as he had now done. Silver-Fox, however, did not reply, until he said, "You eat on that side of the house, and I will eat on this." Then he went on making string, while Coyote, after eating all he could, went to sleep.

When he had finished making string, Silver-Fox got up softly, and measured Coyote's nose. Then he sat down and began to make a net. He had to measure again pretty soon; and then Coyote woke up, and asked what was the trouble. Silver-Fox said that he was only blowing ashes off Coyote's face, so he went to sleep again. Coyote woke up again later, and asked Silver-Fox what he was doing; and he said that he was making a net to catch rabbits in, so Coyote went to sleep once more. Finally the net was complete, and then Silver-Fox told Coyote to eat breakfast, to eat a big breakfast, and then they would go out and get rabbits. They started out, Silver-Fox carrying a big club. Coyote asked why he took so large a one, but Silver-Fox said that it was the right size. By and by Silver-Fox set up the net, and showed Coyote where it was. Then Silver-Fox said, "Now you run off. When you get a little distance away, shut your eyes, and run as fast as you can." Coyote said that he would do so, and started off; and then quickly Silver-Fox took up the net, and put it where Coyote would run into it. Pretty soon Coyote came in sight, driving the rabbits slowly; and when he got only a little ways off, he shut his eyes, and ran as fast as he could. He ran squarely into the net, and this drew up; and Silver-Fox then rushed up and struck him with the club. Coyote cried out, "You are hitting me!" and Silver-Fox said, "Yes, don't mind that." He kept on hitting him until he had killed him. Then he went back to the house, and started off over the world; and wherever Coyote had urinated, Silver-Fox scraped up the ground and smoothed it over nicely. He went everywhere thus, and thought he had fixed every place. There was one, however, on a little island in a lake, that he overlooked. This lake lay far off to the northeast. Then Silver-Fox came back to the house and went to sleep. At dawn he got up, went up and looked out of the house, and listened. For a while he heard nothing, but then he heard faintly Coyote howling far away. He then knew he had missed one place, and felt very sad. He sat down and thought, but did not know what to do. Coyote was too smart for him, he thought. Finally he heard the howling coming closer. Then he thought of a plan. He made a lot of manzanita, wild cherries, plums, etc., grow along the road that Coyote was following. Coyote was very angry, and wanted to kill Silver-Fox. He came to the manzanita, and Silver-Fox thought he would delay him thus; but Coyote only took one berry, and continued on his way. He came to the plums; and of these Coyote ate largely, as he thought he could fight better if he was not hungry. As he ate, he forgot about his anger. Then he started on again. Silver-Fox was afraid, however, and pretended to be very sick when Coyote got back. Coyote told him he had better eat some plums, that they were very good, and that it was useless to lie still all day. Finally Silver-Fox got up and ate some, and so Coyote forgot all about his revenge.

Coyote said next day that he was going out to pick fruit. He went, and picked plums and cherries and manzanita, and brought them back, saying that there was plenty of food. Silver-Fox told him to go and get some wood; and then he went out and caught some rabbits, and they cooked and ate them, and lived without quarrelling any more.

■ ■ ■

Pueblo Indian Folk-Stories, By Charles Lummis, 1910. Located on www.sacred-texts.com

Study Questions for Chapter 7: Trickster Archetype

The Trickster Archetype

1. List the main characteristics of the Trickster Archetype.
2. What are the most obvious characteristics of a Trickster?
3. Why is this archetype associated with change?
4. Why are some Tricksters also considered cultural heroes?

Greek: Hermes

1. Who is Hermes?
2. What are some of the activities that Hermes got involved in on his first day of life?
3. What are some of the inventions he created on his first day of life?
4. How did he get out of trouble with Zeus?
5. What deal did Hermes make with Apollo?
6. What reward did Zeus give Hermes for his cleverness?
7. What characteristics of the Trickster Archetype are evident in Hermes myth?

Yoruba: Eshu

1. Who is Eshu?
2. What are some of the different names for the African Trickster?
3. What kinds of sacrifices were appropriate for Eshu/Elegba?
4. How did Eshu teach the two friends an important lesson?
5. How does Eshu's description fit the characteristics of the Trickster Archetype?

West Africa: Anansi

1. Who is Anansi?
2. How did Anansi gain control of all the stories?
3. What characteristics of the Trickster Archetype are exhibited by Anansi in these excerpts from his myths?

Norse: Loki

1. Who is Loki?
2. What role did Loki play in Balder the Beautiful's death?
3. What happened when Loki cut off Sif's golden hair?
4. How does Loki in the excerpt from his myths demonstrate the characteristics of the Trickster Archetype?

Indian: Krishna

1. Who is Krishna?
2. Where was he raised?
3. How did Krishna distract his adoptive mother from punishing him?
4. Why was Krishna called the butter thief?
5. How did Krishna trick the gopis?
6. What characteristics of the Trickster Archetype are evident in the excerpts from the myths of Krishna?

Polynesian: Maui

1. Who is Maui?
2. Why does Maui lasso the sun?
3. How and why does Maui steal fire?
4. What characteristics of the Trickster Archetype are evident in the excerpts from the myths of Maui?

Atsugewi Native American: Coyote

1. Who is Coyote?
2. How did Coyote inadvertently help Silver Fox create the world?
3. What is Coyote's reaction to food? How does Silver Fox treat his food differently than Coyote?
4. How does Coyote's story demonstrate characteristics of the Trickster Archetype?

CHAPTER 8
HERO ARCHETYPE

Introduction to the Hero Archetype

There are many different ways to describe the Hero Archetype. This chapter focuses primarily on mythological or legendary heroes, not necessarily modern day heroes one would read about in the newspaper. Accordingly many studies have been conducted over heroes in myth and literature. Joseph Campbell conducted one of the best known studies of the hero archetype in *The Hero with a Thousand Faces*. This work lays out a pattern that most heroes follow that consists of three main categories: Departure, Initiation, and Return. Within those three main categories, there are a total of seventeen subcategories. The hero travels from one stage to the next passing through a majority of the subcategories in the process, but perhaps not each and every one. While the categories and subcategories seem to mostly apply to male heroes, they can be adjusted to accommodate a female hero or heroine.

Campbell's study is not the only one that focuses on mythological heroes. Otto Rank and Lord Raglan each studied heroes in mythology and came up with separate lists of qualities or characteristics that most hero myths contain. Their lists include information about the heroes' conceptions and births, along with their heroic deeds. There is often danger to a hero after birth and sometimes there is even difficulty for the mother in the conception of the hero as well as in the birth process. David Adams Leeming seems to combine the aforementioned authors' works when he describes heroes in *The World of Myth*. Like Joseph Campbell, Leeming divides his subject into three categories, however, his categories differ in that the first category focuses on the conception, birth, and childhood of the hero; the second focuses on the journey quest of the hero; and the third on the death of the hero.

Whichever model is used, a pattern tends to emerge of the hero receiving a call to go on a quest or journey of some sort that involves obstacles and possibly monsters that he or she has to overcome. The quest often involves winning a blessing or boon of some kind as the climax of the quest, after which there is a return to the mundane world from which the hero began his or her journey.

The Hero Cycle of Joseph Campbell

In his famous study of heroes, *The Hero with a Thousand Faces,* Joseph Campbell claims that most heroic adventures follow the formula of the rites of passage: separation—initiation—return. Campbell calls this the nuclear monomyth:

> A hero ventures forth from the world of common day into a region of supernatural wonder: fabulous forces are there encountered and a decisive victory is won: the hero comes back from this mysterious adventure with the power to bestow boons on other humans. (30)

Here is the summary of the Hero Cycle and its subcategories:

DEPARTURE

Call to Adventure
> Destiny summons the hero to leave society and enter a region of treasure and danger (dark forest, great trees, babbling spring)

Refusal of Call
> The hero refuses the call and brings disaster on himself and others

Supernatural Aid
> A motherly or fatherly guide protects the hero with the powers of a benign destiny, like a mentor

Crossing the Threshold
> It is the first step beyond the familiar boundaries into the dangerous unknown

The Belly of the Whale
> Transit into sphere of re-birth, symbolized by the womb-like belly of the whale where the hero faces his or her fears about the journey and chooses to go forward.

INITIATION

Road of Trials
> The hero must survive a succession of trials, aided sometimes by advice, amulets, and secret agents (often sent by the Supernatural Aid)

Meeting with the Goddess
> The hero achieves mystical union or has a confrontation with Queen Goddess of the World, in her benign or horrible aspects

Woman as Temptress
> The hero must withstand the temptations of destructive a Mother-Bride or helper-maide

Atonement with the Father
>The hero abandons self and trusts that the terrible Father is, in fact, benign and merciful (usually, not the human father)

Apotheosis
>The hero becomes one with God or the universe

The Ultimate Boon
>The hero receives or captures the key to happiness in the social world

RETURN

Refusal of the Return
>The hero refuses to return and denies his knowledge to social world

Magic Flight
>Having won the trophy, the hero uses supernatural powers to achieve an otherwise dangerous return

Rescue from Without
>The hero's return requires assistance from some other sentient being in order to return home; the hero cannot return home without the help of another being.

Crossing of Return Threshold
>The hero crosses the division from the divine or magical realms back into the human world

Master of Two Worlds
>The hero is able to cross and re-cross the world division

Freedom to Live
>Basically, happily ever after.

■ ■ ■

Source: Campbell, Joseph. *The Hero with a Thousand Faces,* 2nd ed. Princeton, NJ: Princeton Univ. Pr., 1968.

Mesopotamia: Gilgamesh

Gilgamesh is a hero from ancient Mesopotamia, whose origins probably lay in Sumer as far back as three thousand BCE, but whose records come from the later Babylonians and Assyrians closer to one thousand BCE. Gilgamesh was a partly divine king of the city of Erech, where as king he had certain rights and privileges, including sleeping with a bride on her wedding night. Gilgamesh enforced his rights and the citizens groaned under the burden. The gods created a creature named Enkidu, who was equal to Gilgamesh in strength, to challenge the king. Enkidu, who was like a wild

© Watchmaker/Shutterstock.com

man, was civilized through association with one of the ladies of the goddess Ishtar. He challenged Gilgamesh and the two fought. They fought all day, evenly matched in strength, and gained much admiration and respect for each other. They ended their fight as good friends. As friends, they came up with the idea of adventuring to the Cedar Forest to kill the guardian, a demon like creature called Humbaba, so that they could take the cedar wood back to beautify the city.

When Gilgamesh and Enkidu arrived in the Cedar Forest they confronted Humbaba and fought a fierce battle against him, finally overcoming and killing him. Their exploits impressed Ishtar, the goddess of war and love, who desired Gilgamesh and sought him as her lover. Gilgamesh very rudely said no to her, knowing what had happened to her husband, Tammuz. In anger, Ishtar approached her father and asked him to punish Gilgamesh and Enkidu by sending down the Bull of Heaven, who could kill hundreds of men with its fiery breath. When the Bull of Heaven attacked, Enkidu and Gilgamesh sprang into action and soon they had killed the Bull too.

When the gods saw how strong Enkidu and Gilgamesh were and how much they were united in friendship, the gods realized that the two together were a bit of a threat and decided that one of them had to die. They chose Enkidu. He was struck with illness and died to Gilgamesh's grief. In his grief, Gilgamesh wanted to know what happened after death and how to obtain immortality so that he too would not die as Enkidu had died. He decided to visit Utnapishtim, the man who had survived the flood and gained immortality (along with his wife).

Gilgamesh set out on his quest and traveled very far to find Utnapishtim. He traveled across the desert to the Mashu Mountains and there he met two Scorpion guardians who guarded the passage through the mountains that was the path of the Sun.

Mashu the name of the hills; as he reach'd the Mountains of Mashu, Where ev'ry day they keep watch o'er [the Sun-god's] rising [and setting],

Unto the Zenith of Heaven [uprear'd are] their summits, (and) downwards (Deep) unto Hell reach their breasts: (and there) at their portals stand sentry Scorpion-men, awful in terror, their (very) glance Death: (and) tremendous, Shaking the hills, their magnificence; they are the Wardens of Shamash,

Both at his rising and setting. (No sooner) did Gilgamish see them" (Than) from alarm and dismay was his countenance stricken with pallor, Senseless, he grovell'd before them.

(Then) unto his wife spake the Scorpion: "Lo, he that cometh to us—'tis the flesh of the gods is his body." (Then) to the Scorpion-man answered his wife: "Two parts of him god-(like), (Only) a third of him human."

■ ■ ■

The Epic of Gilgamish, translated by R. Campbell Thompson, 1928. Located on www.sacred-texts.com

Gilgamesh had to pass through the mountains in darkness on the pathway of the sun, a test of strength for him. He agreed to the test and the scorpion guardians let him pass them and begin the journey. Gilgamesh walked in darkness for hours, but he stayed on the path and many hours later he arrived at the Tree of the Gods. He met the god Shamash who asked him why he wandered when his task was fruitless, but Gilgamesh asked how he could not wander when he knew that eventually he too would die.

Gilgamesh next encountered the wine-maker, Siduri, who wondered at his haggard appearance and locked up her gates and bared herself from him, because he was intimidating. The two conversed and she shared her philosophy for humans with him.

"Gilgamish, why runnest thou, (inasmuch as) the life which thou seekest, Thou canst not find? (For) the gods, in their (first) creation of mortals, Death allotted to man, (but) life they retain'd in their keeping. Gilgamish, full be thy belly, Each day and night be thou merry, (and) daily keep holiday revel, Each day and night do thou dance and rejoice; (and) fresh be thy raiment, (Aye), let thy head be clean washen, (and) bathe thyself in the water, Cherish the little one holding thy hand; be thy spouse in thy bosom Happy—(for) this is the dower [of man] . . . . .

■ ■ ■

The Epic of Gilgamish, translated by R. Campbell Thompson, 1928. Located on www.sacred-texts.com

Gilgamesh explained to Siduri that he was grieving the loss of Enkidu his dear friend and that he knew one day he too would be dead and sleep eternally, therefore he wished to find Utnapishtim. Siduri attempted to dissuade Gilgamesh in his quest, pointing out how dangerous the journey would be and that only the sun god could make it. There was the Water of Death to cross and a ferry that was sailed across by Ur-shanabi, the ferryman, before arriving in Utnapishtim's land. Siduri warned Gilgamesh to only cross with Ur-shanabi's help, otherwise he should return home and follow her advice.

Gilgamesh continued his quest and traveled to the Waters of Death where he ruined the sails of the ferry before he realized how necessary they were. Ur-shanabi told Gilgamesh to cut down some trees to fashion poles that they could use to pole the ferry across the Waters of Death to reach Utnapishtim. Gilgamesh cut them down and made them according to Ur-shanabi's instructions and together the two poled the ferry across the rough Waters of Death.

Utnapishtim welcomed Gilgamesh and asked after his haggard appearance and Gilgamesh explained his story and his quest for immortality. He asked Utnapishtim how he had gained immortality and he learned of the Mesopotamian Flood and how Utnapishtim was the survivor along with his family and the boat's craftsmen and some animals. Utnapishtim asked Gilgamesh what kind of similarly heroic deed he had accomplished that the gods should reward him with eternal life. When Gilgamesh could not answer, Utnapishtim offered him a trial of strength: let Gilgamesh stay awake for seven days. Unfortunately, Gilgamesh was unable to do so. Each day that he slept, Utnapishtim's wife baked a loaf of bread and lay it next to Gilgamesh's head. When he awakened on the seventh day, there was ample evidence to prove that he had not managed to stay awake. Having lost this chance at immortality, Utnapishtim offered Gilgamesh a consolation prize. He told Gilgamesh of a plant that grew at the bottom of the sea that gave eternal youth to anyone that ate it.

Gilgamesh departed with Ur-Shanabi to retrieve the flower from the bottom of the water. He tied rocks to his feet and sank into the depths where he found the plant and uprooted it even though its thorns tore his skin. After returning to the surface and rejoining Ur-Shanabi, Gilgamesh explained that he would return home to Erech with the plant and give it to someone else and he himself would eat it too and be restored to his youthful appearance.

Unfortunately for Gilgamesh on his journey home, while he was sleeping, a serpent came into his camp and ate the plant and immediately shed its skin. When Gilgamesh awoke, the plant was gone. He had to journey home empty handed, making the most of what he did have: life.

Greek: Herakles

Background: Herakles had a unique conception and childhood and early indicators pointed to the fact that he was not going to be like ordinary men. His father was Zeus and his mother was a human woman, Alkmene, who was actually married to a mortal

Figure 8.1
© delcarmat/Shutterstock.com

man named Amphitryon. Zeus disguised himself as her husband and slept with her in the same twenty-hours that she slept with her actual husband. The result of the double union was twins: Iphikles and Herakles. Herakles was the son of Zeus by Alkmene and Iphikles was the son of Amphitryon and Alkmene. As Herakles grew up he had tremendous strength so his parents gave him an education worthy of any hero. At a young age he killed a lion that was threatening Thebes and as a reward the king of Thebes gave Herakles his daughter, Megara, to be his wife. Hera, who hated Herakles as the illegitimate son of Zeus by another woman, as well as for several more complicated reasons, plagued Herakles on and off from his infancy to adulthood. After he married Megara and started a family with her, Hera struck again. She caused Herakles to have a fit of madness and in his insanity he mistook his family for enemies and killed them all. When he awoke from his attack, he realized his grave sin and went to the oracle of Apollo at Delphi to find out how to atone for their murders. The oracle, probably coached by Hera, told Herakles that he must serve his cousin, King Eurystheus of Tiryns, for twelve years and do whatever he required. Thus Herakles became a sort of servant of Eurystheus (one of Hera's favorite mortals, by the way) and completed the Twelve Labors. There were ten labors originally but Eurystheus refused to count two of them as labors and added two more. When Herakles was first assigned these labors they were part of his atonement process and there was no reward offered for the labors initially, other than purification for killing his family.

(Herakles' story has much more material than included here as he was the most popular of the Greek heroes and was written about extensively by the Greeks and later the Romans, who called him Hercules. He was so popular that side stories called *parergon* were added to each of the labors detailing all the adventures that he went through while on each labor. Due to a limited amount of time and space, this retelling will focus solely on the twelve labors themselves and skip over the side stories.)

The labors grow worse the higher up in number that they go, with the exception of labor number five. It is as if Eurystheus were actually trying to get rid of Herakles, which was possible, as his patron goddess was Hera to whom Eurystheus was devoted.

When Herakles first presented himself at the court of Eurystheus, King of Tiryns, Eurystheus ordered Herakles to kill the Nemean Lion, a lion whose hide was impenetrable by any weapon of man. The Lion was ravaging the flocks and herds in Nemea. Herakles went after the lion with a club that he fashioned from the limb of a tree. When he finally found the lion he stunned it with the club and then choked the lion with his bare hands. In the process of killing the lion, Herakles discovered that the lions' claws were sharp enough to penetrate its hide so he used them to remove its skin. Ever after, Herakles carried the club and wore the lion skin and they became his trademarks.

When Herakles returned to Eurystheus with the proof that the lion was dead, Eurystheus sent him back out to kill the Lernean Hydra. The Hydra was a water snake with nine heads, eight of which were mortal and the ninth was immortal. Herakles had to have help with this labor because every time he cut off a head of the hydra, two more grew in its place. Iolaus, Herakles' nephew, used a torch to cauterize the necks of the Hydra each time that Herakles cut off a head. Finally, Herakles killed the last head and buried the immortal head underneath a boulder. However, when he returned to Eurystheus, the king refused to count the labor as Herakles had had the help of Iolaus and had not completed the deed on his own.

For his third labor, Herakles was sent out to capture the Cerynean Hind. This deer was sacred to the goddess Artemis and had golden horns. Herakles spent the better part of a year tracking the swift creature and had to capture it without hurting it or incur the goddess' wrath. He narrowly missed her anger after capturing the deer when Artemis angrily appeared and asked him what he was doing. Herakles explained that Eurystheus required him to bring back the deer and Artemis let Herakles off the hook provided that he bring the deer back and release it, unharmed, into the wild again. Herakles agreed.

After Herakles had delivered the deer to Eurystheus and returned it to the wild, he was sent to obtain the huge Erymanthian Boar from Mt. Erymanthus as his fourth labor. This boar was larger and more dangerous than the average boar. Herakles captured it and brought it back to Tiryns for the king. When Eurystheus saw the boar he was so frightened by it, even with Herakles present, that the king hid in either a large bronze jar or in a room made of bronze.

The fifth labor was less glamorous than the other labors—Herakles had to clean the stables of King Augeas who had an enormous herd of cattle. It was impossible to muck out the stables in one day so Herakles diverted the courses of two rivers so that the water flowed through the stables, washing them clean in one day, but he demanded payment for the labor, which equaled a portion of the herd. When Eurystheus found out that Herakles had demanded payment for the fifth labor, he declared that the labor did not count.

The sixth labor of Herakles was to kill the Stymphalian Birds, dangerous birds that lived by Lake Stymphalia. Herakles received guidance from the goddess Athena who gave him bronze castanets made by Hephaestos with which he scared the birds to take flight and shot them while they flew. Depending on the source, these birds were sometimes portrayed as man-eaters.

After successfully killing the Stymphalian birds, Eurystheus sent Herakles to retrieve the Cretan Bull, a man-eating bull and the father of the Minotaur, from the island of Crete as his seventh labor. Herakles sailed to Crete where he hunted down the bull and captured it and brought it back to Tiryns for King Eurystheus. Afterward, the bull was released into the wild and eventually made its way north, closer to Athens on the plains of Marathon, where it was killed by the young hero, Theseus.

The eighth labor of Herakles was to bring back the flesh-eating mares of king Diomedes of Thrace. Diomedes had raised the mares himself, and had given them a diet of human flesh. Herakles tamed them by killing Diomedes and feeding him to the mares. When he brought the horses back to King Eurystheus, Eurystheus released them into the wild in honor of the goddess Hera.

The ninth labor of Herakles was to obtain the girdle of the queen of the Amazons, Hippolyta. The Amazons lived up near the Black Sea and this was much further than Herakles had yet traveled. When he arrived, the Amazons were actually honored to meet him and the queen willingly gave him her girdle, which angered Hera. Hera disguised herself as an Amazon and raced through the village telling everyone that Herakles was attempting to abduct the queen. The rest of the Amazons gathered up their weapons and attacked him. Herakles had to fight his way free and in the process Hippolyta was killed.

For the tenth labor of Herakles, Eurystheus sent him to the edge of the known world to take the cattle of the giant Geryon, who had three bodies and lived on an island in the far, far west. Herakles received help from Helios, the sun god, who gave him a giant cup to sail in. When Herakles arrived on the island, he had to kill not only Geryon, but also Geryon's helper Eurytion and their two-headed guard dog, Orthos. After he had successfully killed the monsters, Herakles gathered the cattle and sailed back to Spain in the cup, which he then returned to Helios. He set up the pillars of Herakles, giant rocks where Spain and Africa nearly touched to commemorate his journey. From Spain, he traveled overland herding the cattle before him all the way back to Tiryns.

For the eleventh labor, Eurystheus sent Herakles to the Island of the Hesperides to gather some of the golden apples of immortality from the sacred tree that had been the wedding gift of Gaia to Hera when she married Zeus. The tree was guarded by the Hesperides, the daughters of Night, and a never sleeping serpent, Ladon. Before Herakles could reach the island, he had to capture the Old Man of the Sea, Nereus, who knew the island's location. After arriving on the island, Herakles met Atlas, the Titan who held up the heavens on his shoulders. He learned that he could not approach the tree without Ladon seeing him, but Atlas offered to retrieve the apples for him if Herakles would hold up the heavens. Herakles agreed. But after Atlas had retrieved the apples he enjoyed his new found freedom so much that he didn't take back the sky and told Herakles that he would deliver the apples for him. Herakles seemed to agree, but asked Atlas if he could hold the heavens back up long enough in order for Herakles to find some kind of padding for his neck. Atlas agreed and lifted up the heavens again but Herakles did not return. He took the apples back to Tiryns and showed them to Eurystheus. Afterword, Athena took them away as they were not meant for mortal hands.

For the twelfth labor, Herakles was sent on his most dangerous labor of all, to retrieve the three-headed guard dog, Cerberus, from the underworld. Herakles knew better than to remove anything from the underworld without Hades' permission so he traveled all the way down into Hades' realm and asked the god if he could borrow Cerberus. Hades agreed on the condition that no weapons be used on his guard dog, and that Herakles return Cerberus to the underworld after his labor was completed. Herakles wrestled and subdued Cerberus with his bare hands and brought him back to Eurystheus in Tiryns and then returned him to the underworld. With the completion of the twelfth labor, Herakles' labors ended and he was purged of the guilt from murdering his family.

Herakles took a new wife, Deianira, the sister of a man he had met in the underworld, but he wasn't quite ready to settle down and live a peaceful life. Instead, he chose to visit all those people who had been disrespectful to him while he had been the servant of Eurystheus.

Greek: Jason and the Argonauts

Jason was born to Aeson, the King of Iolcus, but while he was young, his father's brother, Pelias, overthrew Aeson and took the throne. Pelias kept Aeson and his wife imprisoned in the palace and most likely would have killed Jason, but Jason was sent away to be reared by the wise centaur, Chiron. Chiron taught Jason the heroic arts. When he had come of age, Jason set out to regain his father's throne.

The goddess, Hera, became Jason's protector in part because she had a deep hatred of Pelias who had neglected her in his offerings. Before offering her support, Hera first tested Jason on his journey to Iolcus by disguising herself as an old woman

© rook76/Shutterstock.com

who needed to cross a river. Jason kindly took the old woman on his back and carried her across, losing one of his sandals in the process. Jason safely deposited the old woman on the opposite shore and gained, some say unknowingly, the support of the Queen of the Gods.

Jason arrived at the court of his uncle, King Pelias, who looked on Jason with fear for he had been warned by an oracle to beware of a man wearing a single sandal. When Jason identified himself and stated his claim to the throne, Pelias scoffed. What had Jason done to prove himself worthy of kingship? Pelias challenged Jason to sail to the land of Colchis on the Black Sea and bring back the Golden Fleece, an item sacred to Iolcus, but now in the hands of the Cochian king. Jason had little choice but to accept his uncle's challenge if he wished to one day rule Iolcus.

A ship was ordered built and word was sent out that Jason was looking for worthy heroes to go with him on his dangerous voyage to the edge of civilized lands. The call was answered by a number of Greek heroes and even one heroine, Atalanta, according to some versions. The ship was built by the shipwright Argus and named Argo after him. It was endowed with magical abilities by the gods and the sacred wood from Zeus' sanctuary at Dodona that enabled the ship to speak with a human voice. The crew that gathered to man the ship was called the Argonauts.

Finally, the day arrived and the ship, sailed by its 50 heroic crewmen, headed out on its quest to sail to faraway lands and return with the Golden Fleece. One of the first lands that the Argonauts approached was the island of Lemnos, inhabited only by women and ruled over by a queen, Hypsipyle. Only women inhabited the island because in a fit of anger, they had killed all the men. The women had neglected to honor the goddess, Aphrodite, and in turn, Aphrodite had punished them by making them smell unpleasant to their men. The men turned to concubines angering the women. By the time the Argonauts arrived on their shores, the women of Lemnos had realized that without men, their people would die out. Rather than reacting aggressively toward the ship full of men, the women accepted their presence and eagerly offered to share their beds. This great temptation kept the Argonauts on the island for as much as a year, until finally one of the crew reminded Jason of their quest. With Jason's guidance, the men said good-bye to their lovers and their new children, and left the island behind.

The next land that the Argonauts came to was Salmydessus. King Phineus was in a bind. He had offended the gods to such an extent that he suffered daily from their punishment. He could not eat or offer any sort of banquet to welcome his guests because anytime food was set out, the Harpies, foul-mouthed, women-headed bird-like creatures who befouled anything that their talons touched, arrived and ruined the food. Phineus was in danger of starving when the Argonauts arrived. Two of the Argonauts were the sons of North Wind and could fly. They offered to chase the Harpies away from the table and allow Phineus to eat if he in turn told them of the dangers they faced on the rest of their voyage. Phineus agreed. After Zetes and Calais had chased away the Harpies and Phineus had eaten, he made good on his word and warned the Argonauts about the Clashing Rocks, the Symplegades, and how to pass through them.

The Argonauts left King Phineus with many thanks and sailed onward, coming at last to the Symplegades. There, they followed the king's advice and sent a bird to fly first between the rocks. As soon as the rocks clashed together and began to part again, the Argonauts rowed with all their might. They made it through the rocks before they could slam together again only losing the very end of the ship's stem.

The last obstacles lay in the land of Colchis itself. Colchis was ruled by King Aeetes, who was very fond of his Golden Fleece and viewed the coming of a ship full of armed men as a threat. He did not receive Jason and the Argonauts graciously and only agreed to give Jason the Fleece on the condition that Jason complete a series of challenges. Jason agreed. The challenges included yoking together two fire-breathing, brazen bulls, plowing a four-acre field, sowing a serpent's teeth in that field, and reaping the harvest of warriors that grew from the teeth. There was no way that a mere mortal could safely complete these tasks. Aeetes was able to complete them as he was the son of the sun god, Helios, and had superior strength as well as some invulnerability to fire. All was nearly lost until Hera interceded.

Hera had been watching out for Jason. When she realized that Aeetes was not going to hand over the Fleece easily, Hera asked Aphrodite and her son, Eros, for help. Aeetes had a young daughter, Medea, who was a sorceress. Hera asked Aphrodite and Eros to make Medea fall in love with Jason and offer him her help in completing the tasks. Aphrodite and her son agreed. They caused Medea to fall head over heels in love with Jason. She found a way to approach him without her father's knowledge and she offered to help him complete the tasks. However, in turn, she wished for Jason's help. Knowing that her father would kill her for betraying the family, Medea asked Jason to take her with him on his ship. Jason readily agreed and even offered her marriage if she helped him succeed in his quest. Medea gave Jason a magical ointment to rub all over his body that made him impervious to the fiery breath of the bulls and gave him strength. She also told him the trick to defeating the warriors that would spring from the sown serpent's teeth, which was to throw a rock in their midst that would cause them to attack each other.

The next day, Jason went to the field confident of his success. With Medea's ointment, the fiery breath of the bronze bulls felt like a tickle on his skin. He quickly yoked them and made short work of plowing the four-acre field. Afterward, he sowed the serpent's teeth in the field's furrows and watched as the armed warriors sprang from the soil. When all of the warriors had emerged, Jason hefted a huge rock and threw it into the midst of the warriors who began to attack each other. Jason was easily able to defeat those that remained. When all the tasks were done, King Aeetes was not pleased. He had hoped to kill off the stranger, not give away his most prized possession. Stalling for time, he invited Jason and his men to a feast. During the banquet, it became obvious to Medea that her father was plotting ways to rid himself of the Argonauts and keep the Fleece. That night, Medea snuck from her chambers and found Jason. She led him to the grove where the Golden Fleece hung protected by a sleepless serpent. She enchanted the serpent with her magic and Jason was able to grab the Fleece. The two fled for the Argo and the crew sailed away.

The return voyage of the Argo was long and arduous. Medea's father sent her brother, Apsyrtus to lead a fleet of ships in pursuit. The only way Medea and Jason could escape was through treachery. They pretended to meet peacefully with Apsyrtus to negotiate the return of the Fleece, but instead, Medea and Jason, either singly or together, murdered Apsyrtus. To throw off their pursuers, they cut Apsyrtus' body into pieces and dropped those pieces behind the ship as it sailed, forcing their pursuers to slow in order to find all of the prince's body parts.

Medea and Jason fled with the Argonauts to Medea's aunt, Circe, who agreed to help them atone for the death of Medea's brother. After completing the ritual, Circe sent them forth from her island with no other help because of the death of her nephew. Medea and Jason were forced to search for other aid. They landed on the island of the Phaeacians where the king and queen, Alcinous and Arete respectively, offered to negotiate a treaty with Medea's father if Jason and Medea were married first. After they were married, the Golden Fleece became Medea's dowry. Aeetes, while unhappy with this solution, could not fight it and gave up pursuit of the couple.

Medea and Jason and the Argonauts faced other adventures on their long voyage home, including a bronze giant on the island of Crete who threw boulders at their ship as it sailed past. Medea was able to kill the giant with her magic, causing a lot of fear among the Argonauts, and even to some degree with Jason. However, that was the last main obstacle before they reached home. Upon arriving in Iolcus, Jason and the Argonauts were greeted with joy by the citizen who rejoiced in the return of the Golden Fleece with their heroes. However, Pelias was not inclined to give up his throne. It fell to Medea to sort things out.

Medea convinced Jason's cousins, the daughters of King Pelias, that she could rejuvenate creatures and people. She demonstrated her magical abilities by killing an old ram and throwing its body into a cauldron filled with water and magical herbs. She said a spell and out came a young lamb. Pelias' daughters were so excited by this sight that they decided to help their father regain his youthful vigor by performing Medea's spell on him. Unfortunately, the girls did not have all the ingredients. Instead of making their father young again, they turned him into a soup. Jason was blamed for Pelias' death because of his foreign bride. He was exiled and forced to atone for the death of Pelias.

Years passed in exile. Jason eventually found refuge for Medea and himself and their two young sons in the city of Thebes. After living in the city for some time, King Creon approached Jason with an irresistible offer: set aside Medea and marry the king's only daughter. This would give Jason a chance to be the king after all. Jason agreed, but ran into trouble trying to explain his rationale, that he could better care for their children and her if he was married to the princess, Medea. Medea argued with him, but eventually seemed to give way to his plan. In actuality, Medea plotted her revenge. She sent their two children to the new bride with a crown and a robe, both cursed. When the princess put the items on, they immediately began to burn her skin. Creon, her father, attempted to pull the robe off of her, but the fire stuck to him too. Both Creon and his daughter burned up before Jason's eyes. His children were condemned by the angry citizens of Thebes and would have been put to death except that Medea reached them first.

In the worst telling of this myth, Medea herself killed the boys saying that she would rather want them to die by her loving hands than be torn apart by an angry mob. Afterward, she climbed into the chariot of the sun god, Helios, and flew away taking the bodies of her children for burial in Hera's temple. Jason was left alone to live out his remaining years much as he had been willing to leave Medea. He eventually died, a drunkard, sitting below the Argo when one of its beams fell off onto his head. Medea, meanwhile, found refuge for a time with King Aegeus of Athens.

Indian: Rama

One of the most loved stories from India is the *Ramayana,* the story of the hero Rama. There are over three hundred variations to this story depending on where the story is told and who is telling it. The background remains essentially the same. Rama is an incarnation of the god Vishnu, who comes to rid the world of the demon king Ravana who has grown so powerful even the gods feel threatened by him. Ravana has gained immunity from all creatures except man, whom he considers puny, as a result of his austerities and penances, which he performed in honor of the gods. Due to his disregard for man, the gods ask Vishnu to come to earth in human form to kill Ravana. Vishnu agrees. He takes on human form as the four sons of Dasaratha, the king of Ayodhya. One of the sons is more Vishnu than the others. This is Prince Rama.

Figure 8.2
© reddees/Shutterstock.com

Rama and his brother Lakshmana receive special training away from home from Swami Vishvamitra and learn many different mantras that provide them with special powers when they fight. They both become highly skilled fighters and archers. In fact, the two are so skilled that Vishvamitra asks them to help fight off some demons that are interrupting the priests' sacrifices in the woods. Rama and Lakshmana easily do as asked and the priests are grateful to them.

On their way home to Ayodhya, Vishvamitra takes them through the kingdom of King Janaka who happens to be holding a contest for his adopted daughter's hand in marriage. Sita (an incarnation of the goddess Lakshmi) is the daughter of the earth goddess and she was found when Janaka ceremoniously began plowing the fields one year. He raised the baby girl as his own. To find her a husband, Janaka sets up a bow that belong to the god Shiva and say that anyone who can string the bow can marry Sita. Rama competes for Sita's hand in marriage by competing in the contest. Not only does he string the giant bow of Shiva, but he pulls so powerfully that he actually breaks the bow, winning the contest and Sita's hand. Both families are excited about the union and a huge wedding celebration takes place after Rama's family arrives from Ayodhya. Afterward, the happy couple returns to live in Ayodhya where they are deeply loved by its people.

King Dasaratha has raised Rama as his heir, but when it comes time for Dasaratha to step aside and allow Rama to rule, Dasaratha's third wife, Kekeyi, influenced by her maidservant, asks the king to grant her two boons he had given her when she had saved his life many years ago. Her two boons are that Rama be sent into exile for fourteen years and that her son, Bharata, be crowned as king in his place. These requests hurt Dasaratha but as a king he has to honor his word. When the news reaches Rama that his brother is to be crowned and that he is to be sent into exile, he does not question the word of his father, but immediately takes off his princely robes and puts on the robes of a wandering ascetic. Lakshamana begs to accompany him as does his loyal wife Sita. Rama tries to dissuade her as the journey will be difficult and living in the forest will not be easy, but Sita insists that without Rama she will have no life and that she might as well throw herself on the funeral pyre. When Rama sees how determined Sita is to accompany him, he agrees. The three take their leave of the king and his three wives. The king tries to persuade Rama to stay, but he can not go back on his father's words. The whole city turns out to see them off on their journey to the forest.

As Rama, Sita, and Lakshmana make their way toward the forest, they encounter many people who help them and in turn are helped by the presence of Rama, Vishnu in human form. Eventually, after confronting a demon or two and releasing various individuals from their torments, the trio arrives in the forest where they set up a little hut as their house and live a very simple life. Occasionally, Rama and Lakshmana have to fight a demon or two, but for the most part their years in the forest are tranquil ones until the demoness Soorpanakha takes an interest in Rama.

Soorpanakha spies Rama in the forest and falls instantly in love with him. She takes on an appealing human like form and appears to Rama to entice him to take her as his wife. When Rama reveals he already has a wife, Soorpanakha becomes jealous of Sita and wants to kill her but continues to entice Rama and ask if she can be his secondary wife. Rama allows her to tease him but when she threatens Sita and will not leave, he asks Lakshmana to punish her and run her off. Lakshmana disfigures Soorpanakha by cutting off her nose, and in some versions her breasts too, which marks her as adulteress for her advances. Soorpanakha flees to her brothers.

Soorpanakha's brothers are powerful demons, but they aren't powerful enough to punish Rama for his actions against their sister. In fact, Rama and Lakshmana kill Soorpanakha's brothers, which leaves her only one possibility. She has to confront her last brother who is also the king of Sri Lanka: Ravana.

Soorpanakha knows that if she tells Ravana that Rama and Lakshmana have hurt her, Ravana will only laugh at her. She has to take another tactic. She paints a picture of the beautiful Sita that is so realistic that Ravana falls in love without seeing her. Ravana becomes determined to have her and comes up with a plan to remove her from the protection of Rama and Lakshmana. Ravana takes on the appearance of an ascetic and sends another demon disguised as a golden deer ahead of him into the tranquil forest where Rama and Sita and Lakshmana live. When Sita spies the deer, she asks Rama if he will fetch it for her as a gift. He agrees, feeling that it is such a small request after his wife has given up everything to come live with him in the forest. He leaves Lakshmana to protect Sita while he tracks down the beautiful golden deer.

The demon disguised as the golden deer begins to run faster and faster leading Rama further and further from his wife and brother. After they have gone a great distance, the demon casts his voice back toward the forest but made it sound like Rama's voice crying out for help. When Sita hears what she thinks is Rama's cry, she asks Lakshmana to aid her husband. Lakshamana is hesitant to leave Sita but she pleads with him to the point that he leaves her with the reminder that as long as she remains within the protective boundaries of their hut, she will be safe.

Ravana appears a short time later in his disguise as a wandering ascetic. It is customary to offer food to ascetics so Sita goes inside the hut and gathers some food and comes out to offer it to him. Unfortunately, she leaves the protective boundaries of her home and Ravana throws off his disguise, gathers her up and climbs into his chariot and flys with her back to Sri Lanka. The only creature that tries to stop him is a vulture who sees everything and knows that Sita is Rama's wife. Ravana mortally wounds the vulture and keeps on flying until he reachs Lanka where he places Sita in his pleasure garden and refuses her any comforts until she agrees to marry him. (In many of the versions of the *Ramayana*, Ravana has a curse on him so that he cannot force a woman to bed. Thus, Sita must come willingly or not at all.)

Meanwhile, Rama and his brother realize that they have been tricked by the demon disguised as a deer and quickly kill the demon before rushing back to find their hut empty and Sita gone. They search the forest desperately looking for her, but to no avail. Eventually, they stumble on the vulture that had seen her and he gives them the grim news that Ravana abducted Sita before he dies in Rama's arms. Neither Rama nor Lakshmana quite know where Ravana went, so they search and search for many days until they come across a group of sentient monkeys who offer to aid them in return for some aid. After intervening in monkey politics, Rama asks the monkeys to search for Sita for him. One monkey in particular, Hanuman, stands out from all the others. Hanuman recognizes that Rama is the god Vishnu in human form and kneels before him and offers his aid. Hanuman is the son of Vayu, the wind god, and an avatar of Shiva, which gives him amazing powers to transform himself from a minute size to a giant size as well as the ability to leap across vast distances. He leaves Rama with a token he is to give to Sita if he finds her and begins his quest while Rama, Lakshmana, and the rest of the monkey army continue to search more slowly for the missing Sita.

Hanuman makes his way toward the tip of India and the island of Sri Lanka. He transforms into a large size and leaps across the ocean to Lanka, fighting a demon on the way. In Lanka, he resumes a normal size and scouts out the palace of Ravana looking for Sita. He does not find her in Ravana's palace, which is a relief as it means she has not given in to the demon. Hanuman searches the gardens for Sita and finally finds her sitting in her tattered sari with several demonesses keeping watch over her. While he watches her, Ravana arrives and tells Sita that she has twenty-four hours to make up her mind to marry him or be devoured. After Ravana and the demonesses leave, Hanuman slips down from the tree and approaches Sita with a ring of Rama's to prove that her husband sent him. Sita is overjoyed by Hanuman's arrival and the thought of her lord being near, but she will not allow Hanuman to carry her out of the garden. She does not want another man to rescue her let alone touch her, which would dishonor Rama. She tells Hanuman that she will remain in the garden until Rama comes to get her and she gives him one of her jewels that she had hidden in the hem of her sari to take back to Rama as proof of her fidelity.

Hanuman returns to the mainland with the good news but first pays a visit to Ravana's palace to see if he can convince Ravana to send Sita back to Rama. Ravana not only does not listen to Hanuman's good advice to send Sita back before a war begins, he goes so far as to threaten the messenger. He has his demons set Hanuman's tail on fire, thinking that they have him safely bound. Hanuman shrinks to a smaller size and the ropes fall off him. He then increases his size and jumps around the palace with his burning tail, setting many things on fire, before he quenches his tail in the sea and growing large again, leaps back over the ocean to the coast of India and Rama's side.

Rama is overjoyed that Hanuman has found Sita. He quickly gathers his army of sentient monkeys and bears and they build a bridge over to the island that the whole army can march across. The next day they arrive in Lanka and confront Ravana's army. Ravana sends his men but does not fight himself, as he thinks that the humans and bears and monkeys will be easily defeated. He does not realize that Rama is not an ordinary man. To his great dismay, Rama and Lakshmana and their allies defeat much of Ravana's army, including one of his own sons. Finally Ravana decides that he will take the field. He and Rama face off while their armies continue to fight. Rama and Ravana fight on land and in the air. They throw many weapons and shoot many arrows with magical properties against each other, but finally, fortunately, Rama kills Ravana, which ends the war. As Ravana dies, he looks on Rama and sees the god Vishnu and accepts his fate. Dying with that knowledge is a blessing and partly redeems the demon.

© RAMNIKLAL MODI/Shutterstock.com

After the war is over, Lakshmana is found injured. Rama needs a certain herb that only grows in the Himalayas to cure him so Hanuman grows to a vast size and leaps to the top of India. When he cannot find the herb, Hanuman picks up the top of a mountain and returns with it to Rama so that Rama can pick the correct herb to heal Lakshmana, which he does. After Lakshmana is revived he is able to fetch Sita and bring her to Rama. Sita trembles with joy at their reunion, but Rama acts coldly toward her and proclaims that she is free and his obligation to her is over. Sita does not understand. Rama feels that he cannot take Sita back into his house after she has spent so much time in another man's control. Surely she is no longer pure. Sita is devastated by Rama's rejection and tells Lakshmana to build her a funeral pyre to jump in. If she cannot live with her lord, she does not want to live.

In front of the assembled army, Sita throws herself on the funeral pyre. The god of fire, Agni, pushes her back out and hands her to Rama without a burn proclaiming that she is so pure that she has burned the fire god, she thought only of her husband and of his welfare. Having thus proven her faithfulness in front of the army as well as her husband and brother-in-law, Sita is taken back by her husband. They all climb into Ravana's magical chariot, the Pushpak Vimana, which can expand to hold as many as climb into it, and together they all fly back to Ayodhya for the fourteen years of exile are over.

When they return to Ayodhya, Bharata, Rama's brother, gladly turns over the throne to his brother, having refused to rule as king during the many years of Rama's exile, instead taking a position as regent until Rama returned. There is a formal ceremony of investiture and Rama with his wife beside him is crowned King of Ayodhya.

Indian: Siddhartha Gautama, the Buddha

The following story follows the Mahayana Buddhism version of Siddhartha Gautama's life. Mahayana Buddhism is one of the major branches of Buddhism and generally accepts the existence of many Buddhas, both metaphysical and devotional as well as potential Buddhas, called the Bodhisattvas. A Bodhisattva is a person on the threshold of enlightenment (nirvana) who vows to hold off taking that final step into Nirvana in order to help all other sentient beings reach enlightenment first. Bodhisattvas often reincarnate to fulfill that vow. The many various Buddhas and Bodhisattvas can aid a Buddhist practitioner with his or her meditation and even answer prayers. In Theravada Buddhism, which is the older form of Buddhism, there are no gods or goddesses and there is only the one historical Buddha, Siddhartha Gautama. For the sake of clarity, Siddhartha as the historical Buddha is depicted as a normal sized or even an emaciated man, often seated in the lotus position for meditation. The images of the happy, overweight Buddha are not of Siddhartha, but of another Buddha from the Mahayana branch of Buddhism called Maitreya Buddha. He is the Buddha of the Future and is very popular in China and Japan.

Siddhartha's Quest for Enlightenment:

Siddhartha Gautama was an Indian prince (Kshatriya caste: rulers and warriors) born in the Shakya kingdom in northern India (modern day Nepal) in the 6th century BCE. His father was the ruler (raj) of the Shakya clan. His mother, Maha-Maya, was traveling back to her hometown as was customary to give birth to her son when she felt the birthing pains come upon her while yet on the road. She gave birth to the future Buddha from her side, and in some versions, Gandharvas (heavenly angels) caught the baby in a net and lowered him gently to the Earth. The baby took seven steps and said, "Lord of all this am I." The gods above rejoiced at the coming of the future Buddha for he would offer to humanity a new path to reach enlightenment.

As Maha-Maya had given birth along the road, she no longer needed to return to her parents' home and instead took her newborn son back to her husband's kingdom. Sudhodhana was extremely pleased to have a son. He summoned the priests to cast his son's astrological birth chart in order to know what the future held for him. The priests determined that Siddhartha had two possible destinies: he would either grow to be a World Ruler or he would pursue a spiritual life and become a World Savior. King Sudhodhana desired his son to follow in his footsteps and in order that Siddhartha not be tempted toward a spiritual path, Sudhodhana surrounded him with every conceivable luxury. Siddhartha grew up in the palace with all the good things a prince could possibly want and he was surrounded by happy, healthy, and vibrant people. The king did not allow any signs of suffering to appear in Siddhartha's world. He hoped that by sheltering his son, he would grow up to be a great king.

Siddhartha showed some early inclinations toward meditation and was a very kind young man. As he grew older and began to question things, his father arranged a marriage to a beautiful princess for him. However, even marriage to the princess was only able to keep Siddhartha distracted for a time. Eventually, he desired to see what life was like outside the palace walls. He asked his father for permission to explore the town. His father reluctantly agreed, but set a date for the prince's excursion. In between those dates, the king ordered that the town be cleaned up and that only the healthy and able could be out on the streets to greet the prince.

The day arrived for Siddhartha's exploration of the town. As his charioteer drove him through the town's streets, the happy and healthy citizens greeted him with flowers and cheers. However, the gods had other plans in mind. They contrived for Siddhartha to see Four Signs, one after the other: a sick man, an old man, a corpse, and an ascetic. Siddhartha had never seen such things before and had to ask his charioteer what each one was. After each of the first three Signs, his charioteer kindly explained that each was an example of suffering in this world. Everyone could get sick and suffer from bodily ailments and diseases regardless of high or low birth, everyone could lose strength and agility and become wrinkled and shriveled with age, and everyone would eventually die. Each of these things caused suffering not only to the individual, but often to those around him or her as well. When Siddhartha saw the Fourth Sign, the ascetic, he was puzzled by the man's peaceful expression and happy demeanor. The ascetic wore saffron-colored robes and wandered barefoot begging for food and owning no possessions. He spent much time in meditation. Siddhartha's charioteer explained that the ascetic looked so happy because he was a renunciate and had renounced all ties and attachments in order to focus on reaching enlightenment, which would end all suffering.

Siddhartha was deeply impressed by all that he saw, especially the ascetic. He returned to the palace and thought about what he had seen. After he returned, he was greeted with the joyous news that his wife had just given birth to his son. He rejoiced in his son's birth and congratulated his wife. The couple was very happy, but Siddhartha knew that his young son was prone to sickness, old age, and death, just as everyone else. These thoughts plagued him so that he could not return to his former life content. Finally, he decided to leave the palace and become an ascetic in order that he might find an end to suffering and be able to share that knowledge with others.

At the age of twenty-nine, Siddhartha left the palace at night with only his charioteer's knowledge and help. They drove to the outskirts of the town where Siddhartha took off his princely garments and put on the robes of an ascetic. Then he cut off his princely locks and handed his hair and garments to his charioteer to take back to his father and gave him instructions to tell the king that Siddhartha had become an ascetic and would only return to his father's kingdom after he had found the answers he was seeking. Thus, began Siddhartha's quest for enlightenment.

Siddhartha traveled barefoot, begging for a meal each day, and spending much of his time in meditation. He heard of various teachers and gurus who might help him on his quest and he journeyed to where they taught and stayed and studied their techniques. In each case, Siddhartha quickly mastered his teacher's techniques so much so that the teacher often asked him to stay on and become the next leader of the group. However, Siddhartha did not feel that any of the practices were helping him reach enlightenment and politely declined. He had learned wonderful ways to calm the mind and to sit in meditation for long periods and even attained moments of bliss, but none of the teachings offered an end to suffering. After five years studying with a number of different teachers, Siddhartha finally decided to head into the Himalayas to practice a more severe form of asceticism. He planned to live off of one grain of rice each day and drink the dew off of plants. He was joined by five other ascetics who also hoped that this extreme form of meditation practice would help them all break past the veils of illusion (of Maya which means illusion) and achieve Nirvana, awareness of the oneness of all things (enlightenment).

Siddhartha practiced with the five ascetics for a year, but at the end of that year not only was he emaciated and barely alive, he was also no closer to enlightenment. Feeling that the path of extreme asceticism brought him no closer to enlightenment than the life of luxury he had lived as a prince, Siddhartha determined to find a middle path. He left his companions on the mountain, much to their dismay, and returned to the lower lands. After a year of malnourishment, he was so weak that he collapsed by the side of the road. A young woman, Sujata, found him and offered him some rice milk. Siddhartha accepted the food gladly as he realized that in order to meditate comfortably, his body needed nourishment.

After eating the food, Siddhartha found a comfortable spot beneath a pipal (fig) tree and decided that he would remain there at that spot until he reached enlightenment. He sat in meditation for hours and hours. As time passed, his mind stilled and he went deeper into the causes and connections between all things. As he approached Nirvana, Mara, the fiend, appeared with a horde of demons to drive Siddhartha away from meditation. Mara, the embodiment of attachment and fear, did not want Siddhartha to become a Buddha and teach people how to free themselves from their attachments in order to reach enlightenment. Mara needed people to feel fear and desire and have attachments in order to have power over them.

Mara sent his demon horde to attack Siddhartha where he meditated. The demons all cast weapons at Siddhartha, but he was so deep in his meditation that he was not disturbed and as the weapons penetrated his aura, they turned into lotus flowers, falling gently around him. When the first attempt to distract Siddhartha by fear failed, Mara next tried to tempt Siddhartha by appealing to his sense of duty or Dharma. Siddhartha was born a prince and as such was a member of the Kshatriya caste, making him a warrior. His dharma included protecting his father's kingdom. Mara bellowed at Siddhartha that the spot under the tree was not his, but his dharma required him to return to his father's kingdom and help defend it as it was being attacked. Siddhartha, calmly, without breaking meditation, touched his fingers to the Earth. The goddess of the Earth spoke out on his behalf and claimed that Siddhartha had fulfilled dharma in all his many previous incarnations and was no longer bound by the law of Dharma.

When the temptation by dharma failed, Mara turned to a baser one: desire (kama). Mara sent his beautiful scantily clad daughters to dance enticingly before Siddhartha to distract him, but Siddhartha was so close to the unity of all things that he no longer felt the desire. How was it possible to desire that which he already was? He and they were one. The ladies, recognizing the equanimity of Siddhartha, bowed in acknowledgment of his imminent Buddhahood and backed away. Following the ladies' defeat, Mara's entire army bowed in acknowledgment of Siddhartha's achievement and Mara left defeated.

Siddhartha continued to meditate and finally attained the bliss of Nirvana underneath the pipal tree (which, from that day forth, was called the Bodhi Tree or the Tree of Enlightenment), understanding and comprehending the oneness of all things. He stayed in bliss for many days, enjoying the sensation and appreciating the interdependence of all beings. This was because that was. There was no separate self and no separate soul. All things were One. After remaining in bliss underneath the Bodhi Tree, Siddhartha, now the Buddha or the Enlightened One, debated about what to do. He was not certain if his understanding could be taught. As he debated, the gods came down and asked him to take up teaching his new path, the Middle Path, to Enlightenment. The Buddha agreed, and thus his teaching career began.

The Buddha left the area of Bodh Gaya, the location of the Bodhi Tree, and began to travel by foot, begging for one meal a day in order to eat, and practicing meditation. As he wandered he came across the five ascetics with which he had practiced severe asceticism up in the Himalayas. At first, the five men sought to avoid him as they were still disappointed that he had left them. But after they watched him for a bit, they realized that he had a certain glow about him, a calm radiance, and they realized that he had attained what they still sought, enlightenment. They swiftly approached him and bowed and asked him to accept them as his disciples. He agreed. He told them what he had learned during his solitary meditations and this became his first sermon, the Sermon at the Deer Park. It became the foundation for all his later teachings. These teachings together were referred to as Buddhist Dharma, which meant the Way, the Truth, and the Law. The core teachings were the Four Noble Truths, which were among the first things the Buddha taught his new disciples. These were (1) all life is suffering, (2) suffering is caused by desire (or attachment), (3) to end suffering, end desire (or attachment), and (4) to end desire, follow the Nnoble Eeightfold Ppath.

With these teachings, the Buddha set the Wheel of Dharma into motion and the five ascetics, his new disciples, were very pleased. They began to follow the Buddha's regimen of meditation, both seated and walking, with one meal a day obtained by begging. They begged not only because they had no possessions, but also to teach them humility. As they begged in the villages and towns, anyone could approach them to learn about the Dharma. The Buddha's teachings quickly gained new followers and even gained the ears of kings. As time passed, various kings and wealthy men donated lands to the Buddha and his growing Sangha (monastic community) so that they could build monasteries to which they could retreat during the monsoons. During the rest of the year, the Buddha and his monks wandered from kingdom to kingdom, spreading the teachings, the Dharma, practicing their meditation and begging for their daily meals. In this way, the message of the Buddha spread through many kingdoms in India and the Sangha continued to grow.

The Buddha taught until he was 80 years old. During those years, he traveled back to his father's kingdom where many of his family members accepted his new teachings and became his disciples, including, eventually, his aunt and his wife. It took many years before women could be active members of the sSangha and this was achieved only after separate nunneries had been built for them and a very strict code of behavior developed for the nuns. However, eventually all were welcome to join, regardless of caste.

Anyone who followed the Buddha's teachings had the ability, one day, of reaching enlightenment. This was contrary to standard Hindu teachings of that time that said only members of the highest caste, the Brahmins, could reach enlightenment. Hinduism offered hope to its followers by stating that an individual, by following his dharma according to his caste, could eventually earn enough good karma to be born into the Brahmin caste and reach enlightenment. Good karma was achieved only by fulfilling the dharma set by the caste the person was born into during that life. Good dharmic actions (karma) resulted in a better rebirth while bad dharmic actions (karma) resulted in a lower rebirth. Thus, Hinduism was able to justify the caste system and maintain order as well as offer hope for a better life in the future.

The Buddha rejected the caste system because he, as a member of the second caste, the Kshatriyas, had obtained enlightenment. He felt that anyone, regardless of caste, could do the same. Therefore, he accepted people from any caste into his sSangha and expected everyone to be treated equally. When the Buddha died, he left this legacy of equality for his followers, who continued to appeal to all the castes and even the outcastes in India and beyond.

Japanese: Momotaro

Momotaro is a very popular folk story from Japan with several variations depending on where the story is told. The story has numerous representations in cartoon form, as well as several famous sculptural representations.

There once was an old couple who lived a very frugal life. One day while the husband was out cutting wood, the old woman went to wash clothes in the river. As she washed the clothes, a giant peach floated downstream. The woman thought that the peach would make a very nice meal for herself and her husband. She took the peach

© cowardlion/Shutterstock.com

back to their humble home and prepared to serve it to her husband. However, when the couple went to cut the peach open, out sprang a little baby boy. He told them that he had come to be their son. They named him Momotaro, which translates roughly as "Peach Boy," because he had come from the peach.

Momotaro lived happily with the old couple and helped make their lives easier. As he grew up, he learned about an island of ogres nearby. The ogres made everyone's lives miserable and stole whatever they could, which according to some sources was the reason for the general poverty in the area. When Momotaro was a young man in his teens, he told his parents that he was going to defeat the ogres so that the ogres would leave everyone alone. His father gave Momotaro a suit of armor and some weapons. His mother prepared some dumplings for his journey and his parents gave him their blessing before he set off. They were very proud of their young son.

Momotaro left his parents and began to walk toward the coast. As he was walking, he was accosted by a dog. The dog growled and threatened to attack Momotaro, but Momotaro held his ground and offered the dog a dumpling if the dog would help him defeat the ogres of Ogre Island. The dog agreed. They two companions continued on until they came across a monkey. The dog and the monkey were ready to fight each other, but Momotaro stopped them and told the monkey that they were on their way to Ogre Island to defeat the ogres and offered to give the monkey a dumpling if the monkey joined them. The monkey agreed. The three companions continued on until they came across a pheasant. The pheasant and the monkey stood off and would have fought if Momotaro had not explained their important mission to defeat the ogres of

Ogre Island. He offered the pheasant a dumpling if it too would join them on their quest. The pheasant agreed and the four set off toward the coast.

When they arrived on the coast, the found a boat they could use and set sail for Ogre Island. They arrived without difficulty only to find strong gates and towering walls blocking them from reaching the stronghold of the ogres. The four companions came up with a plan. The pheasant flew over the gate and distracted the guards by pecking at their eyes while the monkey climbed over the gate and opened it from the inside. After that, Momotaro and the dog rushed in and the fighting commenced. The ogres were not prepared for the attacks of the pheasant, the monkey, the dog, and the young warrior with his sharp sword. Soon, they surrendered. Momotaro obtained the leader's promise that the ogres would not hunt in his lands again and the ogres offered up much of the treasure that they had previously stolen.

Momotaro and his companions loaded up their boat with the treasures and left the Island of the Ogres behind. They returned to the coast and traveled back to Momotaro's home. His parents rejoiced in his good fortune and everyone rested more easily knowing that the ogres would not be roaming their lands anymore.

The Hebrew Hero Samson

Many people have heard of Samson and Delilah, but not everyone is familiar with the hero's full story. Here it is in translation from the Hebrew Tanach, Judges Chapters 13–16.

■ ■ ■

The *Tanach*, Jewish Publication Society tr. [1917], at sacred-texts.com

JUDGES CHAPTER 13

And the children of Israel again did that which was evil in the sight of the LORD; and the LORD delivered them into the hand of the Philistines forty years.

And there was a certain man of Zorah, of the family of the Danites, whose name was Manoah; and his wife was barren, and bore not. And the angel of the LORD appeared unto the woman, and said unto her: 'Behold now, thou art barren, and hast not borne; but thou shalt conceive, and bear a son. Now therefore beware, I pray thee, and drink no wine nor strong drink, and eat not any unclean thing. For, lo, thou shalt conceive, and bear a son; and no razor shall come upon his head; for the child shall be a Nazirite unto God from the womb; and he shall begin to save Israel out of the hand of the Philistines.' Then the woman came and told her husband, saying: 'A man

© rudall30/Shutterstock.com

of God came unto me, and his countenance was like the countenance of the angel of
God, very terrible; and I asked him not whence he was, neither told he me his name;
but he said unto me: Behold, thou shalt conceive, and bear a son; and now drink no
wine nor strong drink, and eat not any unclean thing; for the child shall be a Nazirite
unto God from the womb to the day of his death.'

Then Manoah entreated the LORD, and said: 'Oh, Lord, I pray Thee, let the
man of God whom Thou didst send come again unto us, and teach us what we shall
do unto the child that shall be born.' And God hearkened to the voice of Manoah;
and the angel of God came again unto the woman as she sat in the field; but Manoah
her husband was not with her. And the woman made haste, and ran, and told her
husband, and said unto him: 'Behold, the man hath appeared unto me, that came
unto me that day.' And Manoah arose, and went after his wife, and came to the man,
and said unto him: 'Art thou the man that spokest unto the woman?' And he said: 'I
am.' And Manoah said: 'Now when thy word cometh to pass, what shall be the rule
for the child, and what shall be done with him?' And the angel of the LORD said
unto Manoah: 'Of all that I said unto the woman let her beware. She may not eat of
any thing that cometh of the grape-vine, neither let her drink wine or strong drink,
nor eat any unclean thing; all that I commanded her let her observe.' And Manoah
said unto the angel of the LORD: 'I pray thee, let us detain thee, that we may make
ready a kid for thee.' And the angel of the LORD said unto Manoah: 'Though thou
detain me, I will not eat of thy bread; and if thou wilt make ready a burnt-offering,
thou must offer it unto the LORD.' For Manoah knew not that he was the angel
of the LORD. And Manoah said unto the angel of the LORD: 'What is thy name,
that when thy words come to pass we may do thee honour?'And the angel of the
LORD said unto him: 'Wherefore askest thou after my name, seeing it is hidden?'
So Manoah took the kid with the meal-offering, and offered it upon the rock unto

the LORD; and [the angel] did wondrously, and Manoah and his wife looked on. For it came to pass, when the flame went up toward heaven from off the altar, that the angel of the LORD ascended in the flame of the altar; and Manoah and his wife looked on; and they fell on their faces to the ground. But the angel of the LORD did no more appear to Manoah or to his wife. Then Manoah knew that he was the angel of the LORD. And Manoah said unto his wife: 'We shall surely die, because we have seen God.' But his wife said unto him: 'If the LORD were pleased to kill us, He would not have received a burnt-offering and a meal-offering at our hand, neither would He have shown us all these things, nor would at this time have told such things as these.'

And the woman bore a son, and called his name Samson; and the child grew, and the LORD blessed him. And the spirit of the LORD began to move him in Mahaneh-dan, between Zorah and Eshtaol.

■ ■ ■

The *Tanach,* Jewish Publication Society tr. [1917], at sacred-texts.com

JUDGES CHAPTER 14

And Samson went down to Timnah, and saw a woman in Timnah of the daughters of the Philistines. And he came up, and told his father and his mother, and said: 'I have seen a woman in Timnah of the daughters of the Philistines; now therefore get her for me to wife.' Then his father and his mother said unto him: 'Is there never a woman among the daughters of thy brethren, or among all my people, that thou goest to take a wife of the uncircumcised Philistines?' And Samson said unto his father:

'Get her for me; for she pleaseth me well.' But his father and his mother knew not that it was of the LORD; for he sought an occasion against the Philistines. Now at that time the Philistines had rule over Israel.

Then went Samson down, and his father and his mother, to Timnah, and came to the vineyards of Timnah; and, behold, a young lion roared against him. And the spirit of the LORD came mightily upon him, and he rent him as one would have rent a kid, and he had nothing in his hand; but he told not his father or his mother what he had done. And he went down, and talked with the woman; and she pleased Samson well. And after a while he returned to take her, and he turned aside to see the carcass of the lion; and, behold, there was a swarm of bees in the body of the lion, and honey. And he scraped it out into his hands, and went on, eating as he went, and he came to his father and mother, and gave unto them, and they did eat; but he told them not that he had scraped the honey out of the body of the lion. And his father went down unto the woman; and Samson made there a feast; for so used the young men to do.

And it came to pass, when they saw him, that they brought thirty companions to be with him. And Samson said unto them: 'Let me now put forth a riddle unto you; if ye can declare it me within the seven days of the feast, and find it out, then I will give you thirty linen garments and thirty changes of raiment; but if ye cannot declare it me, then shall ye give me thirty linen garments and thirty changes of raiment.' And they said unto him: 'Put forth thy riddle, that we may hear it.' And he said unto them:

> Out of the eater came forth food,
> And out of the strong came forth sweetness.

And they could not in three days declare the riddle. And it came to pass on the seventh day, that they said unto Samson's wife: 'Entice thy husband, that he may declare unto us the riddle, lest we burn thee and thy father's house with fire; have ye called us hither to impoverish us?' And Samson's wife wept before him, and said: 'Thou dost but hate me, and lovest me not; thou hast put forth a riddle unto the children of my people, and wilt thou not tell it me?' And he said unto her: 'Behold, I have not told it my father nor my mother, and shall I tell thee?' And she wept before him the seven days, while their feast lasted; and it came to pass on the seventh day, that he told her, because she pressed him sore; and she told the riddle to the children of her people. And the men of the city said unto him on the seventh day before the sun went down:

> What is sweeter than honey?
> And what is stronger than a lion?
> And he said unto them:
> If ye had not plowed with my heifer,
> Ye had not found out my riddle.

And the spirit of the LORD came mightily upon him, and he went down to Ashkelon, and smote thirty men of them, and took their spoil, and gave the changes of raiment unto them that declared the riddle. And his anger was kindled, and he went up to his father's house. But Samson's wife was given to his companion, whom he had had for his friend.

JUDGES CHAPTER 15

But it came to pass after a while, in the time of wheat harvest, that Samson visited his wife with a kid; and he said: 'I will go in to my wife into the chamber.' But her father would not suffer him to go in. And her father said: 'I verily thought that thou hadst utterly hated her; therefore I gave her to thy companion; is not her younger sister fairer than she? take her, I pray thee, instead of her.' And Samson said unto them: 'This time shall I be quits with the Philistines, when I do them a mischief.' And Samson went and caught three hundred foxes, and took torches, and turned tail to tail, and put a torch in the midst between every two tails. And when he had set the torches on fire, he let them go into the standing corn of the Philistines, and burnt up both the shocks and the standing corn, and also the oliveyards. Then the Philistines said: 'Who hath done this?' And they said: 'Samson, the son-in-law of the Timnite, because he hath taken his wife, and given her to his companion.' And the Philistines came up, and burnt her and her father with fire. And Samson said unto them: 'If ye do after this manner, surely I will be avenged of you, and after that I will cease.' And he smote them hip and thigh with a great slaughter; and he went down and dwelt in the cleft of the rock of Etam.

Then the Philistines went up, and pitched in Judah, and spread themselves against Lehi. And the men of Judah said: 'Why are ye come up against us?' And they said: 'To bind Samson are we come up, to do to him as he hath done to us.' Then three thousand men of Judah went down to the cleft of the rock of Etam, and said to Samson: 'Knowest thou not that the Philistines are rulers over us? what then is this that thou hast done unto us?' And he said unto them: 'As they did unto me, so have I done unto them.' And they said unto him: 'We are come down to bind thee, that we may deliver thee into the hand of the Philistines.' And Samson said unto them: 'Swear unto me, that ye will not fall upon me yourselves.' And they spoke unto him, saying: 'No; but we will bind thee fast, and deliver thee into their hand; but surely we will not kill thee.' And they bound him with two new ropes, and brought him up from the rock. When he came unto Lehi, the Philistines shouted as they met him; and the spirit of the LORD came mightily upon him, and the ropes that were upon his arms became as flax that was burnt with fire, and his bands dropped from off his hands. And he found a new jawbone of an ass, and put forth his hand, and took it, and smote a thousand men therewith. And Samson said:

> With the jawbone of an ass, heaps upon heaps,
> With the jawbone of an ass have I smitten a thousand men.

And it came to pass, when he had made an end of speaking, that he cast away the jawbone out of his hand; and that place was called a Ramath-lehi. And he was sore athirst, and called on the LORD, and said: 'Thou hast given this great deliverance by ·the hand of Thy servant; and now shall I die for thirst, and fall into the hand of the uncircumcised?' But God cleaved the hollow place that is in Lehi, and there came water thereout; and when he had drunk, his spirit came back, and he revived; wherefore the name thereof was called b En-hakkore, which is in Lehi unto this day. And he judged Israel in the days of the Philistines twenty years.

Footnotes

314:a That is, *The hill of the jawbone.*
314:b That is, *The spring of him that called.*

JUDGES CHAPTER 16

And Samson went to Gaza, and saw there a harlot, and went in unto her. [And it was told] the Gazites, saying: 'Samson is come hither.' And they compassed him in, and lay in wait for him all night in the gate of the city, and were quiet all the night, saying: 'Let be till morning light, then we will kill him.' And Samson lay till midnight, and arose at midnight, and laid hold of the doors of the gate of the city, and the two posts, and plucked them up, bar and all, and put them upon his shoulders, and carried them up to the top of the mountain that is before Hebron.

And it came to pass afterward, that he loved a woman in the valley of Sorek, whose name was Delilah. And the lords of the Philistines came up unto her, and said unto her: 'Entice him, and see wherein his great strength lieth, and by what means we may prevail against him, that we may bind him to afflict him; and we will give thee every one of us eleven hundred pieces of silver.' And Delilah said to Samson: 'Tell me, I pray thee, wherein thy great strength lieth, and wherewith thou mightest be bound to afflict thee.' And Samson said unto her: 'If they bind me with seven fresh bowstrings that were never dried, then shall I become weak, and be as any other man.' Then the lords of the Philistines brought up to her seven fresh bowstrings which had not been dried, and she bound him with them. Now she had liers-in-wait abiding in the inner chamber. And she said unto him: 'The Philistines are upon thee, Samson.' And he broke the bowstrings as a string of tow is broken when it toucheth the fire. So his strength was not known. And Delilah said unto Samson: 'Behold, thou hast mocked me, and told me lies; now tell me, I pray thee, wherewith thou mightest be bound.' And he said unto her: 'If they only bind me with new ropes wherewith no work hath been done, then shall I become weak, and be as any other man.' So Delilah took new ropes, and bound him therewith, and said unto him: 'The Philistines are upon thee, Samson.' And the liers-in-wait were abiding in the inner chamber. And he broke them from off his arms like a thread. And Delilah said unto Samson: 'Hitherto thou hast mocked me, and told me lies; tell me wherewith thou mightest be bound.' And he said unto her: 'If thou weavest the seven locks of my head with the web.' And she fastened it with the pin, and said unto him: 'The Philistines are upon thee, Samson.' And he awoke out of his sleep, and plucked away the pin of the beam, and the web. And she said unto him: 'How canst thou say: I love thee, when thy heart is not with me? thou hast mocked me these three times, and hast not told me wherein thy great strength lieth.' And it came to pass, when she pressed him daily with her words, and urged him, that his soul was vexed unto death. And he told her all his heart, and said unto her: 'There hath not come a razor upon my head; for I have been a Nazirite unto God from my mother's womb; if I be shaven, then my strength will go from me, and I shall become weak, and be like any other man.' And when Delilah saw that he had told her all his heart, she sent and called for the lords of the Philistines, saying: 'Come up this once, for he hath told me all his heart.' Then the lords of the Philistines came up unto her, and brought the money in their hand. And she made him sleep upon her knees;

and she called for a man, and had the seven locks of his head shaven off; and she began to afflict him, and his strength went from him. And she said: 'The Philistines are upon thee, Samson.' And he awoke out of his sleep, and said: 'I will go out as at other times, and shake myself.' But he knew not that the LORD was departed from him. And the Philistines laid hold on him, and put out his eyes; and they brought him down to Gaza, and bound him with fetters of brass; and he did grind in the prison-house. Howbeit the hair of his head began to grow again after he was shaven.

And the lords of the Philistines gathered them together to offer a great sacrifice unto Dagon their god, and to rejoice; for they said: 'Our god hath delivered Samson our enemy into our hand.' And when the people saw him, they praised their god; for they said: 'Our god hath delivered into our hand our enemy, and the destroyer of our country, who hath slain many of us.' And it came to pass, when their hearts were merry, that they said: 'Call for Samson, that he may make us sport.' And they called for Samson out of the prison-house; and he made sport before them; and they set him between the pillars. And Samson said unto the lad that held him by the hand: 'Suffer me that I may feel the pillars whereupon the house resteth, that I may lean upon them.' Now the house was full of men and women; and all the lords of the Philistines were there; and there were upon the roof about three thousand men and women, that beheld while Samson made sport. And Samson called unto the LORD, and said: 'O Lord GOD, remember me, I pray Thee, and strengthen me, I pray Thee, only this once, O God, that I may be this once avenged of the Philistines for my two eyes.' And Samson took fast hold of the two middle pillars upon which the house rested, and leaned upon them, the one with his right hand, and the other with his left. And Samson said: 'Let me die with the Philistines.' And he bent with all his might; and the house fell upon the lords, and upon all the people that were therein. So the dead that he slew at his death were more than they that he slew in his life. Then his brethren and all the house of his father came down, and took him, and brought him up, and buried him between Zorah and Eshtaol in the burying-place of Manoah his father. And he judged Israel twenty years.

Anglo-Saxon: Beowulf

Beowulf is an old English poem that follows the adventures of a hero of the Geats, Beowulf, who travels to Denmark to help a friend of his father's overcome a monster that has been killing his men. That friend is Hrothgar, the king of the Danes. He had built a mead hall named Heorot to celebrate in with his warriors, but their noisy celebrations disturb Grendel, a descendent of Cain, who retaliated by entering the hall and slaying some of the men. This continued on a regular basis until things were so bad in Denmark that the king abandoned the hall and the news reached Geatland. When Beowulf, who had the strength of many men in his hands, heard the news, he determined to fight the monster and aid Hrothgar who was a friend of Beowulf's father.

© Ron and Joe/Shutterstock.com

Beowulf choses a number of warriors to travel with him to Denmark and they sailed across the ocean and arrive on the coast of Denmark where they were challenged by one of Hrothgar's men. When Beowulf identified himself, Hrothgar's warrior allowed him to land and take his men to Hrothgar's hall for introductions. Hrothgar was happy to host Beowulf and his men and agreed to allow them to sleep in the hall that night. When asked how Beowulf would fight Grendel, Beowulf declared that he would fight bare-handed just as Grendel fought.

That night, after all his men were asleep, Grendel appeared in the hall and ate one of Beowulf's warriors. Beowulf attacked Grendel, and the two grapple. Beowulf grasped Grendel's arm and did not let go, eventually ripping it from Grendel's body. Grendel stumbled from the hall and returned to his lair and was not seen again. The men rejoiced. The next day there was a huge celebration and Hrothgar honored Beowulf. There was much singing and drinking and merry-making into the wee hours of the morning. After everyone fell asleep, a new menace approached Grendel's mother. Grendel's mother was angry at the hurt done to her son and she retaliated by taking Hrothgar's favorite advisor with her back to her mere. When Beowulf learned of the attack on the king's trusted advisor, he declared that he would go after the monster.

Beowulf rode to the swampy waters of the mere. He dove into the waters and found Grendel's mother. The two fought, but Beowulf's sword was not strong enough to injure the creature and he lost it in the dark waters. Entering the lair of Grendel's mother, Beowulf found a giant's sword and used it to fight against the monster. With one stroke he lopped off her head. After killing Grendel's mother, Beowulf saw Grendel's body in her lair. He decided to remove Grendel's head and took it back as a trophy for Hrothgar.

When Beowulf returned having killed Grendel's mother as well as Grendel, there was even more rejoicing. Hrothgar loaded Beowulf down with treasures and all the surviving warriors celebrated long into the night. Beowulf returned home a hero and gave much of the treasure to the king of the Geats. Many years later, around fifty actually, the king and his successor both passed away and Beowulf was given the kingship in honor of his great deeds. As king, he fought new battles, but as these were so many years later they properly belong to a new quest and were not part of his fight against Grendel or Grendel's mother.

Study Questions for Chapter 8: Hero Archetype

The Hero Cycle of Joseph Campbell

1. According to the Hero Cycle of Joseph Campbell, what are the three main stages that every hero passes through on his or her adventures?
2. What are the five subcategories in the first phase of the Hero Cycle?
3. What are the six subcategories in the second phase of the Hero Cycle?
4. What are the six subcategories in the third and final phase of the Hero Cycle?
5. What other scholars have created patterns for heroes based on hero myths?

Mesopotamian: Gilgamesh

1. Who is Gilgamesh?
2. Why did the gods create Enkidu?
3. Why did Gilgamesh and Enkidu decide to go to the Cedar Forests?
4. Why did Ishtar ask for the Bull of Heaven to be sent to earth?
5. Why did Enkidu sicken and die?
6. Why did Gilgamesh seek out Utnapishtim?
7. Why did Gilgamesh dive to the bottom of the waters?
8. What happened to the flower on his way home to Uruk?
9. What did Gilgamesh learn from his adventure?
10. How does the myth of Gilgamesh compare with Campbell's Hero Cycle? What categories and subcategories match Gilgamesh's adventure?

Greek: Herakles

1. Who is Herakles?
2. Why does Hera hate Herakles?
3. Why does Herakles have to serve his cousin, King Eurystheus of Tiryns, for twelve years?
4. What are the twelve labors of Herakles?
5. Which two labors did Eurystheus not count and why?
6. What does Herakles earn at the end of his labors?
7. How does the myth of Herakles' labors compare with Campbell's Hero Cycle? What categories and subcategories match Herakles' adventure?

Greek: Jason

1. Who is Jason?
2. Why was he raised by Chiron, the centaur?
3. Why did Hera favor Jason and how did she test his worthiness?
4. What task did his uncle Pelias give him and why?
5. What was the name of Jason's ship and why was it unique?
6. Who joined Jason on his quest?
7. What was the first place that Jason and his crew visited?
8. Where did they go next and what did they learn about the dangers on their journey?
9. What tasks did King Aeetes of Colchis give Jason and why?
10. Who helped Jason succeed in the tasks and why?
11. How did Jason finally obtain the Golden Fleece?
12. What did Jason have to do to escape pursuit after leaving Colchis?
13. How did Medea help the Argonauts on the voyage home?
14. Why didn't Jason become the king of Iolcus after returning home?
15. Where did Jason and his family find refuge in exile and what offer was he given there?
16. How does the myth of Jason compare with Campbell's Hero Cycle? What categories and subcategories match Jason's adventure?

Indian: Rama

1. Who is Rama?
2. Who is Vishvamitra?
3. Why doesn't Rama become king of Ayodhya?
4. Who goes with Rama into exile?
5. What kind of adventures do Rama and his companions have while in the forest?
6. What happens when Lakshmana drives away Soorpanakha?
7. How does Ravana trick Rama and Sita?
8. Who is Hanuman?
9. How does Hanuman help Rama?
10. What happens during the battle between Rama's forces and Ravana's forces? Who wins?
11. Why does Sita ask Lakshmana to build her a funeral pyre?
12. How does the myth of Rama fit into Campbell's Hero Cycle? What categories and subcategories fit the story of Rama? Which ones do not?

Indian: Siddhartha Gautama, the Buddha

1. Who was Siddhartha?
2. What were his two possible destinies?
3. How did his father shelter Siddhartha from the realities of the world?
4. What Four Signs did Siddhartha see that led him to seek enlightenment?
5. How many years did Siddhartha practice asceticism before reaching enlightenment?
6. Who tried to tempt Siddhartha away from enlightenment and how (three times)?
7. What does the title "Buddha" mean?
8. Who were the Buddha's first five disciples?
9. What was the first lesson that the Buddha gave his new disciples?
10. How does the myth of Siddhartha Gautama, the Buddha, compare with Campbell's Hero Cycle? What categories and subcategories match the Buddha's adventure?

Japanese: Momotaro

1. Who is Momotaro?
2. Who are Momotaro's parents?
3. What quest does Momotaro set out on when he is fifteen?
4. What animals try to attack him and how does he stop them from attacking him?
5. How does Momotaro defeat the ogres?
6. What does Momotaro return home with at the end of the myth?
7. How does the myth of Momotaro fit into Campbell's Hero Cycle? What categories and subcategories fit the story of Momotaro? Which ones do not fit?

Hebrew: Samson

1. Who was Samson?
2. What was his destiny?
3. Who was Samson's intended wife?
4. What creature did he slay with his bare hands?
5. How did he retaliate against his intended bride and her family?
6. How did the Philistines finally defeat Samson?
7. What was Samson's greatest triumph?
8. How does the myth of Samson compare with Campbell's Hero Cycle? What categories and subcategories match Samson's adventure?

Anglo-Saxon: Beowulf

1. Who is Beowulf?
2. Who does Beowulf wish to aid and why?
3. Who is Grendel?
4. How does Beowulf defeat Grendel?
5. How does Beowulf defeat Grendel's mother?
6. What rewards does Beowulf receive before sailing back to Geatland?
7. How does the myth of Beowulf fit into Campbell's Hero Cycle? What categories and subcategories fit the story of Beowulf? Which ones do not fit?

CHAPTER 9
PANTHEONS

Introduction to Pantheons

Pantheons are usually the most important gods and goddesses within a particular culture. The roots of the word are Greek. Pan means all and theon is the neuter plural form of gods. Literally, the word Pantheon means all the gods. However, so many of the polytheistic cultures have thousands and thousands of gods that it would be impossible to name them all. Instead, the word Pantheon has come to mean the most powerful and most important of the gods.

The Greek and Roman Pantheons

In Greece, the pantheon consists of the Olympian gods, described in the Greek Creation of Hesiod's *Theogony,* found in Chapter 2. Most scholars number the Olympians at twelve, because they omit Hades who lives under the earth, and Hestia, who falls out of importance outside of the Greek home. To avoid what I consider hubris, I count both of them, Hestia and Hades, among the Olympian gods. The list includes Zeus, Poseidon, Hades, Hera, Demeter, Hestia, Aphrodite, Ares, Hephaestos, Athena, Artemis, Apollo, Hermes, and Dionysos. Their complicated family relationships are described in the Greek Creation in Chapter 2.

The Greek pantheon was largely borrowed and adapted by the Romans. The Romans had gods, or powers (numinosum) that they recognized and honored, but they didn't necessarily have that many original myths. Instead, they borrowed the myths of the Greek gods and associated them with their own gods, making some adjustments along the way. Usually, mythology books make simple equivalencies between the two pantheons, but in actuality there are some differences. For simplicity's sake, here are the main equivalents.

ZEUS | JUPITER   GERA | JUNO   POSEIDON | NEPTUNE   HADES | PLUTO   DEMETER | CERES   APOLLO | PHOEBUS   NIKE | VICTORIA

HESTIA | VESTA   DIONYSUS | BACCHUS   THEMIS | JUSTISE   APHRODITE | VENUS   HEPHAESTUS | VULCAN   HEKATE | TRIVIA   ARES | MARS

ARTEMIS | DIANA   ATHENA | MINERVA   HYMENAIOS | HYMEN   HELIOS | SOL   EROS | CUPID   PERSEPHONE | PROSERPINA   HERMES | MERCURY   PAN | FAUNUS

© GoodStudio/Shutterstock.com

Zeus = Jupiter or Jove

Hera = Juno

Poseidon = Neptune

Hades = Pluto or Dis

Hestia = Vesta* much more popular and communally worshiped by the Romans with a communal hearth for the city of Rome

Demeter = Ceres

Aphrodite = Venus* becomes Venus Genetrix, the mother of the Roman race via her son Aeneas

Ares = Mars* also a Roman fertility god and much more rational and strategic than his Greek counterpart

Hephaestos = Vulcan

Athena = Minerva* Minerva was honored more for wisdom and handicrafts than war. Bellona was the Roman goddess of war

Artemis = Diana* the Romans sometimes confused Artemis and Selene so Diana isn't always chaste

Apollo = Phoebus or Apollo
Hermes = Mercury
Dionysos = Bacchus or Liber
Persephone = Proserpina
Kronos = Saturn
Rhea = most often Cybele, the Magna Mater
Ouranos = Uranus
Gaia = Terra Mater or Tellus

The Egyptian Pantheon from Heliopolis

In Egypt, according to the Creation myth from Heliopolis, there are Nine most important gods. They are called the Ennead, which simply means "the nine." These gods include Khepri as Ra, the sun god; Shu, the god of atmosphere or moisture; Tefnut, the goddess of cosmic order; Geb, the Earth Father; Nut, Mother Sky; Osiris, the first king

Isis   Anubis   Thoth   Sakhmet   Hathor   Seth   Horus

Nephthys   Ptah   Osiris   Re   Khnum   Sobek   Amun

of Egypt and original god of fertility who later becomes god of the Duat, the afterlife; Isis, the wife of Osiris and the Great Mother goddess of Egypt, in charge of magic and healing. Their brother Seth is the god of the desert and chaos, and he marries their sister Nephthys, the goddess of dusk and death. Not included among the nine, but still considered important gods in their own right are Horus, the son of Isis and Osiris who is associated with the pharaohs of Egypt and the sun, and Anubis, the god of mummification. Anubis is the son of Nephthys by Osiris, raised by Isis. Their family relationships are described in more detail in the Egyptian Creation in Chapter 2, and in the stories of Isis and Osiris found in Chapters 4 and 5.

The Mesopotamian Pantheon from Sumer

In Sumer, the main family of gods begins with Nammu, the equivalent of Tiamat, and Abzu, the equivalent of Apsu. Tiamat and Apsu's story is told in the Mesopotamian Creation the *Enuma Elish* from Babylon located in Chapter 2. Among the many children of Nammu and Abzu are Ki, the Earth goddess, and An, the Sky god. They give birth to Ninlil, the goddess of the air, and Enlil, the god of the air (or storms and the instigator of the flood). Ninlil and Enlil marry and give birth to Nanna, the moon god. Among the children of Nammu and Absu is Enki, the god of wisdom. Enki marries Ningikuga,

© Charis Estelle/Shutterstock.com

the goddess of the reeds, and she gives birth to Ningal, the moon goddess. Ningal and Nanna marry and give birth to three children Inanna, the Queen of Heaven; Utu, the sun god; and Ereshkigal, the goddess of the underworld. Ereshkigal marries Gugulanna, the Bull of Heaven. Inanna, a favorite of her grandfather Enki, eventually marries the Shepherd god, Dumuzi. In the way of the gods, Dumuzi turns out to be the son of Enki by Sirtur, the sheep goddess. Utu or Shamash was the sun god.

The Yoruba Pantheon

Among the Yoruba tribe in West Africa, the pantheon consists of the Orishas. There are hundreds of Orishas. These are some of the most important. The Supreme Being is Olorun, sometimes called Odulamare, the powerful sky father. He is the creator of the universe and seems to rest after that creation and enjoys the perks of rulership. The Creator god is Obatala. He is responsible for making the earth, all its creatures, and humans. He is seen as more of a father figure and looks over the orishas and the humans. Eshu, who is also called Legba or Elegba, is the trickster god. He is also the messenger between humans and the gods. He must be prayed to before the other gods. He is associated with roads, doors, and crossroads. Ogun is the god of iron and

© Charis Estelle/Shutterstock.com

war. He is associated with craftsmanship. Orunmila is the wise prophet of the gods. He is associated with divination. Oranmiyan is a fertility god and creator of dry land. Oko is the god of farming. Aganju is the god of the wilderness. Orungan is the god of air. Obaluaye or Shankpanna is the god of smallpox. Aje Shaluga is the god of wealth.

Olokun is the goddess of oceans and the original marshy waters in the creation myth. Olosa is the goddess of lagoons. Oshun is the goddess of fresh waters. She is considered sweet and is connected to prosperity and fertility. Yemaja is the goddess of the ocean and lakes. She is the Great Mother of All. She is in charge of all things maternal. Oya is the goddess of the winds and the Niger river. She is associated with graveyards and the dead. She is also a warrior and will ride into battle with Shango. Shango is the warrior god of lightning. He is associated with dance and drums and manliness. Oshoshi is the hunter and tracker for the Orishas and is closely associated with Obatala. The sun is Orun and the moon is Oshu.

The Hindu Pantheon

There are millions of gods in India, all different forms and manifestations of Brahman. It would be impossible to go over the whole family of gods because there are so many variations, but wherever one travels in India there are some that remain consistent. These include the Trimurti: Brahma, the Creator god, depicted with four heads and holding copies of the Vedas; Vishnu, the Preserver or Sustainer god (who has ten major avatars) depicted holding weapons and a lotus; and Shiva, the Destroyer god who is also in charge of yoga and meditation. Shiva is often depicted in meditation seated on a tiger skin or as Nataraja, Lord of the Dance.

Each male god has his female counterpart or Shakti. Brahma's consort is Sarasvati, the goddess of inspiration and knowledge. Sarasvati is usually depicted playing a vina or a sitar. Vishnu's consort is Lakshmi (Laxmi, Laksmee), the goddess of fertility and prosperity. Lakshmi is usually seated on a lotus with gold coins pouring from one of her hands into a basin below. Her other hands hold lotus blossoms connecting her to birth and rebirth. Shiva's consort differs according to where one lives in India. He has three possible wives. Shiva's wife is either Parvati, the daughter of the mountain (Himavat, god of the Himalayas) and a yogini, mother of Ganesha and Skanda, or his wife is Durga, the warrior goddess who rides on top of a lion or a tiger and has eight arms, each hand armed with a weapon or a lotus. Durga is one of the most powerful of all the gods and was created to slay a demon that could only be killed by a goddess. The final choice for Shiva's possible consort is Kali, the goddess of Destruction. She is even fiercer than Shiva and is a battlefield goddess. She has ten arms and each hand holds a weapon, no lotuses. She wears a necklace of severed heads or skulls and a skirt made from severed arms and legs. She carries a severed head in one hand that

© KittyVector/Shutterstock.com

represents ego. While she appears fierce, she helps remove attachments and ego that block humans from reaching Enlightenment, an understanding of the oneness of all things, which is called Brahman, and their connection to that oneness.

Other beloved gods in the Hindu family of gods include Ganesha, the elephant headed son of Shiva and Parvati who removes obstacles. Hanuman, the monkey god, is the ideal devotee, completely devoted to the seventh avatar of Vishnu, Rama, and Rama's wife, Sita. Hanuman is a very powerful warrior and he can grow very large or very small. Hanuman can leap far distances. He serves Rama (the seventh incarnation of Vishnu), who is considered the embodiment of righteousness and the ideal ruler. Sita, Rama's wife and an incarnation of Lakshmi, is considered the ideal wife.

Kama is the Hindu god of love, desire and pleasure who rides a parrot. His weapon is a sugarcane bow strung with bees, and he shoots flower arrows that cause people to fall in love. Myths say that Kama once shot Shiva when Shiva was looking at Parvati. Shiva was so angry at Kama that he used his third eye to incinerate Kama. Kama's wife was so distraught that Shiva allowed Kama to return in a new body, although some say he remained bodiless and became even more potent without his body.

Surya is the sun god. He drives a chariot across the sky pulled by seven horses. Chandra (also called Soma) is the moon god and a fertility god. He rides in a chariot pulled by antelope. As Soma, he serves as the vital elixir that fuels the gods. The gods like to drink him so he takes refuge as the crescent moon in Shiva's dreadlocks.

The Norse Pantheon

In the Scandinavian countries and among some of the Germanic tribes, the main gods and goddesses were similar to those of Norse Mythology. The main sources for this pantheon are the prose *Edda* by Snorri Sturlison, and the poetic *Edda*. The Eddas are not the easiest materials to read, and were written rather late, historically speaking, somewhere around the 12th–13th centuries CE.

Odin   Balder   Frigg   Bragi   Thor

Freya   Tyr   Sif   Loki

© Charis Estelle/Shutterstock.com

In this family of gods, blended from the Aesir, the sky gods, and the Vanir, the earth or nature gods, Odin (Woden, Wotan) is the Supreme Being. He rules over the family of gods as the paterfamilias. Odin is the one-eyed All Father, the god of war, who sacrificed his eye to gain a drink from the well of Mimir, which gave him knowledge of the future. Odin also hung himself upside down from the cosmic tree,

Yggdrasil, for nine days and nights in order to obtain the power of the runes. These powers make him the prototype of the magician. He is very wise, and sometimes may be deceitful. As a god of war, he inspires berserkers, warriors who are so filled with adrenaline that they can fight and fight and not realize that they are injured until the battle frenzy passes. Odin rules over the family of gods with his brothers, Vili and Ve, with whom he had fashioned the world from the body of the giant Ymir. Interestingly, Vili and Ve fade into the background and emphasis is given to Odin as king of the gods. Odin is kept informed about the goings on in the world by his two ravens, Hugin and Munin (Thought and Memory, respectively), who fly around the world gathering information and bring it back to him. Odin carries a spear, Gungnir, that never misses, and wears an arm ring, Draupnir, that sheds eight more arm rings every ninth night. His main hall is Valhalla in Asgard, where he receives half of the nobly dead. His daughters, the Valkyries, fierce warrior maidens, are the choosers of the slain who hover over the battlefield on their winged horses and select those souls who die honorably in battle and carry them to Asgard. (Some of the darker Norse tales say that the Valkyries actually choose who will die, not just who among the dead died nobly.) Those who die nobly in battle come to Valhalla to await Ragnarok, the apocalypse, by drinking mead, reliving old battles, and throwing sharp pointy things at Odin's favorite son, Balder, who is invulnerable to almost everything in existence.

Odin's wife is Frigg, the goddess of the Earth. She is a nurturing mother goddess figure best known for her love of Balder, her son. She takes oaths from everything in creation, except mistletoe, in order to protect her son. When he dies, she is devastated. She asks for his return and attempts to have every single sentient thing weep for him. Only one frost giantess, Thokk, will not weep, so Balder remains trapped in the underworld.

Odin and Frigg's other sons are Hodr the blind god, who is tricked by Loki into killing his brother Balder with a mistletoe dart, and Tyr, the god of war and justice. Tyr is a very powerful war god, who also enforces the rules of justice. He lost a hand to the wolf Fenrir, a son of Loki, when the gods chained up the enormous and dangerous wolf.

Odin's best known son is Thor, the god of Thunder, who was also the most liked of the Norse gods. He is the son of the earth itself, and very strong. Thor is described as a big, burly warrior with a red beard. He drives a chariot pulled by two goats, which he slaughters every night for food. The goats are reborn each morning. Thor's weapon is the battle hammer Mjollnir that always returns to his hand when he throws it and can be used to summon lightning. The giants fear Thor and his hammer. He is viewed as the main protector of Asgard against the giants. Thor, while loved, isn't necessarily the cleverest of the gods. He is strong, and a great warrior, but he also loves to drink and eat. He is married to Sif of the golden hair.

Freyr and Freya are the rulers of the Vanir who war with the Aesir for many long years until the two groups of gods finally make peace. Some of the Vanir come to live in Asgard, while retaining ties to their realm, Vanaheim. Freyr is the lord of summer.

He is a fertility god and a warrior. He carries a special sword that is able to fight by itself, but saps the strength of its user afterward. He also has a hankerchief that when unfolded becomes a fast sailing ship. Freyr and Freya together are associated with a golden boar Gullenborsti that is as bright as the sun. Freyr eventually gives up his sword as a bride price in order to marry the giantess Gerdr. When the last battle arrives, he has to fight without his sword, using an antler instead.

Freya is Freyr's sister and the co-ruler of Vanaheim. She is a goddess of love, beauty, and sexuality, much like the Greek goddess, Aphrodite, but she is also a warrior and receives have of the honorable dead when they are removed from the battlefield (the other half go to Odin). Freya drives a chariot pulled by cats, and has a cloak made of feathers that allows her to fly. She is married to Od or Odr, who may be a form of Odin. She is famous for her golden necklace, Brisingamen, for which she had to bargain with the dwarves.

Heimdall is the sentry of the gods and guards the realm of Asgard. He was birthed by nine waves. He can see far distances including down to Midgard and can hear everything, even grass growing. He has a special horn that he will blow when Ragnarok arrives to summon the gods into battle.

Loki is the trickster of the Norse pantheon. He seems to be a frost giant who becomes Odin's foster brother and oath brother. Odin and the other gods must take care around Loki because of Odin's oaths with him. Loki is very clever, and a shapeshifter. He sometimes aids the Aesir and Vanir, and other times causes terrible mischief. He does good things like helping Thor get his hammer back after the giant Thrim steals it. But Loki also tends to be jealous and is often malicious, cutting off Sif's hair when she draws too much attention for her beauty. Loki is also the catalyst for Balder's death, tricking Frigg into revealing her beautiful son's one vulnerability and helping the blind god, Hodr, to aim and throw the mistletoe dart that kills Balder. Loki has many adventures and misadventures. In the form of a mare, he distracts a stallion and ends up giving birth to the eight-legged horse, Sleipnir, who becomes Odin's mount. He has three children with the giantess Angrboda: Jormungandr, the world serpent; Hel, the goddess of the dishonorable dead in Helheim; and Fenrir, the giant wolf that will swallow the sun during the Apocalypse.

Some of the lesser known goddesses include Idun who guards and tends the golden apples associated with youth and immortality among the Norse. Idun is a beautiful goddess with long flaxen hair. She is associated with youth and springtime. She is married to Bragi, the god of poetry. The gods come to Idun to eat the apples and maintain their youth.

ABOUT THE AUTHOR

Jennifer Taylor has an MA/PhD in Mythological Studies with a Depth Psychological Emphasis from Pacifica Graduate Institute in Carpinteria, California. She also has an MA in Classical Civilizations from the Florida State University and a BA in Humanities, Summa Cum Laude, from the University of Central Florida. She is passionate about teaching, the humanities, world travel, the environment, sustainability, and living in harmony with the Earth and each other. She has traveled a number of times through most of Western Europe as well as Japan, India, and Nepal.

Courtesy of David Huff

INDEX

CPSIA information can be obtained
at www.ICGtesting.com
Printed in the USA
LVHW062249070521
686855LV00001B/1

9 781792 409622